SALMON FISHING
IN SCOTLAND

The Haig Guide to
SALMON FISHING IN SCOTLAND

Edited by David Barr

With descriptions of the major salmon rivers and lochs
by Bill 'Rogie' Brown

QUEEN ANNE PRESS
MACDONALD FUTURA PUBLISHERS
LONDON

Created and produced by Robert Dudley
and John Stidolph

Maps by Patrick Frean

Picture research by Tom Williams

Designed by Paul Watkins

First published in 1981 by Queen Anne Press,
Macdonald Futura Publishers Limited, Paulton House,
8 Shepherdess Walk, London N1 7LW

ISBN   0362   00554   0

Typesetting by Inforum Ltd, Portsmouth, England

Colour separations and printing by New Interlitho
SPA, Milan

Frontispiece: Reflections on Royal Deeside

We should like to thank the editor and the writers not
only for their contributions but for the help and advice
they have given us. They in their turn have asked us to
express thanks and appreciation for the co-operation
which they have received during the compilation of this
book from a large number of bodies and individuals.
Apart from those who supplied the illustrations
(acknowledged elsewhere), especial thanks are due to
the following:
Aberdeen City Library, G C Aitken, L L Arden
(E A Hornell Art Gallery & Library), The Ashmolean
Museum, The Duke of Atholl, David Ayres,
W A Baxter & Sons, Ken Bell, I Blagburn (House of Hardy),
H Blakeney, Gordon Burns, Niall Campbell, Grant
Carnegie, Christies South Kensington, A Church,
T R Colin (Stewartry Museum), Stephen Drummond
Sedgwick, Roy Eaton, Erwin Edelman, Kirsty Ennever,
The Field, James Fyfe, Neil Graesser, Sir Reginald
Graham, John Grant, Ralph Harkness, Peter Hay, Jo
Hickson, James Holloway, E Horsfall-Turner, Ian
Hynd, The Viscountess Ingleby, Andrew Lusk, David
Liversedge, Alan Loudon, David MacDonald, Iain
MacKenzie, Jack MacKenzie (Helmsdale), Jack
MacKenzie (Inverness), Harry MacPherson, Dr
Rosalind Marshall, Roy Miles, Dr Derek Mills, Harry
Munro, Dr B Nestall (Highland Trout Co), Arthur
Oglesby, Bill Paton, Jack Paton, Pinneys Smokehouses
Ltd, Piscatorial Society, J R C Proudlock, Punch,
Keeper Ramage, H A Rickett (Flyfishers Club), Bruce
Sandison, Alan Smith, Robert Spiers (Nithsdale Hotel),
John Stuart, David Sutherland, Mr and Mrs Tom Swan,
P J Tait (NFU Scotland), Torry Research Station,
W Tyrwhitt Drake, Andrew Walker, J Watt,
H D Wibraham (Russell & McIver), Rob Wilson
Robert Dudley, John Stidolph

Contents

Introduction

For 800 years, the sons and daughters of the House of Haig have been active in the affairs of Scotland, in war and in peace. For the past 350 years they have given their name to one of Scotland's happiest and best enduring inventions – Scotch Whisky. What could be more fitting therefore than that Haig should be associated with this, a book about Scotland's other crowning glory – the salmon?

The two have much in common. The same rivers and lochs in which the salmon feed and multiply provide the pure spring water which gives Scotch whisky its unique and attractive taste. As with whisky, people throughout the world associate the best salmon with Scotland.

There is much in this book about the lore and custom of salmon fishing. We at Haig understand this well. It was in the twelfth century that the first Haig – one Petrus del Haga – built himself a modest castle on the banks of the Tweed at Bemersyde. The Haigs still live at Bemersyde which was presented to Douglas Haig, the Field Marshal and himself a 'Whisky Haig' after the first world war.

We are proud therefore of our heritage and that is why I welcome 'Salmon Fishing in Scotland'. It is a worthy celebration of a sport that has introduced generation after generation to the beauty of the Scottish landscape and the character of its people. The salmon is a worthy opponent, taxing the mind as well as the body and calling for great patience and skill if he is to be caught and enjoyed. I hope you will enjoy this book and that if you have not already been, you will be 'caught' by the excitement of this most rewarding of sports.

M B Henderson
Managing Director, John Haig & Co Ltd

Glenlossie Distillery, Elgin, Morayshire, the home of Haig Whisky

The Contributors

David Barr's articles on fishing have appeared in leading magazines in England, USA and (suitably translated) France. His regular contributions to *Country Life* have a wide and devoted following that includes many readers who do not fish. He is the author of the (non-fishing) *A Family Way*, a practising Cambridgeshire solicitor, a director of East Midland Allied Press Limited and spends all his spare time fishing. He has a very patient and understanding wife.

Bill (Rogie) Brown has written more words by many thousands on Scottish fishing and Scottish rivers than any other living writer. His entertaining contributions under the pseudonym 'Rogie' have appeared in every single issue of *Trout and Salmon* and there can hardly be a game fisherman who has not referred to Rogie for the latest fishing information. He has found time to catch more than 3000 salmon and also to make a considerable contribution to the well being of Scottish game fishing.

He was appointed by the Secretary of State for Scotland to a 12 member consultative committee dealing with the protection of brown trout and also to the Highland River Purification Board.

He is a superintendent physiotherapist in charge of all the major physiotherapy services in Ross-shire.

B W C Cooke started fishing for trout at the age of six on his father's chalk stream in Hampshire and took his first salmon on the Moy in Ireland when he was 15.

Over the last 30 years he has contributed articles on salmon or trout fishing to all the major sporting journals including *Country Life*, *Rod and Line*, *The Field* and *Trout and Salmon*. He is a long standing member of the Salmon and Trout Association.

Penny Drinkwater is a member of The Circle of Wine Writers, a Member Judge of Club Oenologique, and a member of Les Compagnons du Beaujolais.

She has written five books including the recently published *A Passion for Garlic* (Duckworth), co-authored with her American sister-in-law. She has contributed to magazines including *The Field*, and does a lot of lecturing both at home and abroad.

Drew Jamieson is a geographer by training, an aviator by addiction and an angler by affliction. He has thus observed Scottish rivers from a variety of standpoints.

As a keen student of the Scottish angling scene he has been engaged in research and writing for the past 10 years and has contributed papers to the Water Research Centre and the Institute of Fisheries Management. He is a frequent, if irregular, contributor to *Trout and Salmon* and *Rod and Line* and has been particularly interested in the changes to Scottish fisheries legislation and administration.

He is presently involved in the promotion and development of angling in Lothian region and has made his home in Edinburgh.

Wilson Stephens has a unique status amongst fishing writers. For 26 years, from 1951–1977 he was editor of *The Field* to which he still contributes a regular column under the pseudonym of 'Dabchick'. While editor of *The Field* he was simultaneously editor of *The Salmon and Trout Magazine* for five years. He is a member of the council of the Angling Foundation and a former member of the council of the Salmon and Trout Association. He has contributed articles to a wide range of newspapers and periodicals including *The Times*, *The Financial Times*, and *The Guardian*.

Scotland~
A Paradise for
Fishermen

'Clear dark shadows and bright gleams of light near Dunkeld'
by John Samuel Raven 1829-77

IN Scotland there can be found in marvellous abundance the finest fishing for the Atlantic salmon and for sea trout in the world. And when I write about fishing I include all that goes with it – the power and beauty of the rivers, the quality of the countryside, the ease and comfort and accessability of the fisheries. Comparable rivers in other countries rarely combine all these things. Getting to them demands too often the organisation of a major expedition. They tend to seethe with black flies or mosquitoes. There is no adjacent after-fishing comfort. Nowhere else is there the same numerical concentration of salmon rivers.

Augustus Grimble, in his classic *The Salmon Rivers of Scotland* (well worth buying if you are lucky enough to come across a copy) describes nearly every river – every one of which, nearly a 100 years later, is still fishable, exciting and unique – though admittedly some have been altered by hydro-electric engineering, dams and fish passes. It is worth realising that direct descendants of the fish that were in the rivers Grimble wrote about are still coming in from – and going out into – the sea.

In so tiny a country – not half as big as the American state of Nebraska – such a wealth of this kind of game fishing is little short of miraculous. The choice ranges from rivers that are big and sometimes mighty (by Scottish standards) like Spey, Tay, Dee and Tweed, to the sharp speculative excitements of smaller streams like Urr and Cree. Up all these rivers, whatever their size, between January and November (and there are variations and permutations in the fish-run in each river) there move, whenever climatic conditions allow, large numbers of salmon, grilse and sea trout. It has been difficult indeed to narrow

Cora Lynn, a waterfall on the Clyde, by Alexander Nasmyth

down the list of rivers that have been individually dealt with in this book and there were sorrows at many of the omissions. We have only dealt with mainland rivers and even then have exercised a process of selection – mainly on the grounds of availability or non-availability to the public.

A look at a map will show that the islands off the mainland are dotted with the blue of lochs and their river links with the sea – sometimes it looks as though there is more water than land. There are superb fisheries on many of the Scottish islands, with hotels to match. Certainly some of the world's finest sea trout fishing is to be found there. Alas, a line must be drawn somewhere.

The Rivers The river is the salmon's highway down which he travels after being born in the headwaters and up which he returns to spawn and often to die. The run of fish returning from the sea is miraculously timed so that the fish that reach fresh water in February reach the spawning grounds (where they are at maximum risk) at much the same time as the fast-travelling autumn fish.

On nearly every Scottish river the beats are named, many of the names famous enough to set a fisherman's pulse racing. In answer to the question, 'Where will you be fishing?' the answer is not 'The Spey, 10 miles downstream of Grantown' but 'Carron or Easter Elchies' or wherever else your fortune is taking you. Every knowledgeable listener will then know your prospects and will be aware that your beat fishes well in low water, or in high and low water, or never after April.

Oil painting of Salmon Fishing by R McEwen

Opposite: A gillie in action on the Spey
Below: The late Captain T L Edwards, Spey casting at
Grantown-on-Spey

The Gillies Presiding over the beats are the gillies, men who can lock or unlock the door to a holiday's enjoyment. There are gillies in England, Wales and Ireland, but the Scottish gillie is the real thing, from whose stock all the others have grown. He can be a respected and admired friend and companion – or, rarely, a bad enemy.

No survey has ever been carried out into the origins and distribution of the professional gillies. Sometimes they are poachers turned policemen. Sometimes they are men who have decided that the job gives them their only chance of spending a lifetime fishing. Sometimes they have blossomed from young assistant bailiffs or river watchers into the dignified and formal men that gillies can frequently be. Often they are the third or fourth generation of men who have between them presided over the same stretch of water for more than a 100 years. No wonder they know every eddy, stone and rock. Gillies can preserve – or destroy – the standards of the fisheries on which they work. But while a drunken gillie (and there are a few) with his eyes only on his lunchtime whisky and his standards tuned to his weekly tip can be a menace and a disappointment, the vast majority are stern, attractive men, tolerant of the inadequacies of their fishermen and eager to help. Mostly, they can cast like gods, and catch without effort any catchable fish within their reach. They are also good at ensuring that their guests catch salmon too, if their guests are even half efficient.

Chalk drawing of Scotsman holding a salmon leister,
by Thomas Duncan 1840

They are, by and large, members of a charming and cultured profession, expert in their work, natural conservationists – and diplomatic enough to make fishermen who are not too greedy or too demanding, feel part of the Scottish scene. A gillie will also put up your rod, and recommend the right fly (and never ignore his advice if you want more of it). He will certainly test your nylon (whatever its strength) and break it as if it were cobweb, shaking his head in sorrow at the disaster he has saved you from. He will brush out the fishing hut if you haven't already done it yourself and while the sandwiches are being eaten and drinks shared, he may well come out with a series of sharply funny stories about the ordeals to which he has been subjected by his fishermen. A gillie is half sportsman, half entertainer, but for those who are new to gillie-dom, there are one or two do's and dont's. Never call him by his surname only – unless your own name appears in *Debrett*. Let him put up your rod, if he likes, and carry it to the river – but never let him fish for you. Treat him as the wise and entertaining person that he most certainly is – and he will add stars to your fishing holiday.

Times have even brought changes to unchanging gillies. They are no longer prepared unquestioningly to work 12 hour days and the great characters are men of the past. You are unlikely to meet anyone like the famous Leekie, who ruled over some fishing on Deeside 40 years ago. Beautifully mannered, immensely knowledgeable, he would arrive each morning in immaculately cut tweed plus-fours, shoes burnished, handle-brush moustache oiled and gleaming. Yet when his fisherman hooked a salmon, he would not hesitate to stride into the river, fully clothed, to net it. He scorned the waders he could well have afforded to buy. The next morning he would appear again, wearing, it seemed, the same expensive suit, pressed and fit for a general's inspection.

Techniques Many of the best fishermen in Scotland are Spey casters. Spey casting is the technique of casting a fly off the water without it travelling behind or above the fisherman, a way of casting that is necessary on many of the rivers, not just the Spey. A Spey caster can fish anywhere, among trees or with sheer cliff rising behind him. It is a very easy cast indeed to perfect, provided, of course, that you have been expertly and painstakingly taught and have spent days and weeks determinedly perfecting the skill and fighting the temptation to cast the way you know.

Each July I fish opposite a beautiful girl upon whose face (at 50 yards range, at least) the last eight years have left no etching. She still looks 18 and with faultless technique and no force or violence, Spey casts 30 yards at a time every minute and a half. I started this form of casting when I was over 50, decided that it was too late to change and have continued with over-the-shoulder casting. I cast as well over my left shoulder as my right and so far have not been in the terrible position of being on a good beat but unable, because of the overhanging trees, to cover the pools. Such fishermen would not be asked twice to the best private beats, where results recorded in the fishing book assume notable importance.

Below: The Craigellachie Hotel
Opposite: A sharp day on the Staan Pool at Tulchan on the
Spey

At the End of the Day But where, I hear someone plead, does one stay? In the neighbourhood of all the rivers containing game fish, there can be found hotels, inns and chalets of every size, ready, willing and able to cater for the fisherman and his family. Some have their own fishing for their guests; some will undertake to arrange it; others are glad to welcome fishermen who have made their own arrangements. Among the bigger hotels there comes to mind Ednam House at Kelso, a real fishing hotel if ever there was one, comfortable, food good and the Tweed fishing the sole topic of conversation. It does not at present have fishing of its own. In the evenings in November when that late Tweed run is being attacked by the fishermen, they put a tarpaulin down in the large and lofty entrance hall – and the huge catches are displayed, weighed and labelled as they are brought in. On one night there, I saw four fish over 25 lbs – and slunk quietly away with the 8 lbs sea trout of which I had felt so proud. The Craigellachie Hotel, my favourite, has its own fishing which is booked and rebooked a year ahead. It, too, is comfortable and when the chef is on song, the food is very good. It is also a place where non–fishing families can happily survive. A tiny little pub I have been to many times is the Forbes Arms at Rothiemay, which has the letting of a mile and a half of the Deveron. It can

accommodate up to eight people; the accommodation is very simple and the food plentiful and the guests have the chance to participate in the life of the village in the bar in the evenings. It is a lot cheaper than the first two I mentioned and you get, naturally enough, what you pay for.

Life in the hotels, inns and pubs (or wherever else visiting fishermen may gather) is an integral part of a fishing holiday.

Sundays are normally the days when the change-over takes place. Sunday evenings have their own dramas and anxieties, as the fishermen eye each other suspiciously or greet each other effusively, discovering who is fishing with whom and where. Normally those who are fishing the private (and most likely, better) beats gather in small groups; those fishing the hotel (and, possibly, more crowded) beats skirmish gently among themselves. By Monday evening it will all have become more like a house party, orchestrated possibly to the gentle noises of malt whisky being poured and sipped (one Scottish Highland hotel boasts in one of its bars a stock of 53 different brands). The tales of the first day's adventures grow more dramatic as the hours slip by, the disasters more poignant, the triumphs even more memorable.

The Fishers There was a time when Scotland had a large quota of nationally famous fishing celebrities, men like AHE Wood of Cairnton whose philosophies and skills were the talk of all the rivers. Gone, or almost gone, is that leisured group of people. Their enormous catches were in part attributable to the fact that the fishing was better – and always available to them. They were in a position to choose only the best moments. The majority of modern fishermen fish at times and in conditions in which the old time giants would not have bothered to put up their rods, let alone walk to the riverside.

Most rivers still have one or two local characters, minor celebrities whose skills are envied and admired. One such was the late Tom Tewnion, late and lamented. He earned his living working on the railways and his fame fishing on the Deveron, on many parts of which he was a welcome guest. Like most great fishermen, he was a dedicated catcher of fish; no purist, he would use any legitimate method that gave him the best chance of fish on the bank. Year after year he was among the first to catch a Deveron spring salmon, homing in on it as if on the end of a magnet. I have seen him fishing with two or three competent fishermen, ending the day with twice their grand total. He would never have made a gillie for he could scarcely conceal his contempt for the incompetent, who were, he judged, making his own task harder. All the same he was a charming and helpful companion and in a few outings together, cured me of more fishing faults than a score of lessons. My favourite memory is of the sight of him, shortly before he died, coming down the brae at Rothiemay, half running, like a schoolboy, putting up his rod as he went, and making his first cast (precisely covering a taking-place at the far side of the river) without so much as breaking step.

Rod, reel, line and two fine finnoch

Limitations There are restrictions on most rivers (about which it is wise to enquire in advance) on the fishing methods which may be adopted. Though there are still some where a free-for-all is allowed, most rivers of any eminence tend to become fly-only at the end of April, with remissions for those who long to spin, when the water is over a certain height. The spectacular November Tweed fishing (when the water can be very cold indeed) is, commendably, fly only. A salmon has travelled a long journey before he reaches his river. Comparatively few miles then lie between fish and the object of his journey. Restrictions on fishing methods reflect the sport's conservationist core.

Never on Sundays Visitors should be warned that all game fishing ceases in Scotland on the sabbath; there is no exception of any kind to this rule.

To complete this short summary of the fishing scene in Scotland, I must mention the sea trout which are present in varying sizes and numbers in all the salmon rivers. I have never heard any reason for the variations, but in some rivers the average weight will be markedly higher than others. To some, the catching of sea trout is an objective in its own right. Many enthusiasts prefer them to salmon – but they have their disadvantages. In clear water they are so shy that they are rarely catchable except in darkness and though playing a 6 lbs sea trout that you cannot see, standing in an invisible river, is something to make any pulse race, the lateness has its disadvantages. The only time my wife ever began to think longingly of abandoning her husband, was after a week's holiday in which I had managed to fish all day and most of each night.

How the Rivers and Lochs were Formed

A river is water in its loveliest form;
Rivers have life and sound and movement
And infinity of variation,
Rivers are veins of the earth through which
The life blood returns to the heart.
RODERICK HAIG–BROWN

SECOND in importance only to the salmon itself is the river in which we pursue it. As anglers, we enjoy the river for a far longer time than we enjoy the salmon. We savour its moods and colours from the moment we arrive at the waterside until we leave it, and often, in the mind's eye, for much longer. We may perhaps enjoy the salmon only for those few intoxicating minutes of capture – if we are successful. The river itself is a vital part of the fishing experience and to know about the river is as interesting as to know about the salmon.

How often have we surveyed the river and wondered why it chose this course rather than that one? Why does this part thunder through a narrow gorge and that part sweep across a wide strath? Why does this stream rise and fall with the rain and the other runs steady even in drought? The answers to these questions lead us away from the salmon itself and into the realms of the rocks, the rain and the geological past.

The broad pattern of the main salmon rivers is shown on p 24 and the first step in trying to establish some logic in this pattern is to peel away the vegetation and soils to have a look at the composition and structure of the rocks beneath.

The Regions A glance at the map shows Scotland to be made up of three major physical regions each characterised by different rocks, scenery and rivers. These physical regions are identified as the Highlands, the Central Lowlands and the Southern Uplands, each separated from the other by the great geological cracks known as the Highland Boundary Fault and the Southern Uplands Fault, respectively.

The Highlands are composed of very old, hard rocks of Cambrian and pre-Cambrian age. The principal rocks are metamorphic gneisses, schists and quartzites with igneous granites and other volcanic rocks intruded at various periods of its history. Over the aeons of geological time these rocks have been folded and faulted along a distinct trend from south-west to north-east to form the ancient Caledonian mountain chain. Subsequent erosion and uplift leaves its present shape as a series of high plateaux and ridges exceeding 4000 ft in Ben Nevis and the Cairngorms, deeply dissected by such rivers as the Conon, Beauly, Spey, Dee and Tay.

The Southern Uplands are formed of slightly younger rocks of Ordovician and Silurian age. The characteristic shales, mudstones and 'greywackes' have also been extensively folded and faulted by later earth movements and once again they follow the south-west to north-east Caledonian trend. Uplift and erosion here has preserved remnant plateaux around 2600 ft in Cheviot, Broad Law and Merrick into which have been incised the valleys of the Tweed and Solway river systems.

The Central Lowlands represent a great rift valley which has dropped down between the two great faults to north and south and has preserved much younger, softer rocks like the characteristic old red sandstone of the Devonian period and the important coal

Previous page: October fishing on the Tweed near
Innerleithen
Below: The principal salmon fishing rivers of mainland Scotland

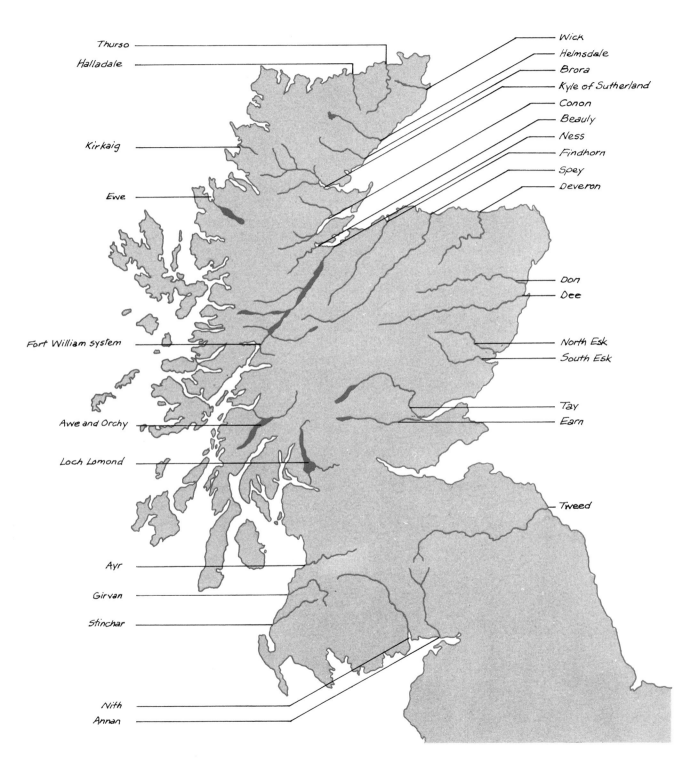

measures and limestones of the Carboniferous. Many of the Highland rivers finish their course in the Central Lowlands, among them, the Tay and the North and South Esks of Angus. Others like the Forth, Teith and Earn are almost completely lowland rivers. One of the largest rivers of this region, the Clyde, is no longer a salmon river although its tributary, the Leven, allows salmon into Loch Lomond and the Endrick.

Apart from the Central Lowlands there are other smaller lowland areas carved out of the younger rocks around the periphery of the mountain areas. The plain of Caithness, drained by the Thurso, is one such lowland, as is the inner Moray Firth drained by the lower reaches of the Conon, Beauly, Ness, Nairn, Findhorn and Spey, both lowlands marking the outcrops of old red sandstone in the north. In the south, these younger rocks are picked out by the Merse of the Tweed and the Annandale and Nithsdale valleys.

Upon this varied structure and shape flow the great salmon rivers, all of them owing something of their character and variety to the rocks beneath.

Drainage How then can we interpret the present drainage pattern? Rivers of all sizes apparently flow in many different directions with the only common denominator being their destination – the sea. However, a pattern can be identified. Two basic threads form the weft and the woof of the tapestry of Scotland's rivers. The fundamental 'Caledonian' grain of the rocks is reflected in a south-west to north-east orientation of many rivers and lochs. Working along lines of geological weakness such Highland waters as the Beauly, Ness, Nairn, Findhorn and Spey, Loch Awe and Loch Tay are paralleled by the Lowland rivers of Isla, Allan, Devon and Tyne and the Southern Upland rivers of Girvan, Stinchar, Ettrick, Yarrow, and Teviot.

However, superimposed upon this structurally-related pattern is a contrasting and much older pattern of rivers which flow across the grain of the land, 'discordant' to the underlying structure. This is a predominantly eastwards or south-eastwards flowing drainage system which is exemplified by such rivers as the Shin, Conon, Garry and Moriston, the Don and the Dee, the North and South Esks, the Tummel/Tay, the Forth and the upper Tweed.

While there is still much discussion about the exact pattern and mechanism for the formation of this original 'discordant' drainage, the widely accepted theory visualises some eastward sloping land surface that was formed, either by an uplifted dome of chalk strata or by some uplifted erosion platform carved into the older rocks by the seas of earlier times.

Upon this generally eastwards sloping surface, the primeval rains fell and coalesced into the early rivers, running from an original watershed, not too far removed from the present one, and out into what is now the North Sea. By subsequent uplift and long erosion any younger rocks have now been stripped off most of the land and the old river pattern is now incised down into the underlying rocks, as a pattern of discordant rivers.

The Ice Age Thus the broad pattern of the rivers was formed. The detailed features which catch the eye and excite the imagination of the curious angler today, date, however, from the last few seconds of geological time – from the last Ice Age or, more correctly, from the last glaciation of the Pleistocene.

During this time a vast ice sheet spread out from a main centre in the West Highlands to cover the whole of Scotland at one stage and then with later contractions and re-advances, the ice affected progressively less of the country. This ice movement and the associated meltwaters are responsible for most of the detailed features which dominate the valleys through which the salmon rivers flow. The high corries of the upper Spey, the loch-filled rock basins of the Ness, Tay and Awe and the steep-sided, flat bottomed valleys of the Conon and Beauly are all evidence of the erosive gouging and plucking of the ice. All this material had to be transported and deposited somewhere else and once again most of the river valleys show evidence of this aspect of glaciation. The retreating glaciers dumped large piles of angular fragments in the form of 'moraines' which often stretched right across the valleys and sometimes formed dams for melt-water lakes. Other debris has been moved and sorted by melt-water streams to form long linear ridges of gravel called 'eskers', or mounds known as 'kames'. Many lower valleys are littered with these features. Variations in post-glacial sea level have left river terraces representing former flood-plains, perched high above the present river levels. These are particularly evident on the Findhorn, Spey and Tay while ice-dammed lakes have left ancient shorelines in Glen Spean and in the 'Parallel Roads' of Glen Roy.

Within these channels of eroded bedrock or deposited gravel runs the water itself, always different in colour, clarity, height and speed. Each day, each hour brings some subtle change in the water or in the reflected sky from where it comes.

The Weather This restless sky is the result of Scotland's position in the battleground between the warm air of the Tropics and the cold polar air from the Arctic; between the moist air of the Atlantic Ocean and the dry winds of continental Europe. Four characteristic air masses affect the Scottish weather. The cool moist polar maritime air mass moves from its source in the North Atlantic on north-westerly winds and, becoming unstable over the Gulf Stream, sets off big showery cumulus and cumulo-nimbus clouds in an otherwise clear sky. From the other direction comes the warm, moist tropical maritime air from the region of the Azores. Cooling and stabilising as it moves from the south-west this usually gives rise to mild, muggy conditions of low stratus clouds, hill fog and drizzle – the apocryphal 'scotch mist' and 'smirr' of rain.

Where these two maritime air masses meet along the Polar Front, a series of warm-sector depressions develop and Scotland's changeable weather can often be analysed as a progression of wet, warm fronts; mild, dry warm-sectors followed by showery cold fronts in seemingly endless procession from the west.

Glen Lyon, Perthshire. One in the net

Settled weather is not unknown in Scotland, when the dry continental air from Europe drifts over as an anticyclone, bringing cold snaps in winter and heatwaves in summer.

The sum total of all this frantic weather activity can be measured, as far as the angler is concerned, in terms of rainfall on the land and runoff to the rivers. Rainfall, or more correctly, precipitation – which includes snowfall – is extremely variable across Scotland. In the western mountains a peak of 5000mm contrasts with a low of 600mm on the east coast. Most of the precipitation on the west coast is in the form of rain from the moist south-westerly winds, lifting and condensing on the high mountain walls with rapid runoff into the characteristic spate rivers of the west coast. In the central and eastern parts of the Grampians by contrast much of the precipitation falls as snow which lies in many areas for more than 100 days in the year and may lie on the high tops of the Cairngorms all the year round. This snowmelt keeps water flowing in the Spey and the Dee well into the summer.

Of an estimated precipitation of 266 cubic metres per day some 66 cubic metres is lost in evaporation and transpiration by vegetation, leaving a mean runoff of 200 cubic metres a day for the rivers. However apart from the salmon fisheries there are many other claimants for this water resource and the salmon rivers have had to adapt to the requirements of hydro-electric development and domestic water supplies.

Modern Developments Hydro-electric developments affect many Scottish salmon rivers mainly in the more remote parts of Scotland in such catchment areas as the Shin, Conon, Beauly, Ness, Awe and Tay. Water supply reservoirs are located closer to the populated areas and although there are numerous impoundments on smaller rivers and in the upland gathering grounds, the main salmon river affected by water supply abstraction is the Tweed. Here, in the headwaters in the Tweedsmuir Hills, the twin reservoirs of Talla and Fruid will soon be joined by the even larger Megget reservoir.

The principal effect of both types of impoundment is to limit access to the headwaters for spawning and for nursery areas. In many cases extensive spawning areas have been flooded by the impounded water and in some cases the dams themselves form a complete barrier or at least a significant deterrent to upstream migrants. In most cases the hydro-electric boards have mitigated the damage to fisheries by installing fish-passes on the main dams and establishing hatcheries to compensate for the loss of natural spawning. Nevertheless, the schemes have changed the character of many river regimes and have affected the salmon populations of individual catchment areas.

Two other problems have a significant effect on Scotland's salmon rivers – pollution and afforestation. The worst of the pollution is now confined to the rivers of the Central Lowlands particularly the lower Clyde and the Forth estuary. Pollution in the Clyde still presents an effective barrier to migratory fish but in the Forth the patches of heavier pollution can be negotiated to allow fish into the upper Forth and the Teith. The most

Before the hydro boards – the Tummel as it was,
from an original drawing by JD Harding

significant pollution outside the Central Lowlands occurs in the Aberdeenshire Don, where determined efforts by the North East Rivers Purification Board are improving the condition of the lower river.

Our awareness of the problems caused by large scale afforestation has only recently developed. The two basic problems lie firstly, in the initial drainage and planting and, secondly, in the establishment of a mature forest. The initial draining of the peat cover of many upland slopes increases run off and erosion, causing flash-floods and siltation of holding pools and spawning gravels. The vast sponge of peat, which absorbs the downpours and releases it gradually into the rivers, is destroyed and rivers rise and fall more rapidly. A mature forest on the other hand increases transpiration through its roots and leaves and thus allows less runoff back to the rivers. If the trees are planted too close to the river banks, a canopy of evergreen branches can reduce the light reaching the water and can seriously reduce the food production of nursery streams.

These then are the rivers – their origins, their nature and their problems. They form a resource which is as valuable and interesting as it is beautiful – a fitting habitat for the salmon.

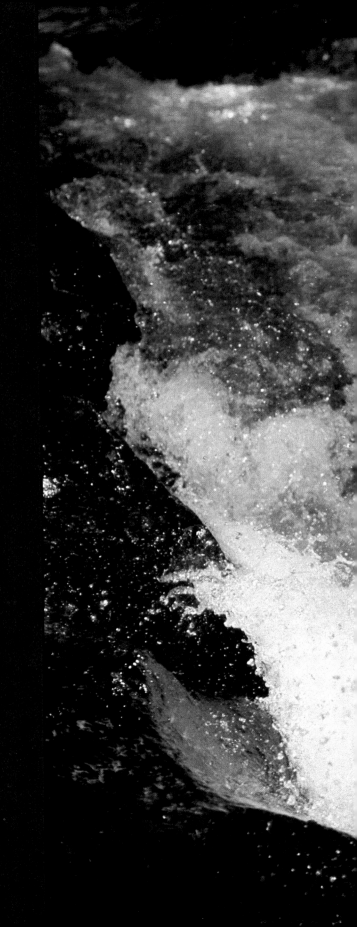

The Life Cycle of the Atlantic Salmon

But at recurring intervals, say three to five minutes, each female would suddenly fling
herself flat on her silvery broadside, usually athwart the stream, and thereupon
followed a sort of convulsive spasm, her whole frame writhing as if in agony,
while her tail, lashing out in vertical strokes, sent the water flying in spray.
ABEL CHAPMAN

SCENES such as those described by Abel Chapman may be found in the headwaters of many rivers from October to January as the Atlantic salmon (*Salmo salar*) gather on the spawning grounds. A suitable spawning area has certain physical requirements. The gravel must be of a size which allows it to be moved by the salmon and must provide a free flow of water through the incubating spawn. It must be free of fine sediment which would clog up the interstices between the stones and reduce the flow. The water itself must be clean and must flow at a speed which is sufficient to provide adequate circulation yet not so fast as to wash away the gravel or spawn. These physical conditions restrict the areas which are suitable for salmon spawning and in any river system there are usually well-defined spawning gravels which are favoured by the fish.

The eggs are laid in a hollow in the gravel, called a 'redd', which is scooped out by the female fish. Each hen fish will produce between 500 and 800 eggs for each pound of her body weight so that a 10 lbs salmon should lay something in the order of 5000 to 8000 eggs. As the eggs are being laid by the female they are fertilised by the 'milt' shed by the male lying alongside. After spawning the eggs are covered with gravel and the spent adult fish are known as 'kelts'.

Although death is not the inevitable result of spawning, as it is in the case of the Pacific salmon, many kelts, particularly the males, do not survive to make the downstream journey to the sea. Observations on the Conon river system suggest that something between 20% and 36% of the upstream run eventually returns downstream as kelts. Once they have reached the sea the kelts are still liable to be eaten by seals, but they have at least the opportunity to regain their condition and to make another spawning run at a future date. Those fish which are spawning for a second time form a variable proportion of the upstream run but figures of between 3% and 6% have been recorded. The oldest known Scottish salmon came from Loch Maree. It had spawned four times and was 13 years old.

New Life The eggs hatch in the Spring to form the next stage of the life cycle, the 'alevin', with a yolk sac attached to its underside. The alevin remains in the gravel until its yolk sac is used up when it emerges as a 'fry' into the nursery stream some four weeks later. This is a period of very high mortality due to predation, starvation and competition for space and it is estimated that less than 10% of the eggs survive to become viable fry. The fry stage lasts for about a year during which time the fish grow until they can be called 'parr'. As a parr the fish remains feeding and growing in freshwater until it is two or three years old and has attained a size of between 10 and 15cm. In the early summer of the second or third year the parr assumes a silvery coat and migrates downstream to the sea as a 'smolt'. This smolt migration generally takes place during May and June and is again a time of high mortality. Fish-eating birds such as the goosander, merganser and cormorant take their toll while predator fish from pike to cod also feed on the smolts in the river and in the sea.

Previous page and below: Leaping salmon returning from the sea

Once in the sea the smolt population appears to divide into two sections. One section remains in inshore waters while the other section starts out on the deep sea migrations for which the salmon is famous. Both sections however feed voraciously on plankton, sprats and sand–eels and grow from smolts of a few ounces to about 5 lbs during the first year at sea. That section of the smolt population which remains in inshore waters returns to the river the following summer as 'grilse'. The average weight of the grilse is around 5 lbs but it is sexually mature and contributes to the spawning stock one year after leaving the river.

The other section of the smolt population will remain in the sea for more than one winter, increasing in weight by about 5 lbs each year and will return to freshwater as 'salmon' proper. Tagging experiments have been carried out on Scottish rivers for many years and indicate that one of the main feeding grounds during this marine phase lies off the south-east coast of Greenland. The salmon will return to freshwater at weights of up to 80 lbs and there is even a legendary report of a fish of more than 100 lbs being caught in the Forth.

Sperm being ejected from an adult male salmon onto eggs to fertilise them

Opposite: Note how the fish on the right has been injured by a net on entering the river
Inset: Sea lice on a fresh run salmon

Both salmon and grilse exhibit a distinct homing tendency and usually return to the river from which they departed as smolts. There are records of fish which have been found in rivers other than their parent stream but it is a general rule that they return to the river of their origin.

When the homing fish return on their spawning run they become the quarry of the angler. They enter the rivers fresh from the sea, silver in colour, with sea-lice on their flanks and full of the strength of their sea feeding. These 'fresh-run' fish represent the cream of the angling. As they approach the rivers the salmon cease to feed and rely on their store of energy to sustain their upstream journey. This poses the controversial

question as to why a salmon takes an angler's lure. There are probably as many theories for this as there are anglers, but, suffice to say, that while all the evidence points to the fact that salmon do not feed in freshwater they can be induced to eat or attack a worm, an artificial fly or an imitation fish.

After some time in fresh water, salmon gradually lose their silvery colour and the rigours of the upstream journey sap their condition. Towards the end of the summer the males grow red in colour and develop hooked underjaws called 'kypes'. The females grow dark and almost black as spawning approaches and the flesh grows soft, pale and barely edible. By the time spawning takes place the fish are a shadow of their former selves. They are scarred, discoloured, often diseased with their fins ragged and torn. The final act of spawning is often fatal and those that survive may not make it all the way downstream to the sea.

Salmon Runs There are salmon running up some Scottish river throughout the year but each river tends to have its own characteristic patterns of movement. There are already salmon in Loch Tay and Loch Ness by the opening day of their angling season on 15 January. These would have had to leave the sea some time previously. There are still salmon running the Tweed and Nith at the end of their angling season on 30 November. Thus each river has its own dates for the start and finish of the fishing season which reflect the movements of the salmon. Even during the close season some salmon still move upstream. A study of the close season migrants on the South Esk in Angus showed that half the salmon were late arrivals which would spawn that winter and the other half were early fish of the next year which would not spawn until the following winter. Although there is considerable overlap, three main runs can be identified: the spring run, the summer run and the autumn run.

The spring run usually lasts from January until May and traditionally represents the best of Scottish salmon angling. Typically these are large two and three sea–winter fish although there is considerable variation between rivers. The spring run is characteristic of most east coast rivers from the Tweed to the Helmsdale and extends around the north coast to the Naver. There are fewer spring fish on the west coast although some are found in the Ewe, the Lochy and the Leven leading from Loch Lomond and are further recorded in some Ayrshire and Solway rivers. While the Tay and the Ness may have spring salmon throughout their length by opening day other rivers may have them confined to their lower reaches. A water temperature of 42°F is thought to be critical before salmon will ascend certain obstacles such as weirs or cruive dykes to continue their upstream journey. There are thus on certain rivers well defined 'temperature pools' beyond which salmon will not pass until the critical temperature is exceeded. There is strong evidence that there has been a cyclical decline in the numbers of spring salmon in favour of an increase in the size of the summer run.

Salmon and Brown Trout, by HL Rolfe

A summer run of salmon is common to all the Scottish salmon rivers. This run will last from June to August although the actual timing will vary from river to river and from year to year. The upstream movement of fish is triggered off by various factors of which water level is one of the most important. The so-called 'spate' rivers of the west coast are particularly sensitive to water level and invariably require a freshet to induce the fish to run.

The upstream movement of the grilse also occurs in summer. They are more regular in their habits and are less dependent on high water levels. The grilse run starts in June, reaches a peak in July and August and tails off through September.

The autumn run is again a feature of many rivers and a marked movement of salmon can be detected in September and October, while in the Tweed and the Nith a later run continues through November and into December. In the latter river a run of very large salmon known locally as 'greybacks' extends the angling season to the end of November.

However, regardless of the date when the fish leave the sea, by the time the winds have stripped the leaves from the trees and the frosts have gripped the upland moors, a keen observer may see, like Abel Chapman:

Broad brown backs clove the torrent, each adorned with a dorsal fin as a gaff topsail, while the flukes of great shovel-like tails sheered to and fro athwart the current . . . .

– the salmon are spawning.

Scottish Law and the Salmon

Flashlight photograph of a gang of salmon poachers in the act

THE salmon is, in effect, the only fish protected by law in Scotland. Within recent times an effort has been made to confer a measure of protection on the brown trout in some specified areas, but this is a very modern development, and applies only to areas in connection with which the Secretary of State for Scotland has made specific orders. For practical purposes the sea trout is linked with the salmon under the general description of 'migratory fish'.

For some years it has been recognised that there is a need to up–date legislation affecting game fish and particularly salmon in Scotland. The current situation is that the Salmon Fisheries (Scotland) Acts of 1862 and 1868 form the basis of Scottish fisheries administration. These Acts established a system of district boards thus providing a local administration for the protection of salmon fisheries. More recent legislation in the form of the Salmon and Freshwater Fisheries (Protection) (Scotland) Act 1951 revised and updated the law on poaching, and the Freshwater and Salmon Fisheries (Scotland) Act 1976 also updated penalties for offences for enactments relating to salmon and other freshwater fisheries. It was this Act which made provision for the possibility of statutory protection of trout in an area where riparian proprietors and others in a position to do so were prepared to offer increased access to trout anglers. This Act again updated penalties for offences against enactments relating to salmon fisheries.

Because of their geographical locations some essentially Scottish rivers have special legislation outside the district boards. The Tweed and Solway Firth are cases in point. The Tweed is governed by the Tweed Fisheries Acts of 1857 and 1859. The Border Esk, although it runs for most of its course through Scotland, falls under the jurisdiction of English legislation.

There is a very great number of rivers and lochs in Scotland and its neighbouring islands and estimates of that number vary considerably. Not all of them have their own district boards, but there are 107 boards, all of which fix their own annual close time for rod fishing and for netting, and lay down rules prohibiting the taking of immature salmon (fish which have not spent at least one period in the sea), poaching and so forth. These boards in most cases are comprised of representatives of proprietors of salmon fisheries in each district. In districts in which boards have not been formed, the salmon fisheries are under the direct control of the proprietors.

Policing the rivers and lochs is very largely a matter for bailiffs who are the servants of the district boards or of individual proprietors, aided by the civil police force where possible – often a matter of some difficulty in the more remote and sparsely populated regions. Bailiffs on salmon rivers have powers of arrest, unlike the wardens who are expected to exercise control over trout fishing in areas for which a protection order has been made. Equipment used in poaching of any kind may be confiscated and fines for the offence have been stepped up steeply in recent years, although the proprietors maintain that they have failed to keep pace with the enhanced value of the fish.

With district boards empowered to lay down close seasons for both netting and angling it is well for the early season angler to check opening dates for the areas he intends to visit. Very generally it will be found that a majority of boards lay down the rule that November to some date in February is to be considered the close season for rods (10 February is very frequently adopted as the final day of the close season). There are exceptions to this general rule, some rivers prohibiting fishing until 15 February, such as the Esk; in West Harris the general opening day is 25 February, whereas on the Brora the close season extends from 16 October to 31 January, and on the Conon it is from 1 October to 25 January.

There is a wide measure of agreement that the basic legislation covering salmon fishing both by nets and rods is well overdue for revision and bringing up to date. Successive governments have acknowledged the necessity for this action, and a number of enquiries have been instituted and consultations with interested parties initiated. The Department of the Secretary of State for Scotland has played an active part in these matters, and readily admits that with much of the law relating to the administration of salmon and freshwater fisheries dating back over 100 years changes are long overdue. The need for change was emphasised by the Hunter Committee which made a long and very detailed inquiry which resulted in a voluminous report as long ago as 1965, but for various reasons, not least the complexity of the many issues involved (the Hunter Committee made no fewer than 127 main recommendations), no substantial changes have yet taken place. Practically the only one of any moment so far as salmon are concerned has been the prohibition of drift-net fishing for salmon in Scottish waters, but this lost much of its desired effect because no similar prohibition applied to such fishing in adjacent English waters. The Freshwater and Salmon Fisheries (Scotland) Act 1976 dealt with only a very limited part of the whole matter of the Hunter Report – the protection and access to trout and freshwater fishings for the most part.

A position has been reached at which the Conservative Government in 1971 published proposals in a White Paper for comprehensive legislation and these have been brought forward again by the present administration. The proposals still being discussed were presented as an integrated scheme designed to open the way to the general improvement of the Scottish fisheries and their administration. Fundamental to these proposals was the proposition that there should be a more up-to-date and more flexible system of local administration. It was recognised that the district boards existed for fewer than half of the salmon fishery districts and were solely dependent for revenue on their members – proprietors of salmon fishings. They have very limited powers in relation to salmon fishing and no real powers or functions in relation to brown trout and other freshwater fisheries.

New factors which have arisen since the issue of the White Paper have emphasised the need for a fisheries administration to replace the district boards with area boards with much wider powers. They would be fewer in number and cover much wider areas than the present boards. They would be responsible for salmon, trout and freshwater fisheries and possibly also for fish farming, and would be constituted on a wider membership basis.

Both the Hunter Committee and the White Paper endorsed the principle that in the interest of the conservation of stocks, salmon should be exploited in or near their rivers of origin rather than at sea. It was recognised that some difficulty might be encountered in changing on a broad basis, especially in estuaries and rivers, commercial netting and trapping practices and in the context of improved management more flexible arrangements were envisaged for changing weekly close times and the introduction of controls on the extent of commercial netting by means of a licensing system.

So far as initial thinking is concerned, the aim appears to be to create about 14 area boards to cover the mainland of Scotland and the islands. There is some support for the idea of having a more limited number of boards with areas broadly co-terminous with those of the existing river purification boards on the mainland and separate arrangements for the Western Isles and Orkney and Shetland. This would involve a total of seven mainland boards.

It is recognised that it is important that the size and functions of an area board should be matched by its ability to be self-supporting from the revenues it would be able to secure. Present thinking is that the boards should obtain their revenue from salmon and trout fishery rates and from fees for local rod and net licences. It is also believed that in their early days the funds would need to be supplemented by Exchequer grants to help the boards become established.

At present, Scotland is unusual in that it does not operate a system of rod licence charges, but it is a practical certainty that the impending new legislation will introduce one and that the boards would retain the new rod and net licence fees applicable to their areas. This is felt to be more desirable than an earlier suggestion that there should be a national licence with the pooling of funds and later distribution to boards in accord with their needs.

Flies and Tackle

William Hardy bringing a fine Tay salmon ashore from the
Wash House Pool on the Pitlochrie Beat

THERE are people fishing today – not by any means in the prime of their youth – who would have fished regularly with greenheart rods, mighty, willowy and very, very heavy. They were muscular in those days; not many of us now would happily stand up to the punishment. Tales are still told of kilted gillies fishing them single-handed; they probably went and tossed cabers on Sundays. Greenhearts were followed by the beautiful split cane rods, light as thistledown by comparison, but not all that light when contrasted to the rods that followed them. Many people still stick to split cane – or built-cane as they became known when made with modern glues – and those who have preserved good split cane rods by good makers have an appreciating asset in their cupboards.

The market was gradually taken over by the far cheaper and vastly improved fibre-glass rods, efficient, light and easy to handle but without the cachet of split cane. They tended to be constructed in brash colours; the line did not run so musically between the rings. It was the difference between the Rolls and the cheaper car – but both would take you to your destination. As they became lighter, salmon rods have tended to become longer, particularly in Scotland where many of the rivers are wide. The standard fibre-glass fly rod is between 13 and 15 ft, and in competent hands will serve nicely on any river. One of the interesting contrasts between American and English game fishermen is demonstrated in the American determination to fish with little wands (they call them poles) no taller than themselves. One or two American anglers, shying from our 14 footers, have performed prodigies on even the big rivers, but they would be impotent on, for example, the Spey with the normal Spey upstream wind; that not only demands power but a steadfast character and an even temper.

The apogee seems to have been reached in the lofty shape of the carbon fibre rod – very supple, extremely light and, despite its apparent frailty, capable of adding another 5 yards to an average cast (all salmon fishermen, wherever they are fishing are convinced that their prey is lying 10 yards beyond their most majestic cast). Carbon fibre rods are very expensive and until recently I fished happily with my 13 ft 3 inch fibre glass rod made cheaply by a small and highly efficient firm in Huntingdon, with my heavier Sharpes built cane Aberdeen lying in reserve in the back of the car. Most carbon fibre rods are particularly well suited to Spey casting.

There are lots of very good spinning rods in fibre glass, which are also most reasonably priced. There are also some powerful carbon fibre spinning rods for the early cold-and-heavy-water spinning. Again the price is formidable but the performance is superb.

The Reels, the Gut and the Nylon. The pageant of fishing tackle has moved fast in the last 80 years when it comes to the mechanics of fishing (the reel) and the sinews (the line). Fly reels have changed little, nor have they improved much. Theirs is a straightforward job, but a very responsible one. A reel that jams, spells total disaster. Spinning reels used

Megan Boyd MBE of Brora, Sutherland, known internationally
for her fly-tying

to be centre-pin reels like the fly reels but lightly made and beautifully fashioned. The flick of a finger would get one revolving like a dynamo. Genuine skill was needed to cast baits any distance unless they were heavily weighted. Some of the over-runs from a badly timed cast could produce 'birds' nests' of such disastrous complexity that the only thing was to cut off the line and start again. The tackle industry has always excelled in stylish packaging. Some of the early reels in their leather cases with the owners' initials stamped on (free) in gold have become real treasures.

Lines came in all sizes and weaves but were mainly silk, untreated for spinning, plaited and enamelled for fly fishing. Those were the halcyon days of the Kingfisher lines, now alas unobtainable, victims of advanced technology. When new they smelt deliciously of turpentine and honey. Because of their finish, they were a joy to use, but at the end of a day's fishing they had to be taken off the reel and dried.

The advent of the plastic lines, which float or sink slowly or sink faster than a stone, has added further problems to the many that beset, burden, perplex and distract the salmon fisherman. At certain times of the year the salmon take the fly at surface level, particularly when water temperatures are 50°F or more. The rule is not absolute and a high swimming fly attached to a floating line catches fish when the water is colder. In the early cold-water fishing the fly should be fished as low as possible. For this, sinking lines are necessary and they are pretty horrible to fish. Casting a floater is easy and relaxed; sunk line techniques are more demanding. In the middle of the season (depending on the weather) the wretched angler faces problems not only of the choice of fly and its size, but also whether to fish it with floating or sunk line. The Kingfisher lines made this problem easier to solve. If you caught fish on them when they were greased, you greased them afresh when they started to sink. Otherwise, the floating line turned quietly into a sinking one. The various lines can be put on interchangeable drums which are alternated by the increasingly unsuccessful fisherman.

Spinning lures have remained quite constant in shape and artistic ingenuity – colourful steel fish and flashing spoons still circulate through pools as they did at the beginning of the century in shapes and colours unknown to nature. Developments in line have, however, given scope for smaller and lighter (eg wooden) baits. But the major development, and without doubt the most significant, was the arrival of nylon; nylon in breaking strains ranging over many pounds, cheap and becoming finer in diameter year by year. By comparison the old gut casts or leaders, or the old thread lines, were clumsy and unreliable. A fishing friend suggested that his wife would please him if she gave him a hundred yards of 20 lbs breaking strain nylon as a modest birthday present. It was so cheap that she returned with a small spool that contained 500 yards. He is still wondering what he can tactfully do with it all.

The arrival of the thin strong nylon was the spur that led inevitably to the fixed spool spinning reel, the reel that revolutionised every kind of fishing and salmon fishing in

Opposite top left: Salmon flies past and present. The treble-hooked
flies are tied by Arthur Oglesby
Right: An assortment of spoons and baits
Bottom: Hardy rods in the making

particular. With such a reel the act (and I, carefully nursing my small prejudices, avoid the word art) of casting can be picked up by anyone of reasonable intelligence in half an hour. Bright people can become masters in half the time. The fixed spool reel has made the distant parts of any pool vulnerable to the novice. It has also converted thousands of less persevering people who might have been daunted by the higher skills needed for fly fishing (and possibly the lower success rate) into supplicants for salmon beats, and has thus contributed notably to the rents that landlords can obtain from a market in which demand exceeds supply. To be fair, it has also opened up the pleasures of the salmon river banks to those who might never have enjoyed them. If my illogical prejudice against spinning as a wholetime occupation is too obvious, it should be appreciated that I do not, myself, enjoy doing it and am an unbelievably incompetent practitioner. In between the old reels and the new are the multipliers which are still used, with panache, by spinning purists.

The Flies These deserve space of their own as well as illustrations. There are more flies, by many thousands, in fly boxes than will ever be cast into rivers. Every fly fisher has his box – or boxes – crammed with his beloved toys, tied for this time or that, this temperature or that temperature. Many of us started our fishing lives with the sensible theory that an all purpose fly like the Hairy Mary, in various sizes, is all that is needed. Then we are lent a fly that is different in every way and it takes a fish with the first cast. Or a tackle dealer whispers – 'No real salmon fisherman can afford to be without a General Practitioner'. Or an expert, known for his huge catches, whispers out of the side of his mouth (as if it were a Stock Exchange tip) 'try a Copper'. Then the Munro Killer (perhaps because of the length of its tail) is said to be irresistible to Spey salmon. Or the pundit cries 'In the colour of our water, the Thunder and Lightning has four times the chance of any other fly'. And on Arndilly they debate at length the choice likely to be most irresistible and usually end the debate by picking out the Arndilly Fancy, a yellow and blue fly that catches more fish than any other on that lovely stretch of fishing. It is just possible that the reason is that it is used more than any other fly – but it will be clear already why the fly boxes become full and confusing.

When fishermen were fewer and labour was cheap, the flies were tied, as works of art, to strict specifications using particular, often rare, feathers and dyes. There was an estate in the north of Scotland at which there was perfected a mutation in the colouring of turkey feathers which resulted in their Jock Scotts acquiring a delicate silvery stripe, which was, I am sure, noted with pleasure by eagle-eyed fish. I would still take some convincing that my universal Hairy Marys would fail me – but who am I to write a contrary opinion with three fly boxes teeming with every known Fancy, Special, Ranger and Killer in every imaginable size? Modern flies, tied with much less attention to complex colour and detail do the job very adequately, if without the same glamour.

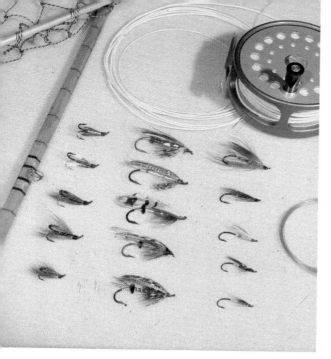
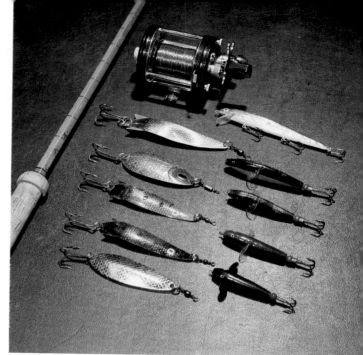

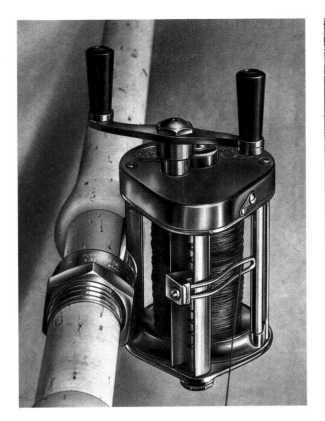

The Rest of the Gear Game fishing has never acquired the top hat, scarlet coat and shiny boot fetiches of the horse world. There is a suspicion of pressure on the more important beats to be seen in tweed breeches, stockings and brogues, but when the waders go on we all look alike. Bright shirts and luminous caps are discouraged, because the more sensitive fish react to them by moving to the upstream beat. The fishing hat has some importance. A degree of eccentricity is permitted and the witty, macabre or original hat (provided that it is not unlucky) is gently encouraged. It should not, of course, look too new or risk being described as 'smart'. Hats can be made to look mature and well-worn in a number of ways, like a night in the dog kennel or a week on the floor in the back of a car. Ear flaps are discouraged except in the coldest weather, not only on aesthetic grounds, but also to discourage tragedies among Aberdeenshire gillies whose ear flaps deafened them to the offer of a dram.

Landing nets, tailers and even gaffs are optional extras, but many salmon fishermen pride themselves on landing their fish without these aids.

Opposite left: Multiplying reel for spinning
Right: Hardy Brothers' Pall Mall shop, as it used to be
Bottom: Esmond Drury hook salmon flies

Below: A selection of hooks (actual size) and the famous
AHE Wood's split cane salmon rod

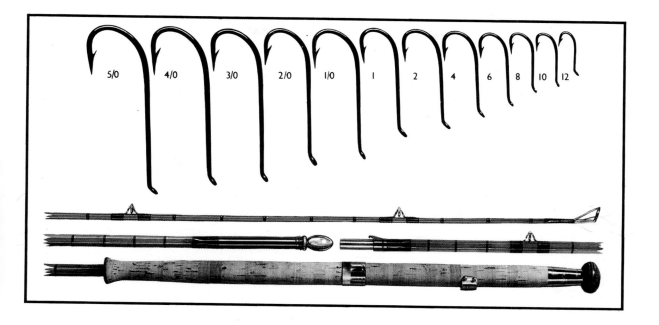

What to Bring It is not possible to be categoric about what tackle to bring. Much depends on the time of the year and the size of the river – and there are no unbendable rules in salmon fishing. Too many times have I been outfished by people whose rod is too small or whose flies seem too large. It is provident to bring spinning as well as fly fishing tackle to make sure that fishing is possible in nearly all circumstances. Chest waders normally prove more useful than thigh waders and a selection of clothing that keeps out Scottish rain can prevent a great deal of misery.

In case it is necessary to buy tackle (and locally tied flies give one a prime feeling of confidence) there should be no difficulty. In the game fishing areas, every small town and nearly every village has its tackle supplier. At Craigellachie, for instance, at the village shop, rods, reels and flies nestle among the groceries, shoes, magazines and clothing. Furthermore, Mr Ironside, a fisherman himself, can detect the river level from his door and can give instant advice as to the day's best flies or baits. In fact, within 2 miles of Mr Ironside's establishment, at Aberlour is a tackle and sporting goods shop, soberly named Munro's. Mr Morrison has it now, but it was from behind those counters that the great Munro himself sold his Munro Killer, a fly that has caught thousands of salmon – and not just on the Spey. These little shops are much of a pattern and nearly all are good. For those seeking a wider choice, Hardy's have their shop (a kind of fishing Mecca) in Pall Mall in London and, in Scotland, Sharpes of Aberdeen (swallowed into a larger empire, officially Farlows but still called Sharpes, whatever the new owners may wish) are invariably helpful and have a mass of tackle available. For further options, the monthly game fishing magazine *Trout and Salmon* carries page upon page of tackle advertising.

A new face on the Tay reflects the changes that have come over fishing in Scotland since Nasmyth painted his picture of salmon leistering

The Changing Scene

THAT the scene should ever change may seem impossible or blasphemous, or both, to those who give part of their souls to Scotland. And outwardly, indeed, the scene does not change. Those contrasting countrysides, from the rich and rolling Lowlands to the stern majestic Highlands, will remain true to themselves as long as Atlantic weather lasts. Centuries turn, times alter, but still the heather glows purple in high summer; in its surrounding vastness the grouse call 'Go-back, go-back', and stags roar from the corries to herald autumn; storm and sunshine chase each other down the glens; and still the greatest of game fish run the rivers. This changelessness, the certainty of returning to find all the same as it ever was, comes as comfort when our stay is over, and motorway or mail train bear us south to those other worlds from which we have taken refuge. We all know the feeling.

We all know, too, that under the surface things have changed greatly, and that the changes have not ended yet. They have not varied the pleasures which we seek in Scotland, but they have varied very greatly the basis on which we find them. Comparison of past and present enables us to assess the future at least in part, and to understand the realities which will govern participation in future salmon fishing.

Paradoxically, the sport ranked both as fringe benefit and sole activity in the two centuries which separated the battle of Culloden from our own day. Only after Culloden were the Highlands opened to travellers; previously the clans had the country to themselves; their endless and doubtless locally enjoyable in-fighting transcended class distinctions, business interests, and all else except the ties of blood. Nobody expected then, or for the next 200 years, to become rich in Scotland. Richness, a strange ambition to a proud and self-sufficient people, was for foreigners; any Scots wishing to indulge in it had to go elsewhere, and indeed did, spreading themselves around the world. At home, where Robbie Burns was enshrining the principle that 'a man's a man for a'that', life was to be enjoyed, however frugal. Each was his own master, however small or great his lot, and there lie the roots of today's traditions.

Returning Scots, their prosperity self-evident, were regarded with admiration or amusement, but never with envy. Well-endowed Sassenachs and other foreigners were tolerated, even welcomed, so long as they behaved themselves. This meant adopting a relaxed and courteous attitude which chimed with that of stay-at-home Scots. Not for nothing was an English gentleman defined as one who, on opening a bottle of whisky, threw the cork on the fire.

The Arrival of Technology Eternal graces survive. But rural Scotland, which for so long existed unconscious of wealth, is now involved in wealth-creation. Technology, by vastly extending the art of the possible, has brought this about, beginning with mechanisation on the land and ending with that valued but distrusted entity 'the oil'. Remote though they may seem, the visible signs of both are but a fraction of what is happening to

Scottish salmon fishing. Like all else, it has become subject to the creation of wealth.

The energy released on to the land from fossilised fuel has extended the exploitation of Scotland for stock-raising, crops and forestry far beyond the degree practicable when the only power available lay in the muscles of men and Clydesdale horses. Contour-ploughing has affected drainage (with consequent effect on fishing), opening up for cultivation areas which previously existed as a kind of sponge, releasing gradually from bog and marshland the summer flow of rivers for which they were the catchment area. Tracked power units have enabled the tree-line to be lifted hundreds of feet uphill on moor and mountain, hastening the return of forestry to what had been open ground since the post-Culloden clearance of the old Caledonian Forest.

These developments have brought real but limited changes to the face of Scotland. The underlying effects have been less limited. Landowners, faced with encroachment on sporting assets, long taken for granted, have been impelled into realistic calculations of what those assets are worth in modern times. Simultaneously, and far away, changes in the face of other landscapes were having different effects, and creating massive new wealth. Destruction of natural environment in the United States had made the Atlantic salmon extinct in its rivers (attempts to rehabilitate the species there make slow progress). Industrialisation is causing similar though less advanced de-salmonisation in Scandinavia. Human populations grow richer in Western Europe; even more so in Japan. Africa's wildlife, and the recreations dependent on it, decline. Travel to and from the ends of the earth has become easier and more habitual for those lacking sporting opportunities at home.

The end-products of these cumulative trends are, first, that the defence of such a natural resource as salmon fishing in Scotland against pressures of agriculture, forestry and industry becomes an expensive business, and the cost must be recouped; second, that a world-wide community of deprived sportsmen has been built up, with immense purchasing power; third, that Scottish sport becomes an internationally negotiable commodity; fourth, that though the Englishman in Scotland undoubtedly has a special relationship, he no longer necessarily has priority, let alone a sole claim to the sport available there, but must bid against all comers. Simultaneously 'the oil', and the heightened standards of living to which it is accustoming the lonely communities of the North, has caused a general rise in expectations, while punitive taxation causes landowners to take the cash and let some assets go.

So the elements of supply and demand are now very different from what they were in those traditional days of simple deals between laird and tenant. Then the laird assented, the financial details were settled by his factor (or, in the case of a duke, by his chamberlain), and the tenant enjoyed the results. No other person was involved.

The key-note of the post-war world has been development. He who develops best, in the end owns most. And the developers have moved into Scottish salmon-fishing. The

Shoulder netting at Tongland on the Dee 1895

ownership of rivers, or rather of the rights to fish them, has become as much an investment as the ownership of any other profit-making security. It is also a safe one. The pressure of would-be fishermen on the mileage of available Scottish salmon fishing is enough to ensure prosperity for years to come for the lessor of rights.

In the United Kingdom and internationally alike, sporting habits become more flexible and less specialised. Sport itself being no longer home-based, the British pressure alone has increased on Scottish salmon-fishing. Many more Britons now fish for salmon than did so before World War II. For instance, two separate migrations of farmers to Highland rivers are now discernible. The first, in May and early June, comes when spring sowing is completed; the second, in September and October, follows harvest. Such farmers are mainly those on large acreages in the corn counties of East Anglia, Wessex, the Midlands and Yorkshire. Yet salmon fishing has only recently become a farmers' sport. Formerly, an East Anglian farmer would stick to shooting and a Midland farmer ride to hounds. Neither would be likely to think of salmon-fishing, and to go to Scotland was considered a major journey. Nowadays ease of travel has made it possible for everybody to do a bit of everything, and the upsurge of middle incomes has brought salmon fishing within reach

Pens used for salmon farming in the Hebrides

of more people. Airline pilots and oil rig engineers now form a recognisable and substantial new element in Scotland's angling community.

The Advent of Big Business Likewise, the prestige of sport has made it a fringe benefit of big business. When taxation makes monetary subventions unreal above a certain level, sporting opportunities form an acceptable way of rewarding executives and paying compliments to influential customers. Financial and manufacturing undertakings in Britain and the United States now own salmon beats and grouse moors in Scotland. Their usefulness commercially is well proved. Their appreciating value makes the investment a sound one.

This is only one facet of the flow of foreign money into the Scottish sporting market. Swiss, Dutch, and Danish proprietors now own substantial salmon rights in the Highlands, together with the hotels which accommodate the fishing parties to whom they are let. The cash turnover is the attraction. Although salmon fishing is as yet less infiltrated by foreign money than grouse shooting and deer stalking, the fundamental fact is that Scotland has what the rest of the world wants and market factors force up prices.

Those who seek to find fishing must therefore go about the business in a different way, first recognising that it is in truth a business. In place of the time-honoured 'grapevine', which relayed semi-confidential information for those in the swim as to where good salmon water might be had, agencies now act as middlemen. Some, old-established, have updated themselves to meet modern conditions. Others have recently come into existence to provide a brokerage service for sports which, in a real sense, have joined Britain's invisible exports. Although most of the major estates continue to manage their own sporting lettings, the agencies in effect act in concert with them.

The result has been to remove much of the uncertainty and tension from the process of obtaining fishing on a rising market. The central fact remains that the market is not only rising, but is likely to continue to do so. Sometimes the agency structure is unfairly blamed for the escalation of rents. The truth is that the actual reasons are not all within human control.

First, in a period of world inflation salmon fishing cannot be excluded from its effects. Second, varied factors external to the sport have reduced the amount of good class water available while, for the reasons stated, the number of would-be participants continues to increase. These factors have included diminished numbers of salmon due to interception at sea by the trawlers of several nations, loss of spawning grounds through the forestry and farming practices described and the intervention of other water sports, such as sailing and canoeing. Only third in the list is the influence of the fishery developer.

Although on a small scale, the development syndrome is as real in respect of fishing rights as it is in other aspects of the property business. The process is simple. Where a length of river has been allowed to run down – perhaps its banks are untended, its pools neglected, its lodge in ruins – a purchaser of the rights has room for manoeuvre. Bank maintenance can make the water fishable again; it can be made more attractive to running fish by improving pools and holding places; accommodation for fishermen and their families is often provided by another development operation on a local hotel. The ultimate benefit, of course, will not stop with the developer, but will extend upstream and perhaps downstream, and eventually improve the total image of salmon fishing in the area. What it cannot do is to reduce prices.

Escalating Prices There is therefore an upward spiral, but no sign yet that the sport is pricing itself out of its adherents' reach. What it is certainly doing is to make more fishermen more seriously aware of the desirability of offsetting, where they can, the continued upsurge. One of the ways of doing this is to sell the catch. Formerly this practice was deplored in theory, though more widely followed in practice than was generally admitted. The chief objection was that it removed salmon fishing from the realm of sport, in which the sportsman would judge when enough was enough, after which the fish he might have killed, but did not, would be spared either for somebody else to catch or to increase the reproductive potential of the river. Continuing to fish for as long as possible or allowable, and killing every possible fish in order to increase the saleable surplus, undoubtedly subordinates sport to commerce.

However, the element of commerce being already there, the practice now seems the less reprehensible for that reason. Moreover it is condoned, even encouraged, by some owners of fishing rights in the interests of safeguarding their investment value. Fishing rights are normally valued on the annual average catch from the water to which they apply. Tenants who, if only to recoup their rent by selling their catch, fish long and successfully also make the more impressive contributions to the game book, thereby helping to keep the average catch satisfactorily high from the landlord's viewpoint.

The Future In spite of commercial attractions and the rising cost of the sport of salmon fishing, a glimmer of hope persists. Thanks to prolonged pressure by sporting and commercial fishermen acting together, exercised chiefly through the Salmon and Trout Association, high seas netting of immature or returning salmon has been substantially reduced. Better understanding of the effects of farming and forestry practices is also spreading. But the brightest potential prospect for sporting salmon fishermen in the future lies, improbably as it may seem at first sight, in the commercial sea-farming of salmon in the Hebrides.

There, and in Norway and elsewhere, techniques have been developed for rearing salmon in large cages through the sea stage of their life cycle, eliminating the transatlantic migration with its losses, stresses and hazards. As experience accumulates and investment increases, the cost per artificially-produced salmon can be expected to drop – eventually to remove salmon from their position in the shops as second only to sturgeon among high priced luxury fish. If this happens the bottom would drop out of the market for netted fish, poached fish, or for sales of the catch. The free-running river salmon would then have two uses only, first as outcross breeding stock for the fish farms, secondly as a sporting quarry. Fishermen would again be able to rent or buy their chosen beat on the value of the sport it offers, instead of the value of its fish when dead, by whatever means.

So the changing scene may change again. Vicissitudes, unsought by fishermen to whom the salmon is more than a quarry, in fact almost the object of a love affair, have swept away the old time foundations of this glorious sport. The fact that salmon fishing has been recognised by so many as something of value, for no matter what motives, has saved it. Already a healthy prejudice grows against forms of fishing other than the fly, effect on the catch notwithstanding. If, as seems possible, salmon fishing's only future is to be as a sport, at least some of its commercial overtones will slip away. Then, inconceivable as it may now appear, even costs may be reduced. What is important is that its spirit is preserved in a manner fitting to Scotland as generations of fishermen have known it, and that future salmon fishing is worthy of its past.

The Rivers and Lochs

NORTH OF THE CALEDONIAN CANAL

This region, north of the Great Glen, takes in some of the most rugged and mountainous parts of Scotland. Amid all the grandeur, each glen, each strath, each fjord–like sea loch has its river or stream up which migrations of salmon and sea trout make their way. Here can be found rivers which contain fish in every month from February to October, some early, some late.

There follow detailed accounts of the region's major rivers – but there are many other rivers of varying importance for which there has not been space for detailed description; the Berriedale, for example, or in north Sutherland, the Naver, an excellent early river but with almost no public access. Then there is the Dionard, a top-class summer river – or below Lochinver, the Polly and its associated lochs. Nearby is the little Garvie, with Loch Oscaig for the dapping enthusiast. Then there is the Dundonnell, a little spate river made famous by *Muriel Foster's Fishing Diary*.

Down the coast to Gairloch can be found the Kerry and the Badachro. Even better is the Carron, another spate river – to say nothing of the Applecross, the Torridon, the Balgie, the Shiel and the Strathmore. Each of these fly-only rivers is capable of producing a memorable day, given the right rainfall. Without it they have little to commend them except the loveliness of their surroundings. None of the rivers that we now turn to is quite so speculative.

Opposite: Fishing on the Dionard

The Thurso

River: Thurso
Caithness
Season: 11 Jan–5 Oct
Best months: Aug
Fly only

The Thurso is one of the very few fortunate rivers, with rod catches in excess of 1,000 salmon per annum, which is controlled by one authority. Thurso Fisheries Ltd own the whole river system and, not only that, they also own the salmon nets as well.

This means that management decisions are made without reference to and discussion with individual proprietors, or even a co-operative of proprietors, as happens elsewhere. The consequences are exciting and those who know their Thurso will agree that it is a well managed and organised river under very capable control. Being a one unit river, owning its own hatchery with a capacity of 1½ million eggs, the proprietors can carry out experiments with the sole object of improving and developing the fishery. For make no mistake, Thurso Fisheries' policy is to open the river to the public and to make it financially viable for the estate. To be successful in that direction there must be good management and there is a superabundance of that on the Thurso.

A striking feature of this river is the dam at Loch More. When the loch is fully impounded, there is two month's supply of controlled river water. Around 1907 a dam was built at Dalnawillan some 30 miles upriver and another at Loch More 15 or 16 miles from the sea as the crow flies – both controlled by sluices. Since then the Thurso has 'fished' throughout droughts which have brought to a standstill other less endowed rivers. This large reservoir is only 300 ft above sea level, so with a fall of only 300 ft dissipated over an aggregate length of about 25 miles, there will be many very long stretches of slow-moving pools which, without a supply of water from the upper reaches, would put paid to anyone's chances of successful angling. So,

especially in the summer months, the dams provide an all-important spur to the success, or otherwise, of the angler.

Over the early part of the season, which opens on 11 January, the Loch More dam, in theory, should play no part in the fishing. But it does. Early salmon usually run quite hard up to Loch More but are stopped by the weir. They then fall back into the pools below, where a stock of spring fish can build up. Eventually they lodge in Loch Beg a little way further down the river. This is just a big round pool through which the river 'flows' – too big to be a pool in the accepted sense of the word – hence 'Loch Beg' (the small loch). But, as happened in the spring of 1979, there can sometimes be so much water in Loch More that it overflows the weir and salmon simply swim over the top, with Loch More having an early season.

Salmon are expected in the river in January but only the odd fresh fish will be caught that month. One of the determining factors will be meteorological. The river can be frozen over with no chance at all of a fish or, in a mild and wet winter it can be in continuous flood for weeks on end. In January there will be just a handful and where in 25 miles of river will winter anglers find even one in that waste of water, bearing in mind the lengthy canal-like pools? So it is a month for the local angler whose enthusiasm for a cast takes him from the fireside and out into winter with little prospect of coming across the first salmon of the season.

February is much the same; too few fish around to be worthwhile. The best February in recent years was in 1979 with 7 fish. But that was one of the mild winters as was 1977 with 6 salmon for the month. It is March before there is any serious fishing and it is then that we note the salmon's propensity for running right through the lower stretches to Beats 13 and 12. From January to April the top beats, especially the Bridge and Weed pools, account for a fair proportion of the early fish. The average catch for March is about 20 but this month has improved over the past few seasons with 39 in 1979 and 31 in 1978. Curiously, these catches were made in what were the severest winters the Highlands have had for many years. The conclusion is obvious – there were more spring fish about.

April is a good month. Sometimes over 100 salmon for the month are grassed but about 60 to 80 is the expectancy. May can be at parity with April and, from examination of the records, in the years when April is good so is May, but also vice versa. It would seem that if a run starts in April then it continues well into May. June is a funny month, as it is in all salmon rivers. The angler is either fishing over stale springers which may be caught if enlivened with fresh rain water or maybe over the grilse runs, coming a bit earlier than usual. It is also the month when the usefulness of the reservoirs begins to be demonstrated, for June is a notoriously dry month over the Highlands.

By July the grilse are on the move in their thousands. They peak in mid-month and between grilse and summer salmon the river takes on a new lease of life and the sport suddenly erupts. Well over 100 are caught but in July 1979, 232 was the total. August is easily the best month, as all the pools in all the beats are now well stocked with fish and, given the right conditions, the sport is fast and furious. In 1979, 346 fish were taken in August. Although the days are shorter, the September fish give good sport. In 1979 the catch was 256. There are still numbers of fresh-run fish going through the river. The first five days in October (the season ends on the 5th) are extraordinary. The fish are very keen to take and as many as 212 have been taken in those few days (1974). In 1979 only 46 were caught in spite of beautiful angling conditions: it is difficult to comprehend the vagaries of salmon.

The total annual catches have actually increased over the past few years. In 1979 it was 1,094 compared to 603 in 1978. Over the past decade 1972 was the best season with 1,262 fish so 1979 with over 1000 fish was a very satisfactory year.

So much for statistics. I wrote that the river was open to the public; that is not strictly so. There are 13 beats, but there is one beat which is kept entirely private. With this one exception, the beats are fished in rotation. Two rods are allowed to fish each beat and a party will fish the odd numbers over a week, and vice versa.

Beat 1 is down at Halkirk, 2 or 3 miles from the top of the tide and Beat 13 is the top beat from below Loch More. Beat 12 and Loch Beg go together. However, all beats can have a go at Loch More anytime they want to. Normally, anglers do not fish the loch until June. Fishing is from the bank, there being no boat. Even so, salmon can be caught from the bank on fly (it is a fly only river, including the loch) and the only reason the loch is

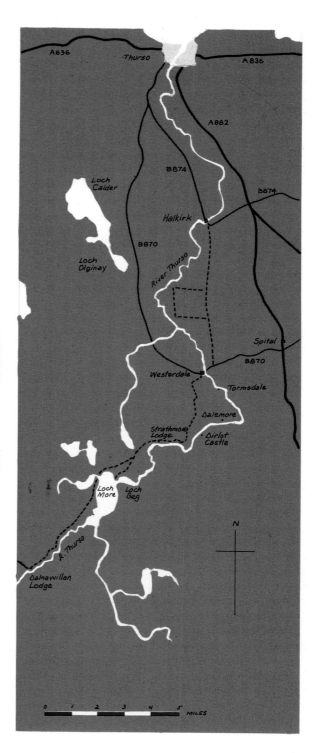

The dam at Loch More

not fished before June is because the best chances are in the river. However, as June is usually the doldrum month, the river sport can be lean and it is then anglers turn to that part of the system where they know salmon are probably in fairly large numbers.

I have mentioned the nature of the river and its very gradual descent to the sea. There are, then, these long, canal-like pools to fish and the way this is done is by 'backing up'. This method is emp-loyed mainly in the spring months but can be done all the year round. In the spring the angler selects, say, a large heavy 2½ or 3 inch tube fly dressed with yellow and black hair; starting at the bottom of his

stretch of the pool he casts it out as far as he can. After a moment to allow it to sink he recovers some line which he lets lie in a semi-loop rather loosely and walks upstream a few paces which causes the fly to progress across the pool. He will recover line as the fly approaches his bank, then will cast again some yards further on upriver. He will repeat this, progressing upstream until he either tires or comes to the top of the pool. It is my own experience that salmon like the fly worked this way. I have fished down a pool, in the spring, and raised nothing – then fished it again by backing, and had two or three fish. I believe the 'secret' is the hair wing of the tube working away and moving like a live thing

– a lively movement which attracts salmon. No matter the reason, it works. Until the end of April big tubes on a sinking line are used. The Tadpole, Black and Tan, Garry Dog and even the all black Collie Dog are the successful flies. I was rather surprised to learn that the big pools fish best with only 12 inches on the gauge. Looking at those enormous lengths of stillish water I had once thought very high water levels a must.

Later on when the water warms, the angler has the choice of a completely floating line or one with a sink tip. I favour the latter, but whatever kind of line is used, the flies for the summer have a common factor in that they should have a fair amount of

black hair for wings. The Stoats Tail, Tosh and other dark patterns such as the Hairy Mary are the most successful. The hook size will be 8 or 10 and only on occasion will a 6 be used. I favour the Esmund Drury trebles, but a double, dressed in the above patterns, will also do nicely. Naturally, individuals will have their own favourite flies but the ones I have listed are the most popular and thus the ones which the majority of salmon take.

How to get a beat is the final question. As with most good salmon rivers open to the public it is not easy to 'get in'. But one can apply to The Secretary, Thurso Fisheries Ltd, Thurso East, Thurso, Caithness. There is one condition of the lease and that is the lessee must stay in the Ulbster Arms Hotel, Halkirk, Caithness.

Big fish, in common with most other rivers everywhere in Scotland, are not so plentiful these days. The average weight of salmon is 9¾ lbs and grilse 6½ lbs. But, recently, the heaviest has been just 23 lbs; precious few manage to get over the 20 lbs mark.

The best individual rod catches, though, can be impressive. It requires a bit of luck – to be on the right beat on the right day and with the levels just perfect for that bit of water. When all those conditions coincide – it happened in 1979 when an angler grassed 15 salmon in one day – someone with this luck together with prowess as a salmon angler, can often get into double figures.

If the prospective visitor cannot get on to the main beats, the 2 miles of fishing from below Halkirk to the top of the tide should not be despised. It is association water and permits by the day are issued from AA MacDonald, Tackle Dealer, 23 Sinclair Street, Thurso, Caithness.

This beat can produce between 100 and 150 salmon per year. Although in the early months, with water temperatures barely above freezing, salmon are held back in these lower pools, the best time of all is, rather surprisingly, in June, July and August. But the criterion for good sport in this lower beat in the summer months is low water conditions. Then, the 'creepers' come in from the sea, scramble up above the tide and cannot go any further – hence the particularly good sport from this beat.

Non-members of the association can get a day ticket. Like the rest of the river system, it is fly only and the patterns, and sizes, described for the main river, also apply here.

63

The Halladale

River: Halladale
Sutherland
Season: 12 Jan–30 Sept
Best months: June–Sept
Fly only

If you drive up through Kildonan Strath following the course of the Helmsdale, across a watershed composed of bleak moor land, you come to Forsinard and the top end of the river Halladale. If the river is in spate you will think it may be an interesting little stream but, as you drive down Strath Halladale to Melvich, following the river, you will soon see on your left an uninspiring-looking canal-like river (I cannot refer to it as a stream) and you would be forgiven for assuming that it would not be worth bothering with. Yet you would be wrong. It has tremendous potential for salmon angling – far more than at first sight.

It is a Sutherland river and flows north, emptying into the Pentland Firth just like its neighbours, the Dionard, Borgie, Navar, Forss and Thurso. It rises in the peat moors not very far away from the source of the Thurso, but it has no big loch to reserve water; therefore it is a true spate river. It is probably about 20 miles long and tumbles down a rocky course near Forsinard, where it looks good in a spate, and then through the strath to the sea at the village of Melvich. More than half the angling stretch consists of slow flowing pools winding through semi-agricultural land.

The estuary is regarded as being from the road bridge at Melvich to the sea – a quarter mile or so – and this tidal water channels its way between sand banks and dunes. Just above the road bridge one will see a very uninteresting stretch of motionless looking water. It is visually uninteresting because, with all the sand banks in that area, the river had to be dredged in order that salmon and sea trout could gain easier access to the river proper. So this part, about 700 yards long, is not much good for angling.

The Halladale is very much a spate river, so the arrival of the first salmon of the year is related to water levels. There ought to be a good chance of a fish in early April and, as a matter of fact, the first of the 1980 season was taken in that month up on Beat 2 in the pool called Forsil. However, there is really not much of a spring run – only the odd fish. The best months will be June on to September and the sport can be excellent just so long as there is water. The season officially starts on 12 January, but this doesn't mean anything, and closes on 30 September. Water is vital for this river – no water, no fishing. With a good upstream north wind ruffling the deep but almost motionless pools, say in July or August, there is always a fair chance.

If there is a spate there will certainly be sport. Spates are short-lived. If heavy rain falls up in the moors and eventually raises the level, then the river will be peat stained and a whole day will be lost. But on the second day, if no more rain falls, angling will be at its best and will last for just two days.

The grilse and summer salmon will run after mid-June (rainfall permitting) and quite big runs will occur throughout July and August giving sport over September until the season closes. The average weight of salmon is quite small at about 7 or 8 lbs and one taken in 1979 which turned the scales at 12 lbs was regarded as being outstanding.

When conditions are perfect, angling can be prolific and this is when the river gives the lie to one's first impression. One angler had 11 salmon to his own rod in one day in 1979. The average catch for a reasonable (wet) year will be 200/300 salmon from the estate water and, in 1979 – a very wet year – it was over 400. These fish came from that apparently unpromising part of the river.

Looking up from the road bridge at Melvich and beyond the dredged stretch one can see the first pool on Beat 4. This is the Weeds – a good and productive pool. Above is Beat 3 with Arsle Pool and Conigal. Beat 2 has Forsil – a likely spot for the early fish – Victoria Pool, Lady Bighouse Pool (man-made) and then Beat 1 with McBeaths, Munro's, Bridge, Jetties and Cemetery. They are all holding pools and anglers fishing the estate water rotate through the four beats, day by day. The estate's agent is Mrs Atkinson, 24 Princes Street, Thurso, to whom aspiring tenants should apply. Melvich Hotel is where estate anglers stay and this is situated overlooking the tidal waters below the road bridge.

Above the estate water are the Forsinard beats.

Unlike the lower water this stretch really needs the spate. With the big holding pools lower down being a bit less dependent on very high water levels, the upper reaches require a good head of water and when this occurs then the sport can be really excellent. Best individual rod catch for one day in 1979 was nine salmon. Forsinard Hotel has 2 miles of river downstream of the hotel divided into two beats, four rods per day are permitted, two per beat. The best pool is reputed to be Craggie and this is confirmed by a glance at the fishing book. Other good pools are Pulpit, Pylon, Gracie's, Majors and Haugh. It would depend, of course, on the amount of water but, not long after salmon are seen and caught on the lower part of the river, the first of the season will be taken on the Forsinard stretch. In 1979, the first of the season was taken on 7 May and from then on the sport was excellent entirely due to the high precipitation over the best angling months. For 1979 the catch return was 56 salmon, 13 grilse and one sea trout. This can be only a guide because a number of day lets do not make returns.

The hotels, while catering for anglers, do not carry any stocks of tackle so it would be wise for anglers to come prepared – the nearest tackle shop being in Thurso.

It is a fly only river and the most frequently used patterns are the Garry Dog, Stoats Tail, Hairy Mary and occasionally, the Jock Scott. The first named fly is a bright yellowish one and the reason for its success is, surely, that it will show up well in the dark waters of this river. I wondered if 'backing up' was used on the big slow moving pools lower down but to my surprise I found that no one employs this method; the pools are fished in the orthodox manner. The Halladale salmon might respond more readily in these big quiet pools, especially in low water and with a good upstream breeze, if the fly was worked across the pool, progressing from tail to head. Just a thought.

Though there is some sea trout angling in the estuarial water below the road bridge, the Halladale is not noted for much of a sea trout run. And although the salmon catch off the river by rod and line in a year of average precipitation is more than one would expect, an enormous number of fish are taken by nets at the mouth and at Sandside and Strathy. I am told they take, on average, 8,000 to 9,000 salmon per year. In addition, many illegal nets take their toll.

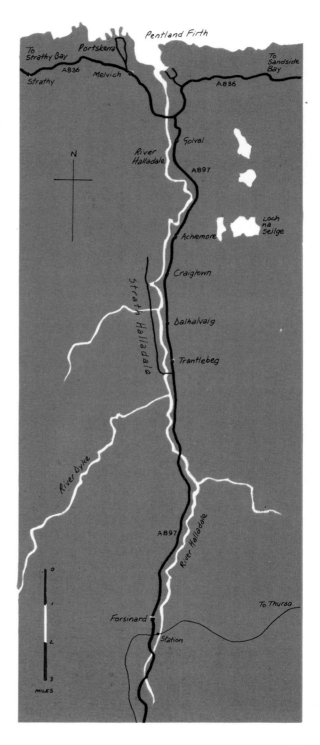

The Wick

River: Wick
Caithness
Season: 11 Feb–3 Nov
Best months: see text

After the Thurso, the Wick river is the next biggest in the county of Caithness. It doesn't have the head of salmon which the Thurso has but it now has a surprisingly good annual catch record. Like the Halladale the Wick looks most uninteresting with its canal-like pools. But looks deceive. It is one of the two major Caithness systems and, although only about 20 miles in length (and that is stretching it a bit by taking into account the feeder burns) it is of reasonable importance as a salmon river with the possibility of fish in March or April and right through to the end of the season on 3 November (it opens on 11 February).

Caithness is a small flat county dominated by extensive peat banks, mosses and wet land grasses. It has no, or very few, trees, and the only hills are in the extreme south and these do not influence the river in any way. The Wick is fed by a number of small burns flowing through the moors but the main river is from Watten to the town of Wick. Between these two points is where the angling is, but the river meanders through well cultivated farmland and between Watten and Wick, some 10 miles, the fall is only 10 ft. So it is a slow, canal-like river and was formed, according to geologists, in the Ice Age. After long periods of drought the peat and mosses become like dry sponges and it can take a lot of rainfall before the river will rise. But when it does it can cause extensive flooding.

The area abounds in a tremendous richness of birdlife – Arctic Skuas, Great Northern Divers, Snowy Owls and many more. Caithness also has the largest number of iron-age settlements in Europe and the fauna and animal life are breathtaking.

The river holds salmon, as I said, but it is dependent on wet weather to provide reasonable fishing.

Salmon can be taken in March (two were caught that month in 1980 before drought conditions put an end to any further chance of sport) but April is usually better, when there could be a reasonable run. There are 24 well defined pools between Wick and Watten and all are controlled by the Wick Angling Association. Only in a good spate will the small tributaries to the south of Watten be fished, and mainly at the back-end. In fact, without good water, they cannot be fished at all.

There is a very tiny communicating stream between the Wick and Loch Watten and there have been occasions when the brown trout anglers in the loch have hooked (but usually lost) leviathans which were, of course, salmon.

Because of the nature of the geography, successive flooding coupled with the very poor rate

Three of the bird species of this wild area
Top: Cormorant drying its wings after swimming under water
Bottom left: Arctic Skua
Right: Snowy Owl alighting at nest beside young

of flow have meant, in the past, that large deposits of sand and silt collected at the river mouth in the heart of the town of Wick. Attempts were made to improve the flow, including the building of a weir, which actually only worsened the silting. So salmon had great difficulty in getting into the river and the annual salmon catch return rarely touched the 100 mark. Then two things happened. One was the formation of the angling association; the other was that oil came to the North Sea – or rather oil-related industry came to Wick, which meant that the harbour was dredged and deepened and the weir removed. Now the water flow rate is vastly improved. The efficacy of these operations has meant a greatly increased number of salmon ascending the river and nowadays they have an easy and obstruction-free run upstream.

With the 24 named pools to which I have referred, all more or less holding pools, the river can accommodate the increased run of salmon and gives much more sport in consequence. In 1979, the salmon catches by rod and line rose from the 100 mark to well over 600. And the Wick AA can take a lot of credit for the way it has exploited the easier access for salmon by good management. It controls the whole river and employs two watchers. The secretary is David Calder, 13 Dunnet Avenue, Wick. Daily, weekly or monthly permits can be obtained from Camps Sports Shop, Wick.

Not only have the catches and runs of salmon improved but so has the average weight. Now quite a number of 20 pounders are being taken. The largest for 1979 was one over 22 lbs by a Watten angler, Willie More. There is also a fairly good run of grilse which average out about 4 to 6 lbs. Sea trout also come into the river. In fact, finnoch can sometimes be caught in Loch Watten by anglers fishing for brownies.

The methods of fishing allowed are by fly, spinning and worm. Probably a little more than half the fish caught are taken on lure or bait but the fly angler does well, though he has the problem of trying to impart movement to his fly.

He does this by employing the technique of 'backing up'. This method can be just as successful as spinning if correctly carried out. In fact, I would go so far as to say that, in the summer, salmon will go for the small fly, say on 8 or 10 hooks, in preference to a spinning lure.

The usual wooden devons are used – brown and gold, black and gold, black and orange and spoons of various hues and shapes. Small flies in the summer such as the Stoats Tail, Hairy Mary, Munro Killer, Tosh all take their toll.

With the river flowing through the town and the first two or three pools within the boundary – Bulls Hole, Durrans, Otter Island, Dyke End, Willies Pool – it is most accessible. Tackle can be purchased almost by the river side and Wick itself is a good shopping centre with plenty of hotels.

This is a success story. Within just a few years the Wick has changed from an uninteresting and mediocre salmon stream to one of considerable importance and all due to the association which took its chance when oil and its related industry came to Wick and 'cured' the barriers which had obstructed salmon from running freely.

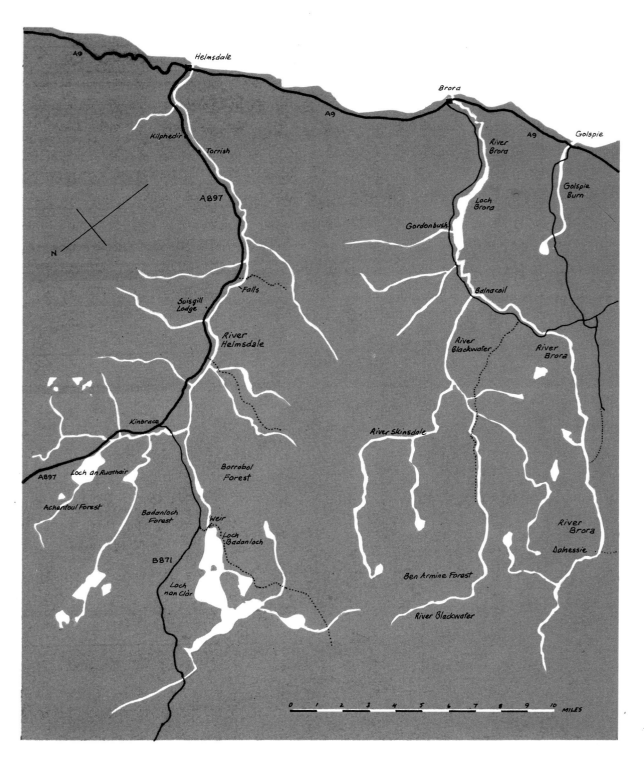

The Helmsdale

River: Helmsdale
Sutherland
Season: 11 Jan–30 Sept
Best months: Apr/July (grilse)
Fly only

A lady spinning on the Helmsdale, known as the 'goldrush river'. Some years ago it was the scene of a miniature goldrush and even within the last few years gold dust has been found

This is a wonderful little Sutherland salmon river which is regarded as being private. In fact it is not entirely private because the very early months are leased to some local, and not so local, anglers who would not in any circumstances give it up. The co-operative of owners tend to keep the river to themselves after April but there are some non-owner leases going. It is rather a closed shop, though. Anyone who manages to fish it after April has got on through a friend of a friend. It is impossible to obtain accurate information on the annual catch returns but it is accepted that in excess of 1000 salmon can be taken by rod and line in a season.

It drains the area of Borrobol and Achentoul forests – a land of lochans and peat bogs. But a look at a map shows some lochs at the top of the river. These are very important. One small one, Loch na Moine, constitutes Beat 6 Upper, and is a very good fishery both from the boat and bank so long as there is a wind.

Away back, well over 70 years ago, Loch Baden-loch and Loch an Ruathair were made into reservoirs because it was common for the river to dry up after April and there would be no more sport that year. Now, even in drought conditions after April, there is enough of a water supply to give good levels until well into August. So these lochs provide valuable water storage.

Halfway down the river, approximately 10 miles from the sea, there is a fall. This is the place which is all-important. Not only does it divide the river into two – six beats above and six beats below – but it stops salmon in their tracks until the water temperature reaches 42°F. So the first salmon of the season will be taken on one of the six lower beats.

The season opens on 11 January and closes on 30 September. Of all the early Highland salmon rivers, the Helmsdale is the one most likely to produce a salmon during the first days or weeks of the

The Helmsdale Beat 4, a 'backing-up' pool

season, though it can be frozen over in January and February. It is widely known, though, that salmon can have run the river well before the opening day. There could be salmon way up as far as Badenloch by 11 January but no one fishes for them because they are, inevitably, thin on the ground. It is a fly-only river and it is great sport to hook a salmon and have to ease it across the ice to the bank. I have seen this happen on a February day on the association water in a pool, frozen over in the morning, a gap opening up after lunch, but closing again by 4.30 pm when the temperature drops.

The six lower beats are the important early ones because it will be the second or third week of March before temperatures rise to allow fish into the upper water. The bottom beat, No 1, has five good holding pools. Beat 2 has a fine holding pool at the bottom, Kilphedir, 300 yards long where one could spend a whole day. Beat 3 has three good spring pools, Upper and Lower Torrish and Tail of Bay. No 4 is all flat water but is wholly fishable and one can actually 'back' it for about a mile. No 5 is mostly streamy water with the Foam Pool a good spring one. No 6 has the great spring pools – Dyke, Church, Manse, Little and Big Rock.

The six beats above the falls are all good after March. Nos 1, 2 and 3 are where the spawning burns empty into the main river and for that reason they are fine productive places because salmon will stay there until spawning time. No 4 is quite extraordinary. In 1979 they had 599 salmon for the season with 94 as their best week and 31 as their best day! This must have been an all time record for the beat. No 5 needs wind and No 6 is the 'Lochs Beat'.

By February the springers are beginning to build up and by March there is usually a good head of fish with the eager ones going over the falls into the upper water. April is the best spring month and fish will be taken from every beat including the lochs. May is still a good month with quite a few late springers coming and this is the month when HRH Prince Charles schemes to be in Sutherland. It is said that the Helmsdale is his favourite salmon river.

In a normal year the grilse runs occur in June, peak in July and tail off in August. These runs are heavy and if there are long periods of good water levels and fish escape the nets then the whole river has a tremendously good time.

In the early months the association water can do better than the expensive beats up above especially in the very hard weather when the river is frozen over or the water is terribly cold. Fish will often stay in the pools just above the village of Helmsdale. One friend of mine has frequently deserted his expensive water, taken a day ticket for the mile or so of association water, and caught more fish there. This water is also good for sea trout and indeed most of the beats look forward to good runs of sea trout in June and July.

The spring fishing means large tube flies and I think the Collie is the best of them. But it was on this river I heard of the Spey Royal from my friend Jack MacKenzie. He uses it a lot with success and gave me the dressing – black and gold body and a black hair wing with a dash of orange. In the late spring and summer, flies are down to 8s, 10s and 12s and most anglers use the dropper, with the larger of the two flies on the tail.

Every year fish over 20 lbs are taken. Recently, big fish have been scarcer but given the right conditions the sport can be fast and furious.

The Brora

Rivers: Blackwater, Brora
Sutherland
Season: 1 Feb–15 Oct
Best months: Feb–May
Fly only

The Brora and Helmsdale, being such near neighbours, are also friendly rivals, particularly over the early months of the season, in spite of the fact that the Brora doesn't open until 1 February. The rivalry is demonstrated as, week by week, month by month, the up-to-date totals are eagerly scrutinised by both camps. The Brora starts off with such a bang in early February that it quickly eliminates the lead which the Helmsdale has built up with its month's start. The Helmsdale however will always

end up with more salmon than its rival. Even so, the Brora is an excellent spring salmon river and for its size, gives very good sport over February, March, April and May,

It is very much influenced by rainfall in the Ben Armine Forest and Borrobol Forest from where the two main tributaries originate. It is not quite a natural river but is lucky in that only the very top of the Brora at Dalnessie is trapped and aqueducted through to the Shin system for hydro-electric purposes. 'The upper river', as it is known, is the combination of the two tributaries – the Blackwater, draining the west side of the Borrobol Forest area and the upper Brora draining the west and south side of the Ben Armine Forest. The two come together at Balnacoil. After a short run they empty into Loch Brora – a loch some 4 miles long and half a mile wide. The lower Brora flows from there to the sea. It is about 3 miles long, and is divided into two beats. In spite of its smallness the lower river fishes very well in February, March and April and I have not known any spring season to be a disappointment, with a hundred fish for February making a good start.

Like all the Sutherland rivers it is fly-only and the big tubes are always used. But they tend to use the heavy articulated ones here and the Pilkinton, Willie Gunn and Collie Dog are most successful. They can experience very high water levels either due to melting snow or heavy rain but this is not a river which suffers adversely from heavy water. Fish will take on the Brora in very high water conditions. It is necessary to have a fair idea of where to look for them in these early months and to be able to cast a long line to get down to them. This is why spring salmon fishing is so satisfying – you've got to work for your fish. In the summer a small fly on a floating line is easily cast and salmon pop up for it – right to the surface. This can happen, too, in the spring given certain conditions. Again, backing up the big flattish pools on the top beat can be extremely productive in the early months of spring.

In order to help the newcomer, Rob Wilson of Brora has written a very good account of the river from the loch to the sea. He describes all the pools and the best method of access. He names all the pools which hold great memories for me like the Rockpool, Donkey, Magazine and the Cruives on the lower half and the Ford Pool and Rallan, two great all-rounders for spring fish, grilse and autumn salmon. The great backing pools are Rallan, Benzie and Upper Fannich and Rob's booklet offers advice on how to employ this method. It is highly recommended for the stranger to this river.

The Brora is known as a spring river but has fish coming all year. The spring runs suffered a set back some years ago but over the past 10 or 20 years they have been creeping back into February, perhaps not spectacularly, but certainly real consolidation has taken place and February and March are pretty reliable months now. By the end of March 200 or more salmon may have been caught. The grilse runs can be heavy and the salmon keep coming in autumn, too. It is also a renowned sea trout river giving good sport in July. They arrive in the middle of May but the first runs go fast and can be away up in Ben Armine in no time at all. The later arrivals do not travel so fast and stocks tend to build up in July to give fine sport on Loch Brora as well as the river.

The lower river beats are owned by Sutherland Estates (south bank) and Gordonbush Estate (north bank). There is a fine rapport between the estates. Letting is so arranged that tenants start each day at opposite ends and fish up or down to the halfway point until 1.30 pm thereafter changing to the other half on their own side. This means that at no time are there any rods fishing opposite each other on the same pool.

There is a tidal stretch of approximatly half a mile which can be fished for sea trout by locals and visitors from 1 May until the end of the season (sea trout and salmon) on 15 October.

Above Loch Brora there is the main river, the upper river Brora, owned by Gordonbush Estate. The Blackwater is also owned by Gordonbush but the Ben Armine water is owned by Sutherland Estates. Salmon and sea trout will penetrate as far up as the Ben Armine water if there is a good spate in June. Some of these upper reaches are leased as package deals – salmon and brown trout fishing together with shooting and stalking and often cottages thrown in. The upper rivers, on average, should outfish the lower Brora once fish start going through the loch. When they do they will arrive up there with sealice and as this usually means the river is in spate then the catches can be heavy – double figures daily if anglers are experienced.

The rate of fall from loch to sea is such that it makes for perfect aeration, so that even in low water the fish tend to take well in the holding pools – quite an advantage. One day in May on the lower beat I hooked five fish in conditions which I had thought quite hopeless. Another interesting feature over recent years has been the steady increase in the average weight of salmon. In 1978 it leapt up by as much as 2 lbs! They still get reasonably heavy fish – salmon of over 20 lbs are caught every year, though perhaps not as many as in the past.

One of the most pleasing conservation efforts I have come across is on the upper river. No hen fish are allowed to be killed after 15 September and on the Blackwater the estate reserves the right to conclude all angling earlier than the statutory date according to circumstances – usually by 1 September. I applaud this action.

The loch is jointly owned by the two estates. No fishing is allowed on it until 1 May and it closes on 15 October. Various hotels have boats on it as well as the estates. There is another conservation effort under way with regard to sea trout. Estates and clubs have all agreed not to fish for sea trout in the river until 1 June and the practice has spread from the Kyle of Sutherland right up to Helmsdale and I know that other sea trout fisheries are thinking of following this trend.

Some good and popular flies have come out of the Brora. One is Kenny's Killer – fine for salmon and sea trout and tied by Kenny Burns who was still employed by Gordonbush Estate when I wrote this. Another is the Willie Gunn (named after its inventor) – and the Loch Ordie is a good loch fly for salmon.

There are a number of well known hotels in Brora catering for anglers and some have boats on the loch or short leases on the river. Mike Waller has teaching courses intermittently throughout the season and, of course, that well known character, Rob Wilson, who has been my own friend, colleague and mentor for many years, has his famous tackle shop in Fountain Square, Brora, and while he does not have his small factory now, he still builds his very famous split cane rods there.

It is a great little river, the Brora, and judging from the fish caught on opening day on 1 February you might wonder why it does not follow all its neighbours on the Kyle of Sutherland and the Helmsdale and open on 11 January. The reason is that the lower river is full of kelts in January and the mortality rate caused by anglers would be great.

The Kyle of Sutherland

*Rivers: Carron, Cassley,
Einag, Oykel, Shin
Sutherland
Season: 11 Jan–30 Sept
Best months:
Carron, Mar/Apr, Jun–Aug
Cassley, Apr/Jun
Oykel, Feb/Mar
Shin, July
Fly only*

When the itinerant angler reaches the summit of Struie Hill he is suddenly confronted with a startling view over Sutherland stretching away north and west from the northern shore of the Kyle. To the ordinary visitor it is a breathtaking panorama but to the angler it is exciting as well, as he gazes up the Kyle and wonders if the river to which he is bound is in ply and the salmon are up. He will be looking towards the Carron (on the south side at Ardgay), the Shin, the Cassley and the Oykel and its tributary, the Einag. If he arrives at Struie Hill early in the morning he may be looking over a sea of mist broken only by 'islands' of hilltops, heralding a good fishing day.

The majority of anglers will not have had the experience of fishing these rivers in January, February or March when they can be completely frozen over or lashed by blizzards. I used the word experience because this kind of fishing is bound to separate the men from the boys! It can be cold – very cold – but all those four Kyle rivers have one thing in common; they can hold salmon in January and February. If one includes the more northerly Helmsdale then, the first Scottish salmon of the year will almost certainly be taken from any of the rivers one can see from the summit of Struie Hill.

This is the land of the Willie Gunns, the Tadpoles, the Collie Dogs, the Garry Dogs, the Black and Tans. All these northern rivers are fly only, and the winter or spring angler has to use large 3 inch tube flies known by such names. Some are built on copper tubes whilst others are on lighter aluminium tubes. Most are used in conjunction with a quick-sinking line but some people use a floater with a sink tip and at least one gillie tends to use a complete floater even in February. These rivers are open 11 January- 30 September.

River Carron

The Carron is a bit different from the others. It flows from south to north and joins the Kyle at Bonar Bridge. By virtue of its substantial tributaries the catchment area is vast, taking in the drainage from the high hills of Dibidale Forest, Freevater Forest and part of Glencalvie Forest. The hydro board 'pinched' a significant part of the headwaters at Gleann Beag which was the most valuable bit of the catchment area. This 'stolen' water now flows into the Conon system. The result of this hydro-electric work has meant that the Carron, always a spate river anyway, is now more so, and at the mercy of short-lived spates. It can rise rapidly and one can actually watch it drop over a period of hours. So, through the season the river level will be low more often than high.

With so many mountains up in the headwaters, the Carron is a 'snow-melt' river and there are numerous periods between February and April when this is a valuable asset. If the river is not ice-bound, there will be salmon in January. They can be caught anywhere from the tide up to the temperature pool of Gledfield. But the pools below the road bridge on the bottom beats are probably the best places for the first salmon of the season. However, I recall the Raven or the Whirl Pool, and even the Gledfield itself, producing that first fish. The spring runs are quite good these days with February and March the most productive months below Gledfield. Snow water does not necessarily make a nonsense of salmon angling. Twice in very high water, due to snow-melt, I have had five salmon in a day from Gledfield Pool. One day was in February and another was in March. Almost every salmon broke surface to take a large Garry Dog tube before it sank. The main ingredient was the high air temperature which is usual during a thaw.

Gledfield will hold the fish until the water temperature reaches 42°F and when that happens they will dash for Braelangwell. There they come to another stop at the famous Morrell Pool. But by the end of April, and certainly in May, they will be through Morrell and well up into the top beats around Amat and Glencalvie. The most productive pools on the Braelangwell Beat are the Washerwoman, the Bottom Pool, and The Keepers above Morrell. Morrell, itself, is well known for salmon but it is also one of the finest sea trout pools in the river and sea trout will be that far by mid-June.

The magic view across the Kyle of Sutherland looking down to Dornoch Firth and Bonar Bridge with the hills of Sutherland beyond

After the spring runs there is a summer run of grilse and salmon but these fish proceed very rapidly right up to Amat and Glencalvie although Braelangwell usually does well as the fish stream through for the higher reaches. The river is not entirely private. Braelangwell can be leased, Gled-field, too, and so can the old Cambusmore Beat. Renton Finlayson, Bonar Bridge, handle some of these fishings and so do MacLeod's of Tain. My own preference for this river would be the lower pools at Gledfield in March and April and then Braelangwell for June, July and August.

River Shin

The Shin used to have an enormous catchment area stretching away above Loch Shin to Merkland but the hydro board have dammed all that great stretch of water at Lairg, at the bottom of Loch Shin; now the river from loch to tide receives a controlled flow which is just enough for salmon to run. That it is also enough in which to catch fish is borne out when the annual catch returns are examined.

The lower river contrasts strongly with the upper reaches. From January to the end of May all the action takes place from the Falls of Shin down to the tidal water – the bottom beats. From the dam down to a little way above the Falls of Shin there is thin water interspersed with deepish slow flowing pools. It does not look too profitable but do not be deceived. The lower half is very rocky and gorge-like and with the normal clarity of the water the salmon can clearly be seen and one is sometimes lucky enough to see the fish start off to take the fly. This is a dangerous moment and it requires nerves of steel not to 'strike' before the salmon turns away with fly securely in its mouth. It must surely be one of fishing's great moments to see the fish, say in the Long Pool or Shoulder of Cromartie or Pipers, move rapidly to your fly and be well hooked.

The Shin has a spring run. It is not a heavy one although there is usually a fish in January, a few more in February and more in March and April. May is the best month before the summer fish arrive. By the end of May the aggregate catch is usually about 100. These will have been taken from the falls down to the lowest pool, the Field, which is tidal. Thereafter, the fish tend to run through the lower beats and be caught from the falls to Rocky Cast. They will ascend the falls – a very high jump for them – in June and go immediately to the pools

Top: One of the rocky pools on the Cassley
Below: Netting a spring salmon on the Cassley at Rosehall
Opposite: Fly fishing on the Shin near Lairg

below the dam at Lairg where the stocks will increase as the season progresses. Nevertheless, the beats just above and below the falls continue to do well with 70 or so for June, 200 for July, over 100 for August; September fades away to nothing.

I like the Shin for various reasons, including the improvements made by the owner of the lower half, Sir John Egerton, and the way he has opened it to the public. Another bonus is a visit to my old friend Hughie MacKintosh, the gillie, at New Year. We have the customary dram, whilst reminiscing on past adventures. Hughie was the first exponent of working the Collie Dog I had ever seen. I used to watch him make those short casts, bringing the big tube round just below the surface, moving it all the time to attract the salmon. He always scolded me for using too long a line and said I would never catch salmon on the Shin that way. How right he was. I know now how to fish the Collie and it's thanks to Hughie.

An interesting theory about the Shin is contained in a little booklet written by Eric Linklater, based on the observations of Andrew Vass. Briefly, the argument is that all the dead kelts provide parcels of food which in the late spring and summer break up and supply fish-meal for salmon. The book contends that after all, salmon do feed in fresh water and absorb some of these particles of food. The book gives the amateur naturalist food for thought and offers very plausible reasoning as to the feasibility of the theory. It seems unarguable that the parr and smolts do feed on the 'food parcels'. How else would they grow in beautiful spawning water which, of necessity, has little else in the way of food?

The local hotel, Sutherland Arms at Lairg, has various periods on the lower and upper beats and, as already indicated, Sir John Egerton leases his water. But, as all good salmon water is at a premium, beats are not readily available.

River Cassley

The Cassley is another Kyle river which though a spate river will, given a chance, produce a salmon or two in January and February. It is at the mercy of the elements, however, and can be completely frozen over in the early weeks of the season.

It is not a natural river, nowadays. The headwaters were tapped for hydro-electric purposes and ever since then the spates do not last long. For

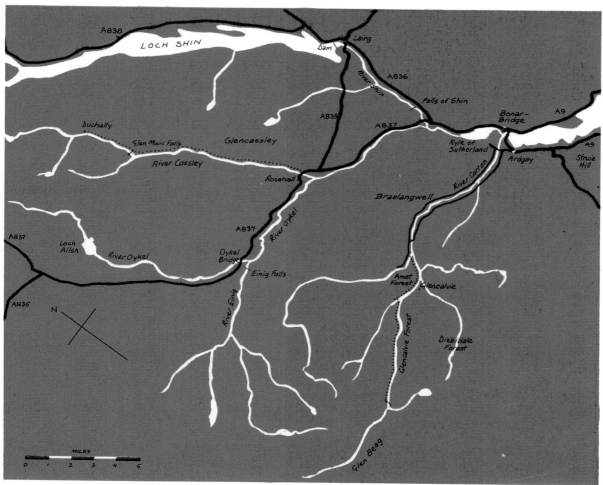

Into a springer below Oykel Bridge

example, the river can show 4 or even 6 ft. on the gauge yet overnight, or throughout the day, the level can drop away to 2 ft. Its source is 6 miles west of Duchally Lodge and above Duchally Dam all the headwater is damned and flows into the Loch Shin system.

Until the very end of May few fish will ascend the falls above the Round Pool and none will go over the Achness Falls before the water temperature reaches 52°F. Thus all salmon fishing from January to June is from the Achness Falls (or the Round Pool) down to the tide. This is the Rosehall Beat owned by Neil Graesser. He lets out this productive spring water through Achness House Hotel, Rosehall, or through Keith Ritchie, estate agents. The main forte of the Rosehall water is that most of the salmon are sea-liced due to the streamy water of the upper section inhibiting any further ascent of the river until about June.

There are some interesting pools such as the rocky Round Pool and the spectacular Crow's Nest where one is perched on a high rock and sees the fish lying like sardines in a tin. It is a thrilling place to hook a fish. But that exciting moment is for later in the season when the water warms up – perhaps as early as May.

Before then all the successes are from the Round Pool down to the very bottom pool at the Kyle. What has always surprised me is that they can catch spring fish in the most uninteresting little pools during periods of low water. Most people would tend to walk past these small productive places without a thought – but they would be missing out. This is no accident. Mr Graesser is a Freshwater Fishery consultant and his own bit of the Cassley is a fine example of how to improve a river and make the most of low water levels.

Big flies are used in the spring. The Willie Gunn, Tadpole and Collie Dog are best as 3 inch tubes but if almost any 3 inch tube is presented to a fresh-run sealiced salmon he will probably go for it. Up to the end of May about 200 to 250 salmon would be expected but weather (temperature and precipitation) has a big influence on success or otherwise. April is always the best spring month. These Rosehall beats average out each year at about 400 fish.

The grilse arrive, sometimes in May, but usually June, and they can give reasonable sport. On the Rosehall water the best month is July but by then they are streaming over the Achness Falls and into the upper river as far as Glenmuick Falls. Some ascend these upper falls and enter the Duchally headwaters. The average number going through this dam is less than 100. So there is no major angling potential here. The Glencassley water can be very productive but it has a shorter season. There are 9 miles of good fishing up to Glenmuick Falls. The left bank is easily accessible but in high water the right bank is more difficult. Access is confined to two bridges although there are one or two boats. The Long Pool is the famous pool and is about one mile long, all productive. Bell Ingram handle the leases which are offered to the public. In the summer, throughout the whole river, tiny flies are employed and most anglers use a dropper which can be as small as a size 10 or even a 12. The Stoats Tail, Munro Killer, Tosh and Hairy Mary are the most popular patterns.

There is a considerable sea trout run commencing in June and one can find these fish away up at the Junction on the top waters.

River Oykel

In any list of favourite rivers I would have to include the Oykel. I don't know it as a summer or autumn one – only as an early spring river and I love every minute of a February or March day when I am up to my waist in freezing water and my fingers are so painful that I have to come ashore and stuff them into my axillae to get the circulation going. A masochist? Perhaps so, but what a thrill it is to feel your big tube fly coming to a halt with a slow draw in its search of the pool out there in the blizzard and your frozen fingers trying to receive the sensations coming from a 'live thing'. Then the fun begins and the pain is forgotten.

It is also a spate river but it is a natural one without any hydro-electric workings. It is big enough to hold a reasonable level for a couple of days but in those early weeks the frost, snow, snow-melt and perhaps just rain, all have a very profound effect on the conditions.

The Oykel rises on the slopes of Ben More Assynt and flows into little Loch Ailsh (a good sea trout loch). Then it winds its way through a flat valley with rather big and slow-moving pools with sandy bottoms. Below Oykel Bridge the main tributary, the Einag, joins the Oykel and, together, they proceed down the valley at greater speed, over

Top: Anglers at the Oykel Bridge Hotel
Bottom: Weighing and recording the day's catch

the temperature pool, the Rock, and down through the early spring beats to Inveroykel where fresh water and brackish water meet.

A lot of improvements have been made to the lower Oykel under the direction of George Ross, the fishing manager, who succeeded his father to that post. One of his best creations, I think, is simply known as The Lower George – on Beat 4. It fishes all season but I know it as a spring pool and have had quite a few salmon out of it in almost any height of water.

If the river is not completely frozen over salmon are caught in January – just a few, but they will be there. February is much better, though, but the interesting thing here is that if the Kyle of Sutherland is frozen over, bank to bank, when the river opens up before the Kyle does, as it is wont to do, fresh run fish can be caught even though the Kyle remains completely iced. The explanation is that salmon travel up to the river under the ice. I suppose they are at home under the ice – after all, they've just come from the North Atlantic! When the river unfreezes, huge floes sail downstream and wading can be a nightmare. I remember hooking, playing and landing a fish in Langwell Pool on a day in February when floes as large as dining room tables were making their way down river. This fish rose to a brass tube fly in a water temperature of 33°F! But the air was much warmer – the essential ingredient.

These first fish can be found as far up as the Rock Pool but only when the water goes over 42°F will the salmon pass through. When they do go there is a fair old race to get up to the Falls of Einag, the Junction or the Island before the fish, because they can be caught up there with sealice the moment the magic figure of 42°F is reached. This usually happens during the first week of March and I remember fishing below the Rock one day that week when George Ross came to me and said that the water temperature had reached 42°F and to go quickly up to Einag Falls. Sure enough, the very first cast there produced a sealiced salmon.

It was on the Oykel that I was taught to 'back' a pool. As described elsewhere (see the Thurso) one starts at the bottom of a pool, casts and walks up a few paces retrieving some line by hand. It is very effective. There was a day on Beat 4 in the Duck Pool which was fished down in the usual way with no result. Then it was backed and by that method

An Oykel salmon comes to the gaff

Opposite: Spring salmon fishing on the lower Oykel
Below: The lower Oykel, the Duck Pool in January

six salmon were caught in an hour! That was during the first week of March. There are many pools on the Oykel where one can employ this method most successfully. For example, the Inveroykel, Duck, Blue, Brae and Langwell, and these are not the only ones.

The Einag Falls is a 'stopper' for salmon until the water goes up to around 50°F. So is the Oykel Falls. Until the end of May or June, the Einag Falls is an exciting place because if you cast a Garry Dog from the Perch you can see your Garry coming round all the way and a bar of silver flashing at it and, if you haven't lost your head and tightened too soon, you are into a fish.

By the end of May, or thereabouts, the fish are up

over both Einag and Oykel falls and well into the hinterland. The Einag banks have been improved and thus the fishing, but it is such a large inaccessible river that it is not over fished. The upper Oykel is different with its made-up road for cars. The Oykel Bridge Hotel has three rotating beats on this stretch. They usually have fish in June and July with fresh-run grilse. August is about the same and September is the best month of all although the fish are, by then, getting rather dark and some will be gravid.

During the summer large runs of grilse and salmon follow the spring fish. The lower Oykel fishings show that April is the best month with over 200 salmon for that month but, in 1978, March was

Fishing lodge at the head of Loch Ailsh

easily the best month with 221 salmon. In the summer, July is the best month with perhaps 150 fish. But the sport during any month of the season is very dependent on the amount of precipitation, be it rain or snow-melt. Langwell is the most productive pool on the lower beats and over 20 fish a day can be taken from that one pool – given the right conditions. The best fly is the Collie Dog. It is normally held to be a spring fly but it can attract salmon even later. I remember one day in May when an angler had a good fish to his enormously long Collie. In fact, it was 9 inches long but I described it as a Collie 'a quarter of a yard long!' Otherwise the usual small hooks in patterns such as the Stoats Tail, Munro Killer and Hairy Mary are

the best.

The Oykel Bridge Hotel's returns for their upper beats indicate an average catch of around 150 salmon and Loch Ailsh should not be despised for sea trout, and even salmon. This hotel, and Achness House Hotel at Rosehall are the two well known angling hotels catering very much for anglers who fish the Oykel and Cassley; Renton Finlayson, Bonar Bridge, are the estate agents who handle the leases for the Oykel and the other salmon streams in the area.

Craigroy Sporting Co, William Street, Nelson, Lancs has the top beat of the upper Oykel (Beat 1), part of Beat 2 and boats on Loch Ailsh. This fishing is available to the public.

The Rock cast on the Eanig

The Conon

Rivers: Alness, Blackwater, Conon

Ross & Cromarty

Season: Alness, 11 Feb–31 Oct
Blackwater, Conon, 26 Jan–30 Sept

Best months:
Alness, Sept/Oct
Blackwater, July
Conon, July–Sept

Fly only (Blackwater)

Time was when the name Conon meant one thing to Scottish fishermen – spring salmon. The very word 'Conon' stimulates memories in veteran anglers of magnificent sport in the lower reaches of this East Ross river in the months of February, March and April. I am the proud possessor of a battered old notebook which once belonged to the late James Anderson of the Conon Hotel, Cononbridge and, in his beautiful copper plate script, he relates the catches, the weather, temperatures, the lures and the best pools. It makes fascinating reading and when I refer to it I am overwhelmed at the amount of information the register contains. It was so meticulously kept that the date of every first fish of the season is recorded, the names of the tenants and even how the estuary nets were doing after they opened in February. The records started in 1921 and ceased just after the second world war.

This information refers only to the present Lower Brahan Beat and the catches for the early months are very impressive indeed. One can only read them and sigh for the good old days. Everything was going for the Conon until the shadow of hydro-electricity was cast upon the waters – waters which as I once described in a guide book to the Conon, 'when used for tea-making tasted of salmon!' In the middle fifties the Conon was harnessed for hydro-electric power and immediately the 'dismal Johnnies' forecast the end of salmon fishing there. To some extent they were right. For some reason in 'hydroised' rivers, the spring fish more or less disappear and they become grilse or summer salmon rivers. This is exactly what happened on the Conon. Whereas the Lower Brahan used to average something like 300 fish over the early months, now this beat is doing well if they have double figures from 26 January when the season opens, until the

end of April. To be accurate, the average catch for those three months for the Lower Brahan over the past decade has been a mere 8.8 salmon! The estuarial nets, which used to do prolific business right from February, now do not open until the end of June and they close after the first week of August. A sad tale but not so sad as it sounds; in spite of everything as many fish are taken now as in yesteryear. They are grilse and summer salmon, of course, and come in their thousands. But what a short season – the end of June will see the grilse runs commence and by mid-August the beats are fishing over 'old stagers'.

Nowadays, the main salmon angling beats are from the lowest dam at Torr Achilty down to the tide at Cononbridge. This stretch incorporates the Coul water on the left bank below the dam to the confluence of the Conon and its tributary, the Blackwater. Over the past 10 years the average annual catch was 186.8 salmon, with 312 for 1979 – a very good year. Best months are August and September and if there is big water, fish will tend to lie well over on the Coul side especially in Gillanders and Big Cast (Chappleton, as it is known on the other bank). In low water the Deer Fence, Clachuille and the New Pool are lovely fly water pools and most productive. Across the way, on the right bank, is the Upper Fairburn water, privately owned by a partnership who still let it in weeks or fortnights to previous lessees. They do rather better than the Coul water because salmon tend to run very fast and stop below the dam on their side. So, very often in low water, they are picking up fish to the detriment of the opposite bank. Their average annual catch was, over the past ten years, 353 salmon – best year 1979 with 492 salmon. This average catch makes the beat the best one on the Conon. Their best months are July, August and September and, in low water, the Glide, Sandbank and Gillanders fish well, with Clachuille (the Boat Pool) very good late in the season and especially in high water.

At the confluence of the Conon and Blackwater there is the Junction Pool which is fished on the left bank by the tenants of the lower Blackwater, followed immediately by the Boat Pool fished by the Blackwater Middle Beat tenants. On the right bank, this side is owned by Fairburn Estate and leased. Below Moy Bridge, Fairburn Estate owns the right hand bank all the way down to where the Orrin joins the Conon (the Orrin is no longer an

The view from the hut at the Upper Brahan Beat on the Conon

angling river thanks to the water extraction by the hydro board). The bottom of this beat ends in the big Kettle Pool normally fished by boat, although I have had fish from the bank or wading in low water on fly. It is a big water pool – the bigger the better. Most people tend to spin it but I and my host, Roderick Stirling, have had salmon on fly there at the end of February and in March. When the water is big, one anchors the boat and lets out rope. The vital factor is where to let down the anchor. Such is the force of current (deceiving in the smooth water) that if the anchor is dropped too low down the pool it may drag. Quite a number of people have shot the rapids and ended down in the next beat. The danger is that the anchor may catch the stones on the way down with an upturned boat the outcome.

The whole of the left hand bank from dam to estuary, and that part from the Orrin to the estuary on the right hand bank, is owned by the hydro board. From Moy Bridge to below the Rowan Pool is the Upper Brahan Beat which is not an outstanding one but can be quite reasonable in August and September when two local hotels have leases on it – Cononbridge Hotel and Strathgarve Lodge Hotel,

Garve. Their average catch, over 10 years, has been 37 salmon and, like the other beats, August and September are the best months. Below this beat comes the second most productive beat on the Conon – the Middle Brahan Beat. They have access to the Kettle Pool on a half day rotating basis with the opposite Lower Fairburn bank. They, too, have a boat but they can comfortably fish from the bank if spinning. In very high water the top pool, the Aquarium, can be good but their best pools are the Lake, Kettle and Rushing Pools in the early months and the Rushing Stream and Ferry Stream in the summer when the grilse head through. They have averaged 342 fish per season over the past 10 years but in 1979 they had the extraordinary catch of 700 fish, with 254 for July, 226 for August and 146 for September. In recent years a few fish are taken in March but between January and the end of May only about 30 to 40 salmon would be averaged.

I have touched on the Lower Brahan Beat and how much it has deteriorated over the early months. But it comes into its own in July, August and September and over those three months the average take is 162 salmon. While the Conon itself

is not a sea trout river, thousands use the Inner Cromarty Firth as their feeding grounds and shoals come up as far as the Lower Brahan to the Junction Pool, the Last Hope and the tidal pool – the Slaggan. May is a particularly good month and these sea trout, up to 3 lbs, are in excellent condition then. The estuary is administered by the Dingwall AC on behalf of the hydro board for sea trout and members and visitors can enjoy reasonable fishing in April and May and again in August and September.

It is fly only here and no breast waders or dinghies are permitted. The most successful sea trout flies are Dunkeld for a bright day, Greenwells, Peter Ross, Grey Monkey, Black Pennell and the Grey or Conon Lure if the sea trout are, or have been, feeding on immature herring or sprats.

Except on the Upper Fairburn Beat and the Coul water where there is the rule that, in low water, it is fly only, spinning lures are permitted – but no worm, prawns or any other bait are allowed.

Above Torr Achilty Dam the Loch Achonachie AC administers the upper Conon for the hydro board. They have four beats allowing for two rods

on each per day. The first salmon come up the fish lift in June and the numbers build up until September which is probably the best month of the season up there. But this part of the river is extremely vulnerable to the vagaries and whims of the hydro board and very often the water levels cause irate anglers to protest vehemently that the conditions for fishing are hopeless – but this is not always the case. The annual catch is something like 30 salmon with as many as 50 a season or two ago.

Most anglers will spin in the early months and the usual Toby spoons and wooden devons weighted with spiral leads are commonly used. All the same, the dedicated fly angler can catch his fish on a large tube fly, possibly a Garry Dog or some other brightly-coloured pattern. After May everyone goes on to the fly and nearly all the salmon are caught on tiny black flies. The silver Stoats Tail is the most popular but the Munro Killer, Tosh and Black Brahan are very successful. The last named fly is interesting. The gillie on the bottom water, John MacKenzie, who ties flies at the drop of a hat, tied a few patterns and handed them to me. I fancied

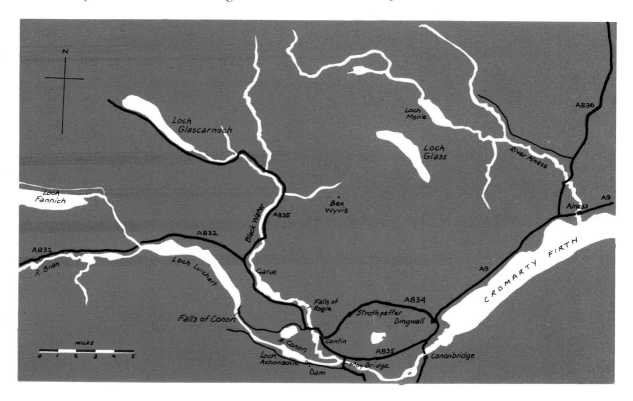

one of them which he called, simply, Red Lurex. I have had great success with it for salmon all over the country and we named it the Black Brahan. I made variants of this pattern which is a marvellous fly for both salmon and sea trout. It has a red lurex body and a black hair wing but I have found that I can use green or pink lurex on the body and a touch of hot orange for the throat hackle. The green bodied one is my favourite and sea trout take it at dusk and early morning in poor light. Also, and more interestingly, salmon can see it in the same conditions and in thick mist. I remember two occasions – one on the Upper Fairburn on Gillanders and the other on the Boat Pool at Moy Bridge when, such was the intensity of the early morning mist that the far bank was not visible, yet I caught five and three salmon respectively on the Green Brahan.

The Conon and Blackwater season opens on 26 January and closes on 30 September. The Conon originates many miles away up above Loch Rosque on the one hand and well above Loch Scardroy at the top of Strathconon on the other, draining some 400 square miles. But this is of no consequence because the whole system is 'hydroised' and the river flow is entirely controlled by the hydro board.

River Blackwater

This is the main salmon tributary of the Conon and was once a wonderful little salmon stream. But it was harnessed for hydro-electric power and all the headwaters were trapped and, by a series of reservoirs, aqueducts, tunnels and so on, the bulk of the river now flows into the Conon. The result has been that the river is nearly always at 'compensation' flow and any local spate lasts for just a day – or two at most.

It had a marvellous spring run of salmon. 40 fish or thereabouts was the take for March (with even the odd one in February, weather permitting); 60 or 80 for April; up to 200 for May and the same again in June. These figures refer to the Rogie or Middle Beat only. In July, there was a heavy grilse run and I used to catch them up at Garve between Achnachlerich Bridge and Wade's Bridge. Now, no fish is allowed past Loch na Croic, not far above the Falls of Rogie. They are kept there until spawning time when they are stripped, fertilised and the eggs put into Contin Salmon Hatchery which has a capacity of nearly 10 million. Now, as a result of being

'hydroised' the spring run has almost died. Not entirely, because there are still a few spring fish making it to Rogie in April and May depending on local spates. The fishery board are also doing their best by introducing Shin eggs but these have not made a noticeable difference to numbers though they certainly have to the size of the fish. A Blackwater salmon used to be about 8 or 9 lbs but now I have seen fish exceeding 20 lbs and even 30 lbs, although few are actually caught. But what a change has come over this river. The first fish of the season may be taken in April up at Rogie if there is enough water. Only a handful will be taken in April and again in May and the first decent runs will be the grilse which will come with the first spate, towards the end of June or July. Once they start coming they keep coming, even in low water. Up to the end of June the average catch was 8.6 salmon over the past 10 years, compared to around 500 just 25 years ago, enough to make a lover of the Blackwater weep! Fortunately the Boat Pool on the Conon goes with the Rogie Beat. This was arranged because of the scarcity of angling water up at Rogie and is a very necessary consolation prize. Nowadays the average annual catch off Rogie is 66 fish but the Boat Pool's average is 46 – so it is a great help.

The Blackwater is a fly only river but one can spin the Boat Pool. In the spring that early fish can be found in the Rogie Pool itself or down in the Square, the Step or the Flat. Big Garry Dog tubes or the Collie Dog will be used to search the small but very rocky pools. The best place of all is the extreme tail of Rogie in high water. The fish lie right on the lip and the fly stops its passage across the tail as a fish takes it. With very careful handling one may manage to 'walk' him out of danger but often he turns and disappears for ever in the foaming cataract between the rocks.

In the summer the same pools produce all the fish. But in low water one 'dibbles' in the white water. This is done with a short line, a loop in your hand, and one's fly stationary relative to the bank but making a V on the surface which means, I suppose, that the fly is travelling against the current. It is an effective and exciting way to fish these little bits of white water and one can see many fish 'nosing' at the fly. But the one which takes it comes with a tremendous bang and is usually well hooked if one has remembered to keep the loop of line in

hand and to let it go at the precise moment. The Pulpit at Rogie is a great place for dibbling. So is the large boulder at the neck of the Turn Pool and the very top of the Square Pool.

The Boat Pool can be spun and the usual lures are the black and gold Toby spoon or the wooden devons in various colours. The fly angler, if he can Spey or roll cast, can get a fish on a large tube. In the summer, and through to autumn, the very small fly will outclass the spinner and I catch most of my fish on the Esmund Drury Tosh on size 10 or 12 trebles. There was a time when I used the Edmund Drury General Practitioner a lot but my method was to recover it very fast and watch for the bow wave of a salmon start out up to 12 yards away. One day in September there was high water and a severe gale. I had on a GP but couldn't keep it in, or on the water and the most interesting thing happened. I actually caught five salmon that afternoon on the 'dapped' GP! They cleared the water and took the GP in the air. I have never seen that before or since!

No waders are required on the Rogie Beat – only rubber climbing boots or even sandals. But on the Boat Pool, if fly fishing, chest waders are essential. However, if spinning one can keep to the bank and fish without waders.

The hydro board own all the salmon rights including the Upper Beat, which is administered by the Loch Achonachie AC and the Lower Beat which is leased to Craigdarroch Chalet Complex.

But over the years the board has tried to sell off their fishings although strong local opposition has managed to forestall such moves. As I write this chapter the status quo remains but may not always do so. Any change would be a pity because the Blackwater and Conon are completely open to the public in one way or another.

River Alness

The Alness has nothing to do with the Conon except that it, too, flows into the Inner Cromarty Firth. It opens on 11 February and closes on 31 October. It rises well up in Kildermorie Forest to the north of Ben Wyvis, flows into Loch Morie and from there down to the tide; it is salmon and sea trout fishing all the way – a distance of around 10 miles.

The future of this river is bright. A tremendous amount of work has gone into improving it and the new pools which have been created have not really 'bedded in' – yet some have started to yield fish. Catwalks, access roads, anglers' stances, notice boards and maps have been created but, most importantly, a dam or weir was built across the bottom of Loch Morie which means that the Alness is no longer a flash spate river. The impoundment of Morie can give at least a couple of weeks of angling water even if there is no further rainfall. Not only that, down near the estuary there was a weir for supplying the local distillery with water. It

The Beauly

Rivers: Beauly, Farrar, Glass
Inverness-shire
Season: 11 Feb–15 Oct
Best months: July–Sept
Fly only

was badly designed and fish found it difficult to ascend. So a fish pass was built into it and now salmon and sea trout can go up in low water levels.

Who can fish this productive little salmon and sea trout river? The answer is everyone and anyone. The whole river is open to the public. Alness AC have five beats one of which Beat 4 was actually bought outright by the Highlands and Islands Development Board and given to the club to administer for local and visiting anglers alike. They lease the others from Novar and Ardross. Novar Estates let all their fishings either through the estate office, with or without cottages, or to hotels in the surrounding area. Dunraven Hotel, Strathpeffer and Coul Hotel, Contin, are two which benefit and they offer the fishing to guests and sometimes to non-residents. So the whole river is open to all.

I have seen a couple of salmon caught in February and one or two in March. All have been taken in the tidal pools or in the Stick Pool below the weir on Beat 4. By April a few more salmon come and this time they will go fast for the middle and upper reaches. A few more will arrive in May but it is really July before the big runs appear and from then on the sport can be good. The Alness AC can have over 200 fish for a season with September and October the best months. It is much the same on the estate beats although there appears to be quite an anomaly here in that the totals of the club's beats are higher than the estate's. There cannot be many rivers with the advantage in favour of association water.

Fifty odd years ago the Alness used to be one of the finest sea trout rivers in the Highlands. Now after years in the doldrums, due to indiscriminate and severe poaching with dynamite and poison, the tide has turned and the sea trout population, as well as the salmon, is recovering. All these nice things did not come about on their own. The estate, the club and the Highland Board have worked in unison in co-operating to improve what was a run-down river and the whole satisfactory and successful outcome has been spearheaded and co-ordinated by Neil Graesser, Freshwater Fishery consultant, supported by Bill Topham, the river superintendent, whose enthusiasm and pride in his job is boundless.

Beat 4 is fly only but all the others are fly and/or worm. Only fly rods are allowed with fly reels – definitely no spinning reels or rods.

About 25 years ago this wonderful salmon river was completely taken over by the North of Scotland Hydro-Electric Board for the generation of 'power in the glens'. There were many objections, of course, but these were over-ruled and ultimately the main river and its two senior tributaries, the Glass and the Farrar, ceased to be normal natural rivers. Great dams were built up on the Glass, the Farrar and, lower down near the tidal waters, on the Beauly at Aigus and Kilmorack. Each was equipped with a Borland fish pass incorporated in the dams. This is the type that contains a shaft with a variable opening at the top to accommodate the reservoir level, and an opening at the bottom. When the lift operates, water is let down the lift shaft and rushes out at the bottom in a great bubbling cauldron, settles down to a good flow and thus attracts the waiting salmon into the bottom of the lift. The bottom gate is then closed, the lift fills with water, the fish rise with the level and eventually swim out at the top and into the reservoir above and so on their way to the higher reaches. There have always been critics of the efficacy of the dams and the lifts, but my feeling is that the Borland lift, operated by experienced people is superior to the conventional fish ladder.

Another bone of contention came from the upper proprietors and lessees who claimed that the hydro board closed down the fish pass for eight months of the year preventing salmon getting into the upper reaches. In order to allay these suspicions the board showed me their programme of operations for the Kilmorack and Aigus lifts. The lift operates as soon as salmon appear at the tailrace of Kilmorack Dam (the bottom dam). But these fish just will not ascend the lift until about the middle of May. Time and time again the lift has operated as

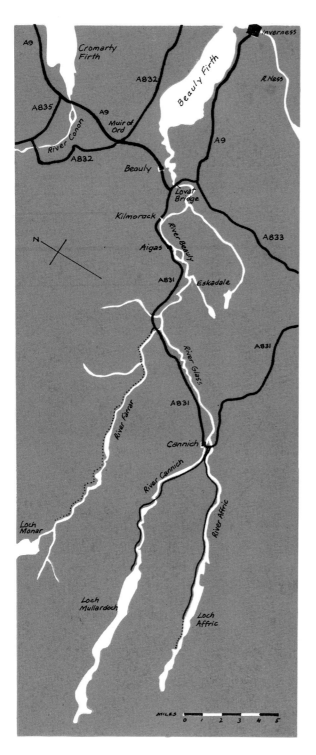

early as 1 April but salmon are stubborn creatures and do not go until they themselves decide the time has come. It is the old question of man interfering with nature.

There was a serious loss of very good angling when the reservoirs were impounded. I am just old enough to remember the magnificent pools at Kilmorack before the dams were built – although I never had the pleasure of fishing them. From Kilmorack right away up past Aigus Dam towards Eskadale was a magnificent stretch in the old days. Now it is a reservoir and, above Aigus, just a long stretch of stillish water – almost unfishable.

The catchment area is vast. It reaches away west to beyond beautiful Loch Affric of the silver birches and gnarled old remnants of the ancient Caledonian Pine Forest, to the gigantic brown trout loch, Mullardoch, some 9 miles long and Loch Monar at the top of the Farrar. But all this is of little significance because of the number of dams, reservoirs and generating stations, which mean that the Beauly and its environs are completely man-controlled and can never be 'natural' again.

As in all hydro rivers there has been the loss of the precious spring run – while the summer grilse runs have benefited. I suppose there are as many fish today as there were in the old days but, as so often happens, they all come in July, August and September. The average number of salmon which ascend through the bottom dam at Kilmorack is pretty steady at about 10,000 – 11,000.

Below Kilmorack Dam is the Falls Beat which includes the pools just below the cruives – Quickshot, Cruives and the Stump. The estate nets the first two pools which is not at all endearing to the fishing tenants, especially in April, when the fish tend to be held up below the cruives in the cold water. After May it doesn't matter so very much. The next beat down is the Home but this beat is slow to fish and it is July before fish seem to lodge in the famous pools of Grome, Charlies and Silver. These two beats have been aggregating anything from 400 to 500 salmon per annum over the past 10 years. While these totals are impressive they are nothing compared to, say, 1967, when over 1,000 salmon and grilse were caught by rod and line from the same beats. The best months are July, August and September, in that order, with the final 15 days of the season in October sometimes extraordinarily good. For some reason the catches over the latter

The gnarled old roots of the ancient Caledonian pines

half of the seventies on the two beats below Kilmorack have been disappointing.

Below the Home Beat is the Downie Beat and I cannot understand why it is not better than it is. It is famous for its sea trout fishing. There is a run of real beauties from February to the end of April and they can catch 800 or 1,000 over those months alone. Then there is a hiatus until July when another run appears which can go on until October. But the numbers have been decreasing somewhat in recent years. The association water is quite good for sea trout with the occasional salmon also. Visitors can be catered for in this stretch from Lovat road bridge right down the tidal pools and well into the estuary.

I did not think and still do not – that colour in a fly is all that important but my belief was shaken by an experience 13 years ago, when fishing the Downie Beat. I was fishing with my friend, Bob Hendry of Craigdarroch, who was unable to come out earlier than 11 am. I started after 10 am with gillie Donald Matheson, selected an all copper-coloured fly, size 6, and started in at the Willow Tree. Soon, I had a sealiced grilse. Then another and another. My friend arrived and promptly asked me what size I was using. 'A six', I answered. So he put on a 6 but caught nothing. Meantime I had moved down to the Fly Pool and caught more fish. My friend caught nothing and asked, 'What pattern?' I told him and he selected something near to it but not quite. But he still caught nothing and I continued to catch fish. Eventually, and reluctantly, he took my rod and I took his. He caught a fish and I didn't do anything with his rod and fly. He was then satisfied that it was not his method of fishing which was at fault and we exchanged rods again. I caught nine fish that short morning – all sealiced – until I cracked off my copper fly. Yes, you've probably guessed the sequel. I caught no more fish even though sealiced fish kept running all day. I still do not understand this success, but it created a record for the Downie Beat for a one rod catch for one day!

The first fish to be taken above the two dams, Kilmorack and Aigus will be on the Lovat Estate's water below the Junction Pool – where Glass and Farrar meet to become the upper Beauly. This could be early in June or even in late May. But the Farrar will simultaneously have salmon, too, and sport will be good all the way to Beannachran Dam. It is the same on the Glass. All the beats up to Cannich will have a smattering of fish in June but it will be July before many are caught. August is better and September is the cream. The season opens on 1 February and closes on 15 October and those last 15 days of the season in October, just like the lower beats, can be tremendously good although we will now be catching red fish. But big baskets are there to be taken in late September and October if you do not mind fish which have long since lost their silveriness.

Lower down, Lovat Estates lease their beats through the estate office in Beauly. Above the Junction some of the upper owners also lease their beats and Glen Affric Hotel, Cannich, acquires quite a number of good beats both on the Glass and Farrar and Murdo MacKenzie will let what he can on a daily basis to non-guests. I love the Farrar. It is such a beautiful glen, tree slopes covered in heather, and if you are lucky enough to fish in September you will never forget the glorious colours of early autumn; up there in October the barking sound you hear reverberating over the glen is from the stags at the beginning of the rut. Here, in this glen, I have the feeling that there is more to fishing than catching fish.

Loch Ness Area

Rivers & Lochs: Garry, Moriston, Ness, Oich
Inverness-shire
Season: 15 Jan–15 Oct
Best months: Garry, see text
Moriston, Ness, Aug/Sept
Oich, Mar
Fly only (Garry)

Most Scottish salmon rivers have a town or city straddling their estuaries. I cannot think of a more beautiful situation than the town of Inverness, where from the high castle grounds you can see the spectacular fault known as the Great Glen, which incorporates Loch Ness and Loch Oich, and the rivers Moriston and Garry. At night the castle is floodlit, as is the cathedral and Eden Court and the lights from these lovely buildings are reflected in the river.

Salmon will pass up the river throughout the year. When the season opens on 15 January (it closes on 15 October) salmon will be found away up in Loch Oich where they can be caught on opening day by trolling a sprat, a Rapalla, a Toby spoon or a devon minnow. They can be caught on the Moriston, too, on opening day and, of course, the brave ones in their boats on Loch Ness can also have luck in January – but it's tough sport on the loch in mid-winter.

The Ness system is vast and probably has one of the largest drainage areas in Scotland apart from the Tay and Tweed systems. With that amount of potential it was not surprising that the hydro board had their sights on some of it and they dammed the Moriston and the Garry. There are actually seven dams and five power stations. No matter what one thinks of the need for electrical power it cannot be denied that the salmon fishing has suffered. Water abstraction on the Moriston and the Garry has meant that these rivers are hardly recognisable to those lucky enough to have fished them in pre-hydro times. Most of these two salmon tributaries

The Moriston at Invermoriston

receive controlled 'compensation' levels and the consequence is low water flows for long periods which do not do a lot for salmon angling.

Salmon get up through the Borland fish lift in the dam at the bottom end of Loch Dundreggan on the Moriston. The average annual 'escapement' there is only about 400 fish. Then they can proceed through Dundreggan and for another 10 or 11 miles as far as Ceannacroic Dam, below Loch Cluanie, where they come to a stop because there is no fish lift. On the Garry the river below the loch of the same name is only a shadow of its former self but nevertheless it is still fishable. Salmon go up the river to the dam at the bottom of Loch Garry where there is another fish lift, up which go some 300 salmon each year. (This number can vary quite a bit; 564 in 1975 or just 290 in 1977.)

Apart from the effect of the hydro-electric works on the Garry and Moriston, the Ness, Loch Ness, the Oich and Loch Oich have not altered much over the years. There was a bit of a scare for Loch Ness and the river when the Foyers pump storage scheme came into operation in 1975/76. The loch

used to rise rapidly and this showed on the river Ness by a rise of up to 2 ft in a very short time. The local club and proprietors protested and very soon the engineers got the hang of it and now there is hardly any rise or fall on the river. I am told by the gillies that a slight rise makes no difference to angling on the Ness.

As I have indicated, salmon go up the Ness all the year round but the angling season is divided into two parts – from January to the end of May and from the end of July until 15 October. This applies to the four beats of the river – a river which is only about 5 or 6 miles long.

The lower, or town water, is leased by the Inverness Angling Club which controls about 1¼ miles of good water above the tide together with a great deal of estuary fishing. It offers the non-member a weekly permit but although it also sells daily permits, these do not cover Saturdays, unlike the weekly ones. Most of the spring fish are caught from the Weir Pool which, although it does not stop fish in the cold early months, inhibits their passage just long enough for a chance. The club

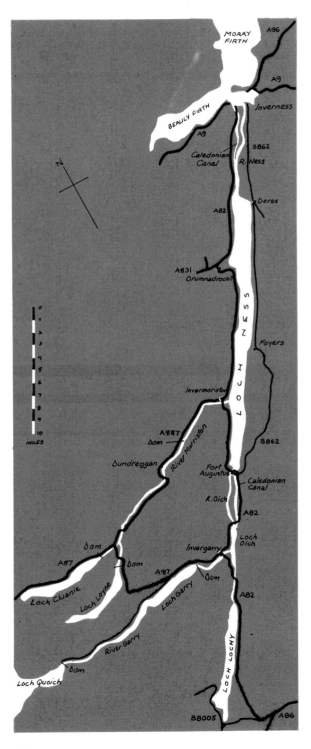

does not do very well over the early season – only about 20 salmon are normally taken during the early months.

As most people know, some very large salmon are taken on Loch Ness each year but, strangely, not on the river, though one of 29 lbs was taken from the Weir Pool in the early days of 1980 by a member. In all, the average catch by the club is around 200 fish and the best times are from the end of July throughout August and September. The tidal stretch of the town water was netted for salmon for a number of years but the lease was, fortunately, retrieved and there was an immediate reaction, with many more salmon gaining access to the river and upper environs.

The club's top pool is Red Braes above which is the Ness Castle water. This is mainly private water and is not really outstanding in the early months. The fish from January to May tend to go right through the club water, the Ness Castle water, the 600 yards or so of another private beat, Laggan (a very streamy water with a nice pool at the bottom), and into the best beat on the Ness – Dochfour.

Dochfour is entirely open to the public but by weekly or longer lets through Dochfour Estate office. However, vacancies do not arise very often. The beat is divided into two, allowing two rods on both, or three if water levels permit. The top beat starts at the weir which is the march between loch and river. The Weir Pool is followed by Burnmouth. The two are fine spring pools but spring fish can be caught on opening day on any of the top water – Netting Water Pool, Gullet and Andrews. The lower beat has the Island and Major and Two Stones which is streamy, swift, shallow and a very good summer pool. But the best pool on this beat is Cul Budhie, which has a streamy neck but slows down to a very big long pool, a fine place for a winter or spring salmon. These are the best of the river over the months from January to May. The weir will hold up the salmon for a little while (but not for long if the river is high).

Bill Paton, for long gillie on this beat, but now retired, told me the early season begins on opening day and ends in early June. The average spring catch is up to 100 salmon in a good year but could be less – only 45 in 1979, for example. But the second 'season' starts at the end of July – there are very few grilse in this river – and the best month by far is September. The annual catch is 400 to 500

The Ness at Inverness

salmon. The pattern for the Dochfour Beat applies to the rest of the river – August and September are the best months – and although enormous salmon pass up into Loch Ness, few are caught in the river. Bill Paton told me that a 30 pounder would be very exceptional but that 20 pounders could be reasonably common.

On all the beats spinning is the only method used in the high and cold waters of January and on to April (never prawns or shrimps on the Ness). Toby spoons seem to be popular but wooden devons are equally used and most people say they hook better than the big spoons. In the summer, up and down the river, small flies are the successful 'lure' such as the Hairy Mary, Tosh, Stoats Tail and the Munro Killer. According to Bill Paton sparsely dressed flies on No 4 hooks are most successful throughout the season.

As I indicated earlier, Loch Ness has fish in it in January, but it can be a rough place. It is 25 miles long and enormous waves build up. It takes years to get to know the drifts, because the salmon only lie by the rocky shoals near the shore-line; with 30 yards of line out the boatman's expertise is all-important, as he manoeuvres the boat to get the lures over the lie at the right moment. Normally

two rods are used, a 'shore' and a 'deep'. The former has a short line to keep the lure near the surface and the 'deep' is longer and the bait fishes at a greater depth. Different coloured Rapallas, Toby spoons, gold-dyed and natural sprats are all successful. Each year quite a number of fish well over 30 lbs are taken from almost any of the famous drifts down the south bank, around Foyers, Invermoriston and Fort Augustus. It is not known how many, but the number is considerable.

The Moriston offers early salmon fishing from 15 January, but only the 500 yards of river from the tailrace of the generating station to the loch will produce fish early in the season. Glenmoriston Estates let this water out, accommodating six rods per day. If Loch Ness is high a peculiar thing happens. The first time I fished this river with my friend Don Keegan, everything was normal – there was a good flow from the electricity station and the river pushed its way out to the loch. Suddenly they stopped generating; the flow slowed down and stopped. I could hardly believe my eyes when, within a few minutes, the river started to flow upstream! When the thrust of water from the station stopped, the river and loch merely found parity of level and, in fact, after another few minutes, river and loch became one – as far up as the generating station.

Realistically, the estate refers to the beat as the Estuary Beat, one that can be quite a productive little bit of water. It is mainly spinning water but there is a nice stream opposite the tailrace where a salmon or two have been taken on fly in January or February. The estate claims the average catch between 15 January and 1 March can be as high as 100 salmon and from then on to early June another 100 fish can be taken. This would include those fish taken from the two boats which fish the loch. An average weight of salmon at 20 lbs is impressive and often fish over 30 lbs are taken, with eight such monsters on one recent day.

The whole of the Moriston is open to the public through Glenmoriston Estate. All their fishings from Loch Ness, the Estuary to the lower and upper Moriston are available. Tenants leasing cottages, chalets or staying in the hotel are charged at a reduced rate. Gillies and Landrovers are also available. Spinning is permitted on Loch Ness and on the Estuary Beat but it is strictly fly only on the lower and upper Moriston.

Salmon move up out of the Estuary by May and, by early June, are through the dam at Dundreggan. From the dam to Torgoyle Bridge is 5 miles and this is the Dundreggan Beat which is not particularly outstanding for salmon. But the Upper Beat from Torgoyle to the fish heck at Ceannacroic is about 6 miles and produces around 30 to 40 salmon per annum. Best months in these upper beats are August and September and the flies used are no different from those of other salmon waters at that time of the year; Hairy Mary, Stoats Tail, Garry Dog etc and in very small sizes. Although large salmon are caught in the Estuary the average weight in the top waters is only 8 lbs. Obviously the large fish are wary of the low water levels.

The Garry was sold by the hydro board a few years ago and the new owners let it through the Rod and Gun Shop, Fort William. The leases are pretty permanent and the best is not available to the casual enquirer. It is a fly only river except for that part from the generating station to Loch Oich – a very short distance – where spinning is allowed. Boats on Loch Oich go with the Garry and very often the first salmon of the season for the whole of the Ness system will be taken off the loch. Lures are just the same as for Loch Ness.

The Oich is the communication between Loch Oich and Loch Ness and it is only over the past five years that this river has been opened up to the public. Alex D MacDonald, Fishing Tackle, Fort Augustus, issues tickets for three rods per day for a $3\frac{1}{2}$ miles stretch on the left hand bank, terminating at Fort Augustus, on behalf of the local estate, and also two rods per day on a $2\frac{1}{2}$ miles stretch of the same bank, where Loch Oich empties into the river.

There are no restrictions as to permitted lures and if there are good water levels the fishing can be excellent with as many as four fish to one rod. But one has to be lucky because the records indicate that only around 40 salmon are caught on the lower stretch per season and far fewer off the Upper Beat, although the latter's figures could easily improve if it were fished more often. Best fish over recent years was one of 34 lbs from the Boat Pool by Alex MacDonald himself, and I know he has had the first fish of the season quite frequently. This can be on 15 January but the best month is March.

Fort William Area

Rivers & Lochs: Cour, Eilt,
Lochy, Moidart, Morar,
Nevis, Roy, Shiel, Spean
Inverness-shire
Season: 11 Feb–31 Oct
Best months: July/Aug

This is a gigantic area of the Western Highlands stretching from the tail end of the Great Glen to include Loch Lochy, the river Lochy and its tributaries, Spean, Roy and Cour, and the Nevis at Fort William. Then away north west to Mallaig it takes in those famous sea trout and salmon lochs, Loch Eilt and Loch Morar. These areas are enormous in themselves but, in addition there is Morvern with the salmon and sea trout fishings on the Aline, Rannoch and Arienas (on the Ardtornich Estate) and Moidart with the famous Shiel and Loch Shiel for salmon and sea trout.

Few would deny that this is the grandest and most scenic part of Scotland. The ratio of water to land is very high indeed and the country is rugged and mountainous with a vast number of deep long sea lochs – almost like Norwegian fjords. In conse-

quence the rivers are short and nearly all have a fresh-water loch at their head. To this there is one exception, the Lochy system, the largest and most prolific salmon river in the whole area. It is mainly a private river but there is one stretch to which the day anglers have access and an excellent stretch of water it is if you consider 400 to 500 migratory fish taken for the season to be satisfactory. This is the return given in a small, concise, but useful little booklet *Guide to Fishing – Fort William Area* by the Rod and Gun Shop. The extent of this public stretch (Beat 7) is from about one mile north of Fort William back down to the tidal waters. The part of the beat from the railway bridge to the junction with the tailrace of the power station is reserved for fly fishing only. From the tailrace down to the first set of overhead wires (300 yards) spinning is permitted provided the water level is above the marker. Below this there is another large pool reserved at all times for fly fishing only. Worm, prawns and bubble floats are forbidden. One other condition has been added since the guide was printed and that is the bag limit is set at two salmon per day! 12 fish in a day are known to have been taken – but by dubious methods. Enquiries can be made at the Rod and Gun Shop, Fort William, where a number of fishings throughout the whole area are handled.

A few salmon start to run the Lochy in late April – and these pass quickly through upriver. But the

public water can start to fish in May with best months July and August. There is no real run of spring fish but salmon can be quite large – up to 30 lbs with quite a number each year between 20 and 25 lbs. There is a reasonably good run of grilse but the Lochy is a spate river and if conditions are good the sport can be excellent. There is some water abstraction for the pulp mill at Corpach (doomed to closure as I write) but this has never made any noticeable difference to the flow.

The main tributary is the Spean. There are a number of beats on this small sporting river. Beat B is handled by the Rod and Gun Shop, Fort William, and consists of the left hand bank from Cour Pool down to the road bridge at Spean Bridge – a distance of about half a mile. It is very rocky and is definitely not for the aged or handicapped. There are good holding pools here, the Cour being the top one and large salmon over 20 lbs can be caught. It is fly and/or spinning only. Numerous bits and pieces have been given over to local angling clubs for their own use but some private stretches are sometimes available. Spean Bridge Hotel leases a half mile of interesting water – rocky, but with good pools. It is half a mile away from the hotel and stretches from the old railway bridge to the 'high bridge'. Fly and/or spinning is permitted but no worming or prawning and only two rods per day are allowed. The Roy flows into the Spean 4 miles up beyond the village and Roy Bridge Hotel offers tickets for this part which can often have fairly large salmon in it. Fish of 23 to 26 lbs have come out of the Roy. The Cour is similar and it, too, is very much a spate river. The whole of the Spean, and its small tributaries, comes into its own from late June but August is the best month.

These rivers are all badly poached but there is evidence that the local owners and clubs are taking the situation seriously because there are more arrests followed by successful convictions nowadays. Since netting has been curtailed there has been a marked increase in the runs of salmon. Where spinning is permitted Spean salmon seem very keen on a spun lure. I think the reason why they go for a 4 inch silver or gold Toby spoon is that the Spean will colour up after a spate and these big spoons can easily be seen (and heard?) by salmon. It is the favourite weapon. For the fly angler the Shrimp, Hairy Mary and Stoats Tail patterns are best, but the local anglers favour them as tubes.

The other Fort William river is the Nevis. It runs down off Ben Nevis and flows through the town to the sea. The Fort William AC controls this water which is about 7 miles long. Six tickets are available daily and angling is with fly only except when the river is in spate, when worm is permitted. Spinning is not allowed at any time. It is a back-end river and a spate river. The first of the salmon could be well upstream after a spate in July. Like a lot of those West Highland rivers the water is usually crystal clear except immediately after a spate and one can see the fish in the pools from quite a long way off. The trouble is – if the angler can see the fish . . . the fish can see the angler! So, like the little Croe, with its open banks, cast as long as you can with lightish tackle. The best of the salmon are only about 10 lbs.

Morvern is a wild bit of country bounded on the south by the Firth of Lorne and on the north by Loch Sunart – a sea loch. All the while the mountains of the island of Mull watch over this beautiful and quiet backwater of the Highlands. The main salmon and sea trout fishings belong to the Ardtornich Estates who open them entirely to the public. Details of what is available, cost and maps can be had from the estate office. All their fishings are fly only and the main fishings for salmon and sea trout are the Aline, divided into three beats, and the White Glen Beat, a spate beat. There is also the Rannoch and Loch Arienas for salmon and sea trout. The expected salmon and sea trout catch returns are from 50 to 60 salmon and 200 sea trout, each year. But all the little rivers in this part of the world are very much dependent on rain.

Moidart means Loch Shiel to me, with very good salmon and sea trout fishing. Salmon run up the little river Shiel at Acharacle, enter the loch and the early fish tend to go right up the 23 miles of loch to the top end at Glenfinnan. They are taken on the trolled lure whilst the sea trout stick to the fly. Salmon will rise to the fly later on in August and September and dapping is successful for sea trout as well as salmon. Nearly all the hotels from Glenfinnan to Acharacle provide boats. The Shiel is less than 3 miles long and the early fish (in May) tend to run straight through followed by grilse in June and July. The many sea trout run in May and, as ever, the early fish will be the largest, with the smaller ones following on in July.

The river Moidart shares the same sea loch as the Shiel and is not readily available but it is a spate

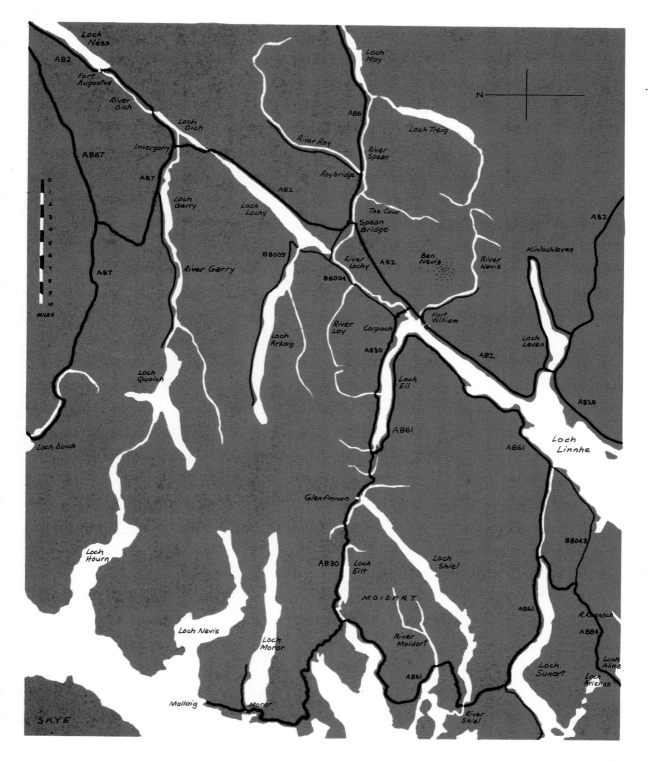

A salmon trap on the Polly

river and has a reasonable run of sea trout and salmon, especially in July. Salmon are small – a few larger ones in May, perhaps, with 6 lbs grilse in summer from the top water but an average of 8 lbs from the lower beat. Sea trout are numerous late in the season (August and September) but are small-ish.

For me the pièce de résistance is Loch Eilt to which the very large sea trout run from May/June. For the past few years sea trout up to 15, 16 or even 17 lbs have been taken fairly regularly. It is fly only, but dapping is permitted and it was here that I first tried out the tube dapping fly. The chosen pattern is built on a polythene tube for lightness and a small treble hook is threaded through. When a fish is hooked the 'fly' slides up the cast out of the way. I prefer the tube dap to the conventional single hook, but there has always been controversy as to the merits of the hooking qualities of the tube dap compared to the single hook. An enquiry at Morar Hotel could be made, but the answer is likely to be that there are no vacancies – such is the popularity of Loch Eilt.

Last, but not least, of course, is Loch Morar. This is the deepest loch in the UK and has its own monster and I don't mean salmon or sea trout! Salmon average out at a modest 9 lbs. Both salmon and sea trout will be in the loch at the same time – from May on. Salmon do not seem to rise to a fly but will take a trolled bait and sea trout only go for a fly, so the best bet is to troll a spoon or minnow up to your drift and then fly fish for sea trout, trolling your bait all the way home. Boats can be hired from various places but the Morar Hotel may be worth contacting. Sea trout can be as heavy as 4 or 5 lbs and the best places are in the numerous bays round the periphery of the loch and in the region of the islands. A word of warning – don't go steaming up the loch with a powerful outboard. There are plenty of dangerous rocks and ridges just under the surface!

The whole area west of Fort William abounds with numerous small sea trout and salmon rivers and lochs. There are far too many to name and if you happen to be going into this beautiful region then consult the various guide books which give a comprehensive run down of these little fisheries. But, remember, they are mostly spate fishings, marvellous for a few hours after rain – unfishable much of the time.

The Kirkaig

Rivers: Inver, Kirkaig
Sutherland/Ross & Cromarty
Season: 11 Feb–15 Oct
Best months: July–Sept
Fly only

What a challenging and sporting little salmon river this is – and what a good one. It is one of the most exciting rivers I know, though one has to work hard for one's salmon. It is a physical river in the sense that a considerable degree of energy is expended getting to the Middle and Upper beats and when they are reached the angler has to descend from the path, down very steep heather-covered rocky banks to the pools and, frequently, in order to fish the next pool down, has to climb back to the path and do the whole exercise again. There are also high rocks, cliffs and banks behind, making life difficult for those unable to roll out a line or cast over the left shoulder.

Only for mountain goats then? No one should be put off. Every step of the 2 mile long path up to Kirkaig Falls is a wonderful experience and although fishing the top beat may be for pretty fit anglers, Commander Swann, who has fished this river every year for the past 15 years and can usually pick up nearly 20 salmon during his annual stay in July, was in his middle seventies in 1980 when I renewed my acquaintance with him away up on the top waters! The one serious problem for the lone angler is the carrying of salmon all the way back to the car at the road bridge!

The catchment area covers about 80 square miles, but the Falls of Kirkaig, just over 2 miles from the tide, is completely insurmountable to salmon and the Falls Pool is the top of the river for practical angling purposes. I used to wonder why this fall was never eased for the passage of salmon but when I saw it, I could understand the impossibility of such a task. It could be classed as a spate river but with the series of lochs above the Falls of Kirkaig the peat content is quickly filtered out and the river can run clear in no time at all.

The pier near Little Assynt on the Inver is in very deep water and great care is needed by all who use it

The Culag Hotel at Lochinver has the river for guests although non-residents can often be accommodated for a daily permit. The river and hotel are owned by Assynt Estates. Peter Hay, the factor, an expert angler of great experience and one who knows this river intimately in all its seasons has written an extremely helpful guide for anglers who do not know the Kirkaig. It describes every pool in each of the three beats, how to fish them and where the best lies are in the varying water levels. He gives a list of the successful flies and warns the angler of the danger of fishing with nylon too light for this rocky and swift river. It is a fly-only river and only the right bank is fishable. Beat 1 commences at the Kirkaig Falls Pool down to the Mac-Kenzie Stream – 13 named pools. The Falls Pool is a spectacular place because the angler cannot possibly land the fish on his own. His companion, or gillie, slides down from the fishing stance by a rope to a ledge where, with luck, the fish is gaffed and recovered. This beat includes the Little Falls which is reckoned to be the best pool on the river. Red Lump is just below and is a good place but as the current flows so swiftly through this narrow pool fish usually have to be walked down to Barbara's Pool to be landed. The Bow Pool is a small but deep pool and has a reputation for producing the big fish. This beat is one mile long and is hard work and a great beat for those with a weight problem!

Beat 2 (the Middle Beat) consists of 10 pools and requires a bit less of the gymnastics although there are steep banks of rock and heather behind one's back. The Upper Red Pool is a good pool at all times and I found that 'dibbling' was a profitable method here, fishing from the high rock. Little Kirkaig is a pool which holds fish in all heights and, the next one down, the Hazel, is another which holds fish in any height.

Beat 3 (the Lower Beat) has seven pools. The top one, the Heather, which is probably best, holds a lot of fish and yields a lot, too. The bottom pool is the Sea Pool which can be good for sea trout but only the occasional salmon. Apart from the Heather Pool the remainder are adjacent to the road and very accessible. The trouble with this beat is that the banks are open and are always populated with tourists and tents although something is being done about this problem. In all, there are 30 named pools on the Kirkaig with many more un-named places where fish can be caught when they are running.

Although the season opens on 11 February and closes on 15 October, there will be no more than the odd fish in the river from March until June, and then only if there is water. The first real run of salmon occurs at the end of June and certainly with the first spate of July. This summer run is usually heavy, with grilse as well as salmon. They will run throughout August and bigger fish come in September. The occasional fresh-run salmon will be taken in the lower stretches in October, but do not depend on it – by then most of the stock will be pretty red. It is surprising how many large salmon

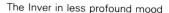

The Inver in less profound mood

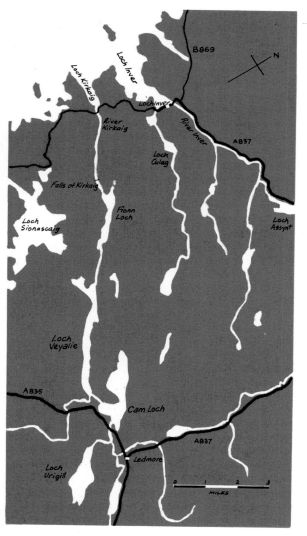

can be taken in this small river – fish well up in the teens and even over 20 lbs. I remember a few years ago fish of over 30 lbs being taken. But it would be fair to say that only a small proportion of the big fish ever get grassed. To reiterate, it is a grand, sporting river. Its rockiness, the swiftness of the current and the impossibility of following fish from a number of pools, demand that heavy nylon casts be used. In a flood, even in high summer, large flies are presented such as 7/0s and even 1/0s and 3/0s in medium water. That is not to say that small hooks are not successful. I have had successes on No 4s and 6s. A number of people use the dropper. Peter Hay fishes a 1/0 as the dropper and a 3/0 on the tail. Of course this is in high water. He gives a number of fly patterns in his guide such as the Silver Grey, Silver Doctor and Thunder and Lightning but a fly which I found very effective was the Blue Elver with its long 'wings' making it look really like a live thing in the bubbly water.

Waders are hardly necessary – certainly not at all on the Upper Beat. I have fished from the Falls right down to the estuary in one day, wearing only rubber soled climbing boots. I find these more secure than rubber knee boots and less tiring.

To meet the ever-growing demand for salmon angling by hotel guests, Assynt Estate on occasion, gives the Culag Hotel its top beat of the Inver which flows out of Loch Assynt and empties into the sea at Lochinver village. The beat starts at the sluice at the bottom of the loch and extends to the Grilse Burn. There are two stretches of river which widen out into lochans with a boat on each of them. Their best pools are the lochans Loch na Garbh Uidhe and Lochan an Iasgaich – pronounced 'Loch na garve oo ye' and 'Lochan an Ee-as-kech' respectively. Lochan an Iasgaich means 'Loch of the fish', or 'the fishing loch' – very apt!

Some of the pools in this top water are very thin and do best in spate or high water conditions. Much smaller flies than those used on the Kirkaig have to be used because of the slower flow. It is best fished in July and right on to the end of the season but the odd fish can be up there in May or June. There is not much between the Kirkaig and the Inver with regard to the first fish of the season. But the Kirkaig usually has that distinction although an April Easter will see the Inver with a fish or two. There are other beats lower down the Inver but these are not easy to get on to.

The Ewe and Loch Maree

Rivers: Ewe, Loch Maree
Ross & Cromarty
Season: 11 Feb–30 Sept
(Loch Maree 11 Feb–12 Oct)
Best months: June/July
Fly only

The Ewe is one of the smallest rivers in Scotland, for practical purposes little more than a mile long. Any reader though, who doubted whether so Liliputian a stream merited much attention would be making a grave mistake. In fact the Ewe and the loch which feeds it, Loch Maree, are famed throughout the world. The whole system is renowned for its salmon and grilse but, most of all, its sea trout. Where the angler can catch a sea trout larger than a salmon we must make an exception and include the prince of game fish along with the king.

Many miles away, up in the rugged mountains above Kinlochewe lies Loch Coulin with its small communicating outlet to Loch Clair. The burns which feed these two lochs are the main source of the river system and what a catchment area that is. The rainfall for the month of November 1979 was 14 inches! There are two other main feeder streams, the Heights River and the Glendocherty Burn that combine with the countless burns which throw themselves off the steep slopes of Ben Slioch and other high ranges, to swell Loch Maree. Maree itself is roughly 14 miles long and is one of the six largest Scottish lochs. It is certainly the best sea trout and salmon loch in the British Isles. Though deep in places (366 ft) there are many acres of water at just the right depth for angling and it is this as much as anything that has contributed to its international renown.

Strangely enough it is sometimes at the top of the system, some 16 to 20 miles from the sea where the first salmon of the season is taken. Coulin and Clair are two picturesque lochs which have as a backdrop the mighty Torridonian range of mountains. Out of Clair tumbles the Kinlochewe river for a length of some 6 miles before it dissipates into the top end of Loch Maree. There are those who say that Loch Maree is the most beautiful loch in all Scotland. I agree with them – perhaps because I see it in winter with its centuries old Caledonian pines scraping a living from the bare rock and snowclad Slioch towering above in magnificent isolation, like a great cake capped with icing. Opposite Loch Maree Hotel are the Islands. All have names, but more importantly the channels and passages between them bear the famous names of the beats; Ash island, Steamer Channel, Hotel Bay, Back of Island, Salmon Reach and so on.

After 14 miles the loch narrows at Coree and Tollie Bay and as the sides of the loch gather towards each other we begin to find the semblance of a current flowing in the direction of the sea. But it is not quite the river yet. This part is still the loch

and is known as A Beat. Nevertheless, in times of high water there is a draw, especially around the area of the Garden Pool and many a salmon has been hooked just there when the water is high.

River Ewe

The river starts officially just below the Garden Pool at a place called the Top Narrows. From here to Lower Narrows the river is hardly worthy of the name and only these narrows help to make it worthwhile – Top Narrows, Middle Narrows and Lower Narrows with large tracts of 'loch-like' water between them. There is hardly any descending gradient between the three narrows so there have to be high water levels to create a flow in these 'pools'. The other most important ingredient is, of course, wind.

But, here again, one can be deceived. Although they look pretty useless places Top Narrows and Middle Narrows are two very good pools for salmon from the beginning of the season on 11 February to 30 September. Sea trout, of course, do not arrive until sometime in June. Even Lower Narrows is a fine pool at its very tail in high water.

The river completely changes its character immediately below Lower Narrows. From a frustrating stretch of angling water, when it is low, quite suddenly it descends to the sea in a turbulent jumble of white water with very fine angling pools at intervals on the way down. This stretch of 'normal' salmon river is, quite absurdly, less than a mile long but within it there is the Tee Pool followed in quick succession by the Macordies, the Hen, the Manse and the Flats impounded by a weir with a

Previous page: 'Into him' on the Cruive Pool

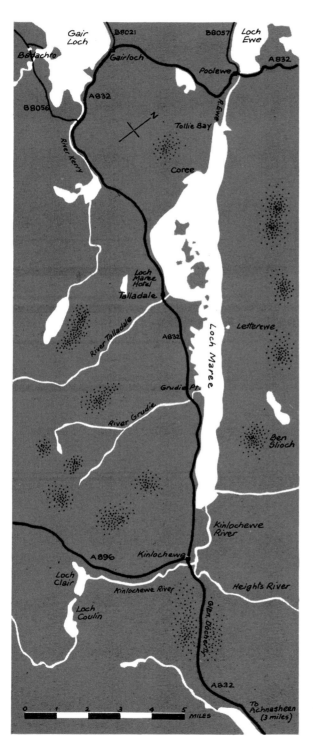

gap in the middle – a famous gap where salmon and sea trout stop for a few moments on their way up and can be caught!

Just below the Flats the river divides into two because of a man-made island built a century or so ago to form cruives for the netting of salmon. On the left side is the Hen House Pool and the other holds the Old Cruive Pool. Both streams come together and the whole lot thunders down to the Sea Pool, which is an excellent fishing pool in low or medium water. The tide reaches up to the Sea Pool on most occasions, but, if not, then the whole of the river system disappears in a foaming mass into the sea under the bridge at Poolewe.

With the river being so short and with the vast area and depth of Loch Maree behind it, four interesting features arise. Even in February the river never ices up and conversely in the summer it never really gets too warm. Second, the loch acts as a filter and the water, even in an enormous spate, remains crystal clear; third, it has no peat content to sicken and 'put off' fish. Finally, when the loch fills up after prolonged rainfall, the river 'fishes' for at least two weeks.

The best part of the season is July. Not only salmon and grilse come streaming up the river into Loch Maree but literally thousands of sea trout also. More salmon have come off the river in July recently than in August and September, but the exciting feature of July is that the same small fly will attract a salmon, a grilse, a sea trout or even a small sealiced finnoch. When your fly stops mid-way round its semicircular journey so does your heart. Is it one of the big chaps, a salmon of 20 lbs perhaps, or better still is it a specimen sea trout of 10 lbs or over? Or is it just a little finnoch? This is what makes July the best month – not simply the fact that there are more fish about than other months. Of course in August and September there are more salmon in the river but there is a subtle difference. In July they are all streaming through, salmon and sea trout, and every fish caught is sealiced. But after July, the salmon still come, probably in greater numbers, while the bulk of the sea trout are now in the loch. The salmon slow down and even take up residence in the pools. Now one is fishing over stale fish – getting staler all the time and therefore a bit more difficult to catch.

Back to July; this month seems to have been improving progressively over the last few years. In

1978 100 salmon were caught in July. In 1979 the score was 130. This was very good fishing. In 1978 I personally had seven salmon to my rod in one day. In 1979 I had nine fish. This kind of daily total is about as good as you will find anywhere. I have already mentioned all the pools in this small river but, particularly in high water, there is no doubt that the Flats is the best of all. This is not just my own choice. More fish come from this pool than any other. I have cause to be biased however. I once caught a 16½ lbs sea trout there which was the best-ever sea trout for me and is also still a record for the river. Strangely the same pool also gave me my best-ever salmon taken anywhere, at 28½ lbs. You will understand therefore that I have strong feelings on the subject!

The next best pool is the Middle Narrows. I find it an exciting place to fish. The two groynes directly opposite each other create a V. Even with a wind, one can always see the salmon come at the fly – the boil, perhaps the dorsal fin breaking surface and the tail going over, the loose line tightening and then that most thrilling of moments when the rod bends and you are into him (a salmon is always a 'him' for some reason). The Upper Narrows is exactly the same. A beautiful V as the current draws together as the result of its two groynes and here too the same sensation can be experienced with fish showing as they take the fly. The turbulent Macordies is not quite the same, but what a fine man-made pool this is, with its weir at the bottom, its three groynes from which to fish and the line of large stones, parallel and well out from the right bank to enable anglers to cast without catching the heather. The famous Tee Pool is just above the Macordies. But what a difficult pool this is with its enormous backwater which brings your fly round until it is going back upstream! The secret here is to cast in the usual way but then keep in touch with the fly by recovering line all the time. Both sides have groynes and one must start off by first fishing a short line to cover the salmon or sea trout which are lying just feet off them.

The Manse Pool has four groynes and, here too, one can catch a salmon or sea trout virtually at one's feet. But down on the Flats the men are separated from the boys! If the water is too big for wading one has to make the 25 yards or more to the gap from the lower groyne. It is a long cast from the right bank. The groynes on the left side are shorter

and if one can Spey cast so much the better. But while most of us are trying to cover as much water as possible the tyro can pick up his first-ever salmon almost at his feet off any of the groynes.

The Sea Pool is the Mecca for most anglers. They can almost cast from their car on the right bank! But it is a lovely pool to fish with the first really good taking place opposite the door of the church. However, both salmon and sea trout rest at the very brink of the pool after they have struggled up the heavy white water from the sea and they often take just there. The trouble is, as you may have already guessed, the big salmon or sea trout tend to go back to where they came from – the sea. And there is not a thing one can do about it except reel in the slack or broken line.

I have mentioned July because it is the most exciting month but salmon will certainly pass through the river in February, March and April. Not many will be taken – just a handful. May is the first good salmon month and by mid-June the grilse, the summer salmon and the early sea trout will start off the real fishing in earnest. August and September are two good salmon months but although salmon are numerous they are getting progressively more red and a little dour. But sea-liced salmon can still be caught right up to the end of September.

The Ewe is controlled by one estate and enquiries could be made to The Factor, Scatwell Estates Office, Muir of Ord, Ross-shire. The Kinlochewe river is sometimes available to the public, especially during the early salmon season and enquiries could be made to The Estate Manager, Kinlochewe Estates, Kinlochewe, Achnasheen, Ross-shire.

Officially the salmon and sea trout season opens on 11 February and closes on 30 September. These dates apply to the river and, of course, there are very few sea trout about before mid-June.

For the loch the same dates apply except that the season for both salmon and sea trout continues until around 12 October. Here, again, there will be no sea trout in the loch until mid-June.

Loch Maree

The Kinlochewe Chalet Complex and Kinlochewe Hotel put out their boats in April and at once they catch salmon by trolling along the top shore and near the river mouth. But the loch is more famous for its sea trout and after anglers stop thinking of

Slioch towering over Loch Maree

salmon at about the end of June, up come the first of thousands of sea trout. The big ones tend to arrive first – fish of up to 10 lbs. In the middle sixties sea trout up to 20 lbs were abundant but then came disease and other environmental problems and, suddenly, we had no large sea trout left. But there has been a steady increase in both number and the size of sea trout and, in 1979, Loch Maree Hotel's boats were responsible for a total catch of 1,448 sea trout at 4,434 lbs, an increase in the average weight of 1.6 lbs over 1978. Very many sea trout between 6 and 10 lbs were caught in 1979 and the same story of success was confirmed from the Kinlochewe end.

Loch Maree Hotel leases the largest and most productive area of the loch. Their beats extend round the beautiful pine clad islands and as far up as Grudie Point. They have nine boats all rotating through the beats with a tenth boat from Shieldaig Lodge Hotel, down the road near Badachro.

Nearly every angler uses the Loch Maree method for catching sea trout, which is by dapping. These sea trout, and the salmon too, go for a large dapping fly attached by a nylon cast to a terylene 'blow line' which catches the wind and extends well out from the boat like a spinnaker. In a big wave and strong wind the fly should dance about from wave top to wave top in a semicircular pattern and now and

The Croe

Rivers: Croe
Ross & Cromarty
Season: 11 Feb–31 Oct
Best months: July–Sept
Fly only

This little spate river in the Kintail area of south west Ross can be surprisingly good for salmon and sea trout. But the essential ingredient is rain and it is sad just how little there always appears to be in the summer when one is looking for it!

The Croe water is gin clear most of the time and it pays to fish 'fine and far off'. I have cast out a tiny No 12 Tosh into the Elbow Pool and seen a salmon start out for it quite a number of yards away. So, if you can see the fish don't let him see you!

Some time at the end of the sixties I did a survey of this little river for the estate which has the right-hand bank and for the National Trust for Scotland which has the opposite one. The troubles stemming from the fact that both sides shared small pools with crystal clear water were legion and, arising out of the recommendations I made the river is now fished by the owners on alternate days, which means they have both banks and no arguments!

The National Trust for Scotland issues permits through the agent, Mr R MacLean, Morvich Farm, by Kyle of Lochalsh, but it must be said that it is such a popular little river from mid-August to mid-October (the end of the season) that there may not be any vacancies. Only four rods are allowed.

I have known salmon to be in the river, and caught, in May but normally July sees the beginning of both the sea trout and salmon runs. It is such a small stream that I am always surprised when I learn that salmon well over 12 lbs can be caught and sea trout up to 6 lbs. A 19 lbs salmon was taken in 1980 from the Elbow Pool and the record is 19½ lbs. But the average weights are 6 or 7 lbs for salmon and 2 or 2½ lbs for sea trout. I have caught a beautiful silvery grilse of 6 lbs as late as mid-October and even a 12 lbs salmon on the last day of the season.

again a Maree monster will torpedo through the waves and grab the fly. At other times, it is fair to point out, they will only 'inspect' the fly. Wet fly fishing is not practised much around the islands but at the Kinlochewe end more fish are probably taken on the wet fly than the dap. The heaviest sea trout off Maree was one just an ounce or two short of 20 lbs and the heaviest salmon weighed in at 33 lbs. Casts of these can be examined at Loch Maree Hotel.

The sea trout season on the loch continues a little longer than on the river – boats stop around 12 October. Dapping equipment, flies and rods, boats and engines, can be hired locally.

NORTH EAST SCOTLAND

This is a stimulating and easily accessible part of Scotland; Aberdeen station when the night train arrives is still thronged with passengers carrying their rods and tackle. Aberdeen is an easy drive from Edinburgh, with motorways almost all the way to Perth and good roads from there. It is the bustling and booming centre of the North Sea oil industry and just as it is said to be difficult to look at the Spey without seeing a salmon jump so it is hard to miss Aberdeen's fetching and carrying helicopters.

Moving across the area from Aberdeen the scenery becomes more and more rewarding, rolling to begin with, growing more mountainous and majestic with every mile. No one should miss the chance of exploring the upper reaches of the Don or of a journey up the valley of the Spey.

In addition to the rivers described in detail within, there are the Nairn, the Lossie (with its angling club centred on Elgin, where there is also a first-class golf club), the little Ugie, flowing into the sea at Peterhead, and finally, closer to Aberdeen, the Ythan estuary, by Newburgh, famous for its sea trout and occasional salmon.

It is an area that contains some of the cream of Scottish salmon fishing combined with every other facility that the most discerning tourist could demand.

The Findhorn

Rivers: Findhorn
Nairn/Morayshire
Season: 11 Feb–31 Oct
Best months: Mar/Apr/Sept

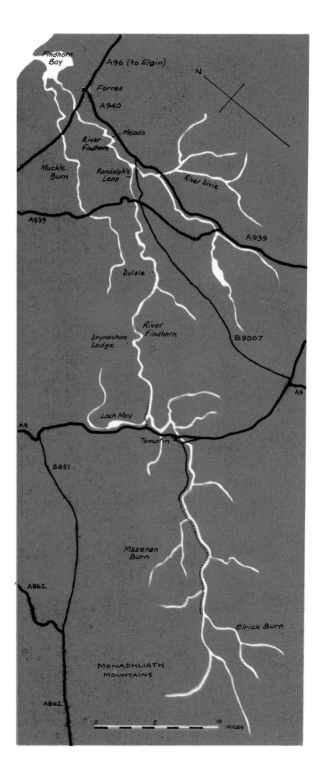

If the Spey is said to be the swiftest flowing river in Scotland then the Findhorn must surely come second. This is not surprising because its source is high up in the Monadhliath Mountains. It is approximately 65 miles long and drains some 400 square miles. The river is fed by a few tributaries but the burns up in the headwaters are excellent spawning streams. The Funlack Burn attracts spawning salmon up to Loch Moy where they use the feeder streams for that purpose. The Mazeran Burn is important, too. Then away downstream comes the Divie Burn which is a very fine spawning stream but its fishing is private.

From its source to just above Dulsie Bridge the river is very open with shingly pools and reasonable streamy, although thin, water. The deep drainage systems up in the higher rough grass lands with stunted juniper trees and heather create those awful flash flood conditions which are not good for angling and are damaging to the spawning redds in the small feeder streams. The top half of the river can experience a 4 ft rise in less than 15 minutes.

At Dulsie Bridge the character of the Findhorn quite astonishingly changes when it suddenly and rapidly drops and plunges down through redstone cliffs which are 200 ft high in places. It is a beautiful but awesome part of the river with some of the white water rapids descending 20 ft. In the middle of this stretch is Randolph's Leap, a very narrow pool where the whole volume of the river pours through a gap in the rocks less than 10 ft wide. I saw this extraordinary place one day in a high spate and couldn't believe that all the water I had seen up at Dulsie was pouring through such a small gap. This place is part of the 'gorge' area, over 20 miles long, and has an important bearing on the upstream movement of salmon. There is another natural phenomenon a little further down in the gorge area – the Poolie – where the gap is also just about 10 ft.

In the spring with low temperatures, and the snowmelt keeping it that way, salmon will move slowly up from the estuary and come to a halt in the gorge area. If not too cold around mid-April, and just for an hour or so each day, the big fish may move through these temperature pools but in very cold water this movement may not take place until May. In 1980 there was an exception. With very little snow the fish moved up in mid-April before the drought stopped all further runs. So one gets the picture. Above Logie, salmon fishing is not usually productive until late April whereas below that area the early sport can be reasonable. But once fish start going through the gorges they go at speed and within three days they will be right up at, and above, Tomatin, on the A9 Perth/Inverness road.

In its lower reaches the Findhorn is the most beautiful, wild, rugged and sometimes fearsome salmon river one can hope to see. But what about its salmon and sea trout? The spring runs suffered as a result of disease but, like most others, there has been some improvement over recent years and this is in no small measure due to the good husbandry of Ralph Harkness, the now retired river superintendent, who enlarged the hatchery which eventually had an average capacity of 500,000 eggs.

All my angling life I have heard many complaints of the way the estuary and adjacent coast are netted. In fact, it reminds me of the North Esk with all its bag and stake nets along the coast and the intensive estuarial netting. Anglers often grouse that the Findhorn is a salmon river at the mercy of the commercial netsmen. But, to be fair, although the netting season opens on 11 February they now limit the netting to two or three sweeps per week until 11 March. This agreement was reached between the fishery board and the netting interests in order that more spring stock should escape to spawn naturally for the ultimate benefit of both rods and nets.

However, after 11 March the nets are hard at it for the remainder of the season; if there is plenty of water there will be a good 'escapement' and the rods will be happy and have a good time. Over the last three years of the seventies, there was precipitation and fine stocks of salmon in the beats as a result. But if the season is dry then the river suffers and the local anglers say that they have to rely either on a good head of fish getting into the river before

the nets start or on late fish after the nets cease on 26 August. The only other hope during a dry season is a river rise over the weekend when the nets are off. I have heard it said that the aggregate catch of the river, estuarial and immediate coastal nets, averages 4,000 salmon and as many as 10/15,000 grilse per annum. Some say this is a very conservative estimate (why don't they say what their catch is?). In the low water of summer a few grilse can pass upstream over the fords of the netting pools.

The early run is in February and March and these are the bigger fish – up to 30 lbs and many between 15 and 20 lbs. Heavier runs occur in April but smaller fish at 8 to 10 lbs.

In late or mid-June the grilse run and then there are limited numbers of summer salmon of 10 to 20 lbs in weight. Finally, there is a run of late salmon but these do not travel fast or very far. Most are taken low down the river from the estuary pools, upstream for about 10 miles. These late comers are just in from the sea and are a mixture of silvery and coloured fish – but good enough to keep compared to the gravid fish taken higher up with the worm and other lures.

It is my own experience that the top beats above, say, Dulsie, do not have many fresh-run fish after August. It was up at Drynachan that I first became aware that the fly in August and September was far more productive than the worm or spinner. I was fishing that beat one September and using a No 8 Copper King. I came across the pool, Quilichan, to get to which one has to cross the river in the famous 'bucket bridge'. This is literally a bucket suspended from wires and one has to pull oneself across the river swaying like mad if it is a windy day. From that pool I had nine salmon, two of which I kept for smoking and the rest went back. I saw no fresh run fish up there – they were all coloured. But the other bank were spinning and using all kind of lures without success. I never forgot that experience and have since proved to my own satisfaction that the small fly in the summer and on to the end of the season will do the damage. I am not referring to late October or November, of course.

The Findhorn is a nightmare to describe by beats. There is an enormous jungle of them that conforms to no easy pattern. The Forres Angling Association (GG Lilley, The Tackle Shop, 97 High Street, Forres) has a nice bit of water stretching from above the main Forres/Inverness road bridge to the tidal

waters of Findhorn Bay. Their best months are in March or April and again after 26 August when the nets come off. During the netting season the association does not have access to the pools which are netted, except on Saturdays from 10 am. Their best pools are the Collins and Antons in low water from April. From 26 August all the pools fish well as they get stocked up with fish. Cloddy and the Blondin, away down near the Bay, are best for finnoch fishing if one keeps an eye on the tide and fishes at the right time. An average year for them would be about 100 salmon and 80 grilse although in 1979 they had 200 salmon in addition to grilse. Each March they record a few fish between 25 and just over 30 lbs.

Above the club water it is either private or with small stretches like the Meads which are let to people on a long-term basis. We are now into the 'gorge' area and it is hereabouts that the early fish are held up by these temperature pools and don't go through until May. Hereabouts is the best of the Findhorn angling, hence the difficulty in finding a beat.

In the top reaches of the gorge there are the well known beats like Logie, Dunphail, Lethan, Glenferness, Cawdor, Shennachie, Moy, and many more. Most of those are on long term leases and some can be leased with cottages. Freeburn Hotel on the A9 at Tomatin leases two beats, one mile each bank, overlapping, with three rods each side. Salmon can be up there by the end of May, given a spate, and the annual catch can be over 70 salmon. No prawns are allowed, otherwise any legal lure is permitted. It is very much a spate river in the upper half with big floods arriving unexpectedly and very swiftly. There are sometimes permits available for non-residents.

Around 1969 the sea trout population suffered badly with disease and the stocks were virtually wiped out. But Mr Harkness put in 70,000 sea trout fed-fry in 1970/71 and eventually the sea trout runs were resuscitated. The fish are not large – around $1\frac{3}{4}$ lbs. They can be found all the way up to Mazeran and the Funlack Burn as well as the Muckle Burn, which is not exactly a tributary of the Findhorn but flows into Findhorn Bay.

The Spey

Rivers: Avon, Dulnain, Spey
Inverness-shire/Banffshire
Season: 11 Feb–30 Sept
Best months: see text

The Spey is unarguably one of the best salmon rivers of Scotland with prolific runs of salmon and sea trout. It is not the longest salmon river in Scotland. It is about 100 miles in length and drains some 1,000 square miles – but it is the fastest flowing river in the country. A great deal of the late spring or summer fly fishing, to be successful, should be done in breast-waders and every angler who wades to any real depth would be well advised to use a lead-tipped wading staff.

Where is the source? Well, it used to be in the vicinity of Loch Laggan but a little of the Spey catchment area was utilised for hydro-electricity and now flows the other way. So what about up at Dalwhinnie? The little river Truim flows down past that station halt and joins the Spey at Newtonmore. But, really, the Spey has so many tributaries, all plunging down from either the Cairngorm Mountains on one side or the Monadhliath (monaleea) Mountains on the other side that one can take one's choice. These hills are over 4,000 ft and 3,000 ft respectively, so the Spey is very much a snow-fed river and the snowmelt in spring has a vital bearing on the success (or otherwise) of the angling.

The notable tributaries, with big runs of salmon and sea trout, are the Avon (pronounced ann), the Fiddich, the Livet (which joins the Avon) and the Dulnain. These are the main ones but there are numerous smaller streams, important either for spawning purposes or angling, or even both.

From around Boat of Garten, below Aviemore, it is a big river. With so much snowmelt coming off the most massive bulk of mountainous country in Scotland the Spey will be 'big' well on into May, and even June. Only rarely will this river be down to summer level in May as it was in 1980 after a very

dry and mild winter. The Cairngorms come as near to giving a 'continental' climate as is possible in this country. So the high Cairngorm plateau has a very positive influence on the character and the flow levels of the Spey, and on the runs of salmon and sea trout.

When the season opens on 11 February salmon will be in the river all the way up to Grantown and perhaps even to Nethybridge. This would indicate that salmon run over the winter and when you learn that the season closes on 30 September you wonder why this great river should have one of the shortest seasons. The main spring runs are in March and April and these early fish can reach as far as Grantown with sea lice. It has to be said, though, that the spring runs are not quite what they used to be. In the fifties and early sixties they were colossal. All the same, over the past two or three years there has been a tendency towards an increased spring run together with a small but progressive return to larger fish. This improvement was to be seen in 1978 when the spring runs began to resemble those of the pre UDN years. It was the same in 1980 which turned out to be even better than 1978. So, perhaps the 'old days' of big spring runs are returning. At the time of writing the average weight of these early runners is from 10 to 12 lbs with a best of 29 lbs in the Grantown area and one of over 38 lbs lower down the river. There are still a few big fish around. For example, in the Gordon Castle area, 40 pounders are still taken, but these are late fish which do not travel far up the river. They are the remnants of the autumn run for which the Spey was, very many years ago, as renowned as the other Scottish back-end rivers.

The famous beats of Delfur, Orton, and Gordon Castle, on the lower part of the river, provide the best of the sport in the spring because the water temperature is usually low and fish will take their time in reaching the middle and upper waters. But, in a very mild spring, as in 1980, they can fairly shoot through the river system and the upper beats score. Nonetheless, Arndilly, Aberlour, Rothes, Knockando and Tulchan will have good stocks of fish from February building up to April and May and, while the Castle Grant fishings and the Strathspey AA fishings will always have fish in February, the bulk of the stocks over those early months will be well down the river. If you can get a rod (and if you can pay the price) and you want to fish in

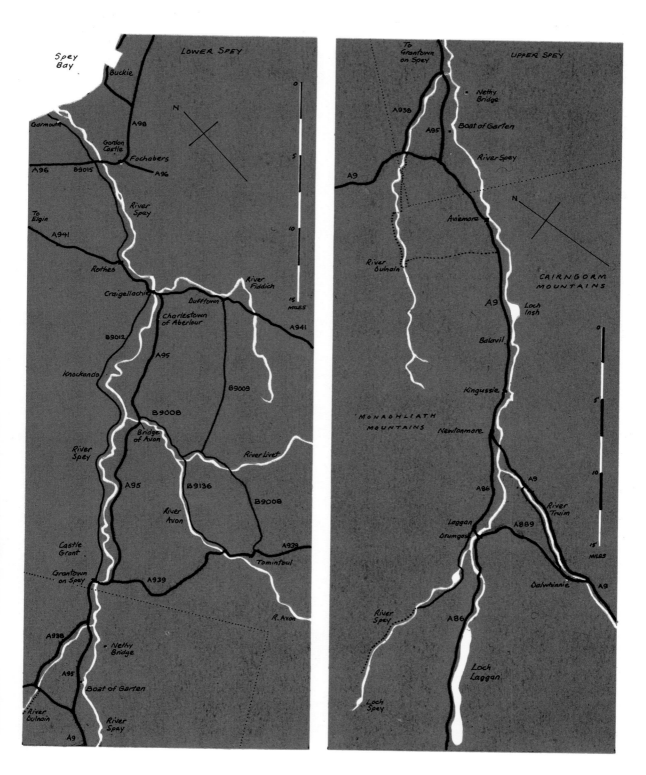

Salmon netting at Spey Bay

February, March or April then you'd best try from Fochabers up to the middle reaches in the area of Knockando or thereabouts.

The early angler in spring (are February and March spring?) will probably decide to fish with a lure. It is the most popular method and the usual multi-coloured wooden devons with lead weights and various spoons of numerous hues and shapes are used. Still, a few anglers will persevere with the fly, but these will be brass tube flies dressed with black and yellow hair or yellow, red and blue hair. Tubes are easily made, so the angler will tie up his own, using the colour combinations of his own fancy. There is no doubt, though, that spinners will take more salmon in the cold months than flies. This is not because of the cold alone but also the sheer bulk of river. The spinner can cover more water and more effectively than the fly.

Come May the water temperature will still be low (melting snow) but May anglers will now be using the fly in preference to the devon or spoon. It can be hot in May and the flies will have shrunk in size to 6s or 8s. I remember one day in late May when the air temperature went over the 80°F mark. It was a sweltering day and nothing was caught all morning on my beat just above Aberlour. I like the Tosh (black and yellow) and finally I put on an Esmund Drury Tosh, size 10, in the middle of the afternoon in what were hopeless conditions. I hooked the biggest fish of my life at the tail of the lowest pool of my beat and there I played it until it went out of the pool and into the beat lower down. Alas, I lost that fish but a few thoughts remained. When all else fails it must be a good idea to change down to very small flies. Perhaps the fish will be lost but at least you may have sport. Also, have plenty of backing. The Spey is still a big river in May and June and 200 yards of backing is essential. I was given a ticking off by my gillie because I didn't follow the fish into the next man's water. He was quite right, of course!

There are private beats on the Spey but many estates let their fishing on a weekly or fortnightly basis. The trouble is that salmon fishing is at a premium and an aspiring lessee would have to put his name on the waiting list for the choice, and even the not so choice beats. Bell Ingram of Perth and Edinburgh handle a large number of fishings on the Spey and other Scottish rivers. But there are plenty of hotels and angling associations with leases and

these fishings should not be despised. Craigellachie Hotel, below Aberlour, is one such hotel with good water which can fish early in the spring and right through the season. They have two beats and anglers change beats at one o'clock each day. The best months are May, June, July and August and the average catch over the last seven years was 322 salmon. The best year was that great one in 1978 when they had 529 salmon.

The main salmon angling associations are at Aberlour, Grantown and Nethybridge. Because of the extent of their fishings and their impressive annual returns, the Strathspey Angling Association is probably the most important, with 7 miles on the Spey, both banks, and 12 miles on the Dulnain, both banks. However, there are some restrictions. The itinerant angler must reside in the Grantown area in order to qualify for a weekly permit. But

that should be no hardship. Grantown-on-Spey, and the surrounding pine-covered countryside dominated by the massive Cairngorm, is a most beautiful part of the Highlands. The association produces a useful map indicating the pools and showing clearly the stretches reserved for the fly-only angler. There are 31 named pools on the Spey and 30 on the Dulnain. It is a well organised body and provides shelters at strategic places, looks after its banks and polices the river. Each day in the tackle shops' windows the river level is recorded – a useful practice which could be employed elsewhere to advantage. There are other rules laid out in the permit. One is that there will be no prawn fishing and only fly fishing is allowed when the water falls below normal summer level. Hence the usefulness of the day to day reading of river levels in the shops and hotels.

The Strathspey AA's fishings are quite prolific. The annual catch will vary from year to year but in 1978 they had a good year with 762 salmon, including grilse, and 564 sea trout (averaging 2.2 lbs). But in 1979 the total was down to 402 salmon although 817 sea trout were taken (averaging 2.14 lbs). No doubt at all, this association offers remarkably good angling. Although March and April will produce salmon the best spring month is May. July, August and September usually break even but the fish of September are by then pretty red. The best months of the year for catching sea trout are June and July.

Angus (John) Stuart, the tackle dealer in Grantown, is responsible for some of the more successful flies on the Spey. His little Stuart's Special for sea trout is a winner, with its silver body and red and white hair wing. His Stuart Shrimp is very

Anglers on the water near Grantown-on-Spey

attractive to salmon and the other flies which are
extensively and successfully employed are the
Toucan and Brodee (predominantly dark ones)
and, of course, the Munro Killer. John's Munro has
my preference because he makes it with the hair
wing extending well beyond the gape of the hook. I
think the longish tail makes it more attractive to
salmon and most of my own flies are dressed this
way.

Out of the association's 31 pools the Long Pool
and the Lurg are the two best. The first named is the
great spring pool. It holds a lot of spring salmon
because, I am sure, the rough white water just
above will be a deterrent for salmon when the
water is cold. The Lurg is above the Long and is
good all season once fish come up in numbers. In
fact, the association's water is mainly good except
for the slack parts and the only other pool I would
single out would be No 12 on the map – the Tar-
rigmore which is very good in summer and
autumn. A 'best' day on this water could be with up
to 20 salmon and although sea trout average 2½ lbs
John Stuart had one recently of 7½ lbs on his Stuart's
Special.

Down the river at Aberlour the angling association there has two pools in the village. They are
large pools and can accommodate plenty of rods in
big water. They, too, have a restriction in that a
permit will only be given to those staying overnight in Aberlour and only two per day to each
hotel. They average around 200 salmon per year
and the Boat is the better of their two pools. Salmon can be caught on opening day but April is best.
Six or seven salmon can be taken in a good day and
J M Morrison of J Munro, tackle dealer, Aberlour,
had the most recent largest salmon at 28 lbs in 1979.
The average weight is 10 lbs.

Up at Nethybridge the Abernethy Angling
Improvement Association has 14 named pools on
its stretch which extends from above Boat of Garten to Nethybridge. They have the usual rules such
as fly only when the river level drops to the red
marker; no prawn fishing and, along with Strathspey AA, no salmon may be sold but must be kept
by the angler for his own personal use. Salmon
have been taken in February as far up as this stretch
but not regularly. A few are caught in March, more
in April but May is the best spring month. Their
average catch is under a hundred but in spite of
appeals for returns to be made it is quite certain that

many more fish are caught each year and not
declared. Sea trout are not plentiful but sometimes
June can give reasonable sport. The two really good
fly pools are Millers at the top of the beat and the
Nethy Pool at the bottom. The association gives
out a map of its fishing showing the pools and also
offering advice on the best flies to use. Above Boat
of Garten the salmon angling is not of any great
consequence according to the returns. It is true that
salmon are taken at Aviemore, Loch Insh, Balavil,
Kingussie, Newtonmore and even on the Truim
but not in any numbers. The upper Spey is becoming more of a brown trout river and a good one at
that, thanks to the efforts of the Badenoch AA.

Both the Strathspey AA and the Abernethy AA
lease their fishings from the Strathspey Estate.
They are very valuable fishings in terms of the
economy of the tourist industry in that part of
Speyside. With an average of something like 600
salmon between them a large number of anglers
will come to, and depart from, Speyside very
happy people.

The main fishing tributary is the Avon and it is a
surprisingly good little stream with salmon going
into it in April. The Dalnasheugh Hotel has both
banks for 2½ miles plus another 2½ miles on one
bank and they get quite a lot of sport from April on.
Best months are from then to July. In 1978 they had
401 salmon and 406 sea trout which is more than a
satisfactory catch for a year. There is a good spring
run and a run of grilse in July, if wet, but September
fish are coloured. A best day would be up to 10
salmon and, in 1978, a good fish of 28 lbs was taken
on fly from the Factor's Pool. They keep two beats
for fly and/or spinning and one section for all legal
lures including the worm. Higher up, the Rich-
mond Arms Hotel and the Gordon Arms Hotel at
Tomintoul also offer stretches to guests and the
Post Office Stores in the village dispenses permits
to the public.

The Spey is now well known for the number of
angling schools at Aviemore and Grantown, etc.
These are well advertised in the angling press. As
for tackle shops every village and town on Speyside
has an abundance of them and there are very many
hotels which make a feature of catering for anglers.
The Waverley Press publish a pictorial map of the
Spey depicting the beats and pools from source to
sea. And, of course, there are plenty of guide books
which are mines of information on angling matters.

Top: The public water at the mouth of the Spey
Bottom: Arthur Oglesby's fishing course at Grantown

Spey casting on the Polchrain Pool at Castle Grant

The Deveron

Rivers: Blackwater, Bogie, Deveron
Aberdeenshire
Season: 11 Feb–31 Oct
Best months: see text

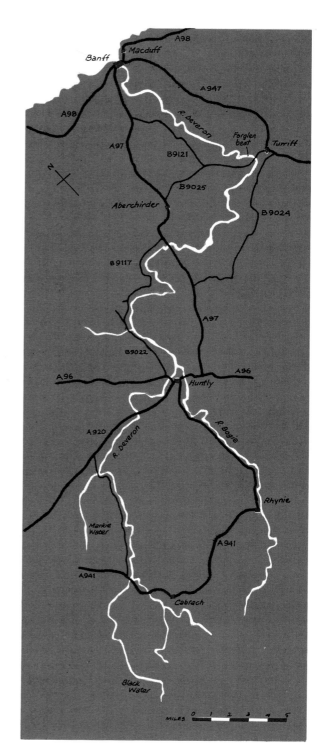

This north-east Aberdeenshire river is about 61 miles in length and most of it gives good salmon and sea trout angling. It is a nice looking river with a bottom of shingle and rock and far more 'Highland' than its near neighbour, the Don. It rises up in the snow clad Strathbogie Hills together with its main tributaries, the Blackwater and the Bogie, and the snow-melt has quite a bearing on the water heights in the vital months of March, April and even May. Thereafter, it has to be rainfall which will influence the river levels and here we have that problem of flash spates arising from the vast amount of afforestation. But because the river is rocky with plenty of white water, quite a number of beats can fish well in fairly low conditions.

Salmon angling is prolific as far up as Cabrach Lodge leaving three miles above unfished and regarded as a sanctuary for spawning. The Blackwater is the best spawning tributary. Only salmon enter this stream, which is spate controlled, and if there is rain in June, July and August they will go right upstream in a mad rush. They are small, 7 to 9 lbs, but a few can reach 10 to 12 lbs. The Bogie on the other hand is hard fished, a gift from the Duke of Gordon to the people of Huntly. It is run entirely by the Huntly Angling Association on behalf of trustees. There are 27 named pools over about 20 miles. It enters the Deveron at the Meetings, a mile below Huntly. Sea trout run the Bogie in June if water allows. It has a sandy bottom which the sea trout like. Salmon come late – in September and October. All legal lures are permitted except in October when only fly and minnow are allowed.

Out of the 27 pools shown on the association's map the best are No 2 (Rapping Gate) – excellent for fly, Brander's Pot, Junkin, Auld Brig Pot, Black Corner, good and productive, and Leslie's Pot

which has more of a flow than the others and is therefore good fly water too. No 25 on the map is the Old Bridge Hole and is big in relation to this tributary stream – about 500 yards long. There is no need for waders and if using a wooden minnow the best way to fish is to take a 2 inch brown and gold (plastic will do) and cast out but not wind in. Just leave it to come round on its own and the fish will take it. If wound in, it will not be so appealing or attractive to salmon. Whilst still in the Huntly area the same association has a 6 mile stretch of the Deveron – also given by the Duke of Gordon. On the same map referred to above, 38 named pools are shown, all numbered for easy identification. Permits can be purchased at the Huntly tackle dealers.

Deveron water in spate is very dark or black, but

by the following day it thins out to that lovely golden brown which I associate with a typical Highland river immediately after heavy rainfall. The dark or black colour is caused by the peat stain but, when golden brown, the fly angler comes into his own.

Since the disastrous years following 1966, when disease came, the Deveron has been gradually improving. The spring runs have shown an increase in recent years with a number of big fish once again being caught. In 1980, Mr Henderson, Ardmiddle, had a 33½ lbs fish on fly in March. Two of 35 and 32 lbs were taken from Inverkeithny Beat, also in March.

Opening day is 11 February. How far up can one find a salmon then? Mr Brown, Craighead, on the Conieheugh Beat has taken two or three salmon as early as 11th February and this beat is only 4 miles below Huntly which is about 28 miles from the estuary. From there down to Banff, there can be salmon in all the beats; in particular there are the 2 miles of Montcoffer which has the George Pool where 19 salmon were taken in one day on the Pebble fly (or Collie Dog) – or Forglen, reckoned to be the best beat on the Deveron, with Banff Stream the best pool on the beat, followed by the Stepps and Cheukel.

There are so many beats that it is impossible to name them individually but, after February, the stocks build up and in May when water levels become low, the 'low water' beats come into their own. Forglen fishes very well in low water, especially if the river is only about 1 ft above normal – it is a first class fly water then. Rothiemay is the same. In fact, from Forglen down to the tide, all the beats fish well in low water and, in a dry season, lots of fish will be caught. But the reverse is true. In high water, up go the fish to benefit the top beats.

Above Turriff, the Lower and Upper Netherdale Beats are both very good spring waters, have good holding pools, and also fish well all the season round. The Heron, Lower and Upper Haughs are the best pools on the Lower Netherdale and on Upper Netherdale the Lower and Upper Log, Kelmlyn, Burnmouth and Boat Pool are the best.

There are marvellous runs of grilse. These started in 1975 when, suddenly, larger numbers started to run (maybe at the expense of the spring salmon). There is also a run of real autumn salmon, 18 or 19 lbs fish, but a lot come in after the season

closes on 31 October. The thing about the Deveron is that an angler always has the chance of a lifetime – the possibility of that big fish over 30 lbs and taken on fly.

Over each 'normal' season about 4,000 salmon will be caught by rod and line and it depends very much on the rainfall throughout the season as to where these fish will be taken. If a dry year then the lower half of the river will be favoured – and very well favoured – but if wet, as in 1979, then the upper beats, right into the hills, will do better. It is much the same for sea trout of which about 1,500 can be taken in a good year.

There are a great number of beats over the length of this river but the great majority of them are available one way or another – weekly or fortnightly leases, directly from owners, estate agents, hotels, and in some cases from tackle shops. Hotels with fishings are listed in the tourist publications. Bell Ingram, 7 Walker Street, Edinburgh handle some of the best waters available to the public.

Although fish are taken on fly in March, usually it is April before many anglers employ their fly rods. They are thinking then in terms of water temperatures of 44° or 45°F and big tube flies. But, later, the small Stoats Tail, Hairy Mary, Munro Killer and Badger and Blue are the popular ones. A salmon angler is usually reluctant to go below a size 10 but one angler on the Deveron had a 5 lbs grilse on a No 12 dry fly Greenwell's Glory whilst upstream fishing for brown trout!

Mr J Watt of Huntly, is the river superintendent and he told me about an idea of his which I had heard about only once before. He used to take out all dead fish in the spawning areas, as far as possible, anyway. Now he doesn't. He contends that as the dead fish break up the particles suspended in the water are the source of food for the alevins after they have lost their sac. He has seen the alevins in swarms feeding off the dead fish. Another reference to this theory, together with an even more thought-provoking one, is quoted in the river Shin chapter. Mr Watt is a dedicated river man. His annual reports are most interesting and I do not think I have ever seen such detailed accounts of how many spawning fish have used this or that redd. He and his bailiffs certainly get around – from the redds up in the hills down to the sea where they are always on the look-out for illegal nets and so on. The Deveron is fortunate in its bailiffs.

The Don

Rivers: Don, Urie
Aberdeenshire
Season: 11 Feb–31 Oct
Best months: see text

It was not only salmon disease which brought the Don to its knees, but also pollution. It was a downright disgrace the way in which industry in the lower Don was allowed to discharge its life-killing effluent into the river with consequences which came within an ace of finishing off a beautiful salmon, sea trout and brown trout river. Below Inverurie to the sea, sewage works and paper mill discharges, which entered the river within a comparatively short distance of each other, reduced the Don to nothing more than a stinking poisonous canal. Only in times of high flood could migratory fish manage to penetrate this barrier. The Aberdeen AA took the initiative in putting pressure on the Dee/Don River Purification Authority and, over recent years, the situation has improved considerably. But it took a lot of pressure from organised anglers to get something done.

The results of this clean up are clearly reflected in better runs of salmon and sea trout. Above Inverurie, of course, the upper reaches always showed a high standard in water quality. There is a lot to do yet to get the Don into a satisfactory condition because when there is drought it does not take long for the problem to rear its smelly head again.

The Don is about 70 miles long and its source is away up at the top of Strathdon above Corgarff and Cock Bridge (the refuge of many travellers in the winter when the snows block the infamous Cock Bridge/Tomintoul road). Up there, and down to Monymusk, it is a nice clean swift flowing river with pools which attract the fly angler. This stretch is susceptible to fluctuation in level by weather, snowmelt and rainfall, but lower down the Don becomes slower flowing, with deep holding pools. It might be described as a spate river but after a good rainfall the upper and middle reaches will surely give three or four days of very good angling conditions.

Its main tributary is the Urie (which can pour in

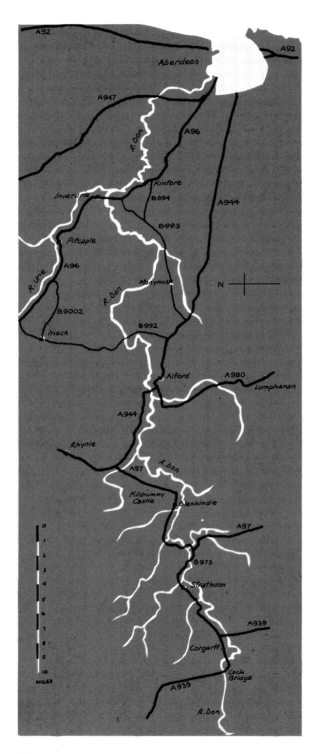

coffee-coloured water to the Don) and there are many large burns all of which will influence the total flow. The Urie offers 8 to 10 miles of angling and salmon can be in this stream early in the season.

With the gradual improvement in the pollution situation two features have emerged. Over the past five years the spring salmon have progressively improved and now the sea trout have returned in significant numbers. These are two encouraging landmarks and, as for the spring salmon, the 1980 runs were the heaviest for 20 years! This good news was tempered by the return of disease. This was a pity, because disease (UDN) had recently started to become less virulent since its first outbreak in 1968. We know about UDN and Furunculosis but over the later part of the seventies there emerged another rather peculiar salmon disease. It manifested itself in only a handful of Don salmon and only in the very early months of the season. In 1977 two cases of 'jaundiced' salmon were reported, peaking in 1979 with 60 cases – all caught by anglers. Scientists examined the fish but could offer no explanation except that their bile system had gone wrong. The salmon showed a golden tinge to the scales, a reddish hue to the fins and the flesh had an oily taste. The difficulty for the scientists was the small number of fish involved and the fact that the affected fish were found only in March and April.

Salmon, for angling purposes, will penetrate as far as Edinglassie, but very late on, and they will eventually spawn there, although the Urie is also a vital spawning area, too. However, when the season opens on 11 February salmon can be found as far up as Kemnay. Irrespective of conditions, however, the bulk of this early fishing will be from the Grandholm fishing, not far above the influence of the tide and up to Inverurie. Inverurie is a prime holding area especially the Manar fishings but the Kintore fishings also hold salmon and give good sport. These fishings do well very early in the season and extraordinary well if the levels are low and the water cold. 1980 was so mild that salmon were actually up in the Kildrummy Castle Hotel water before March was out.

So far I've referred to some specific beats. As they do for the Dee, the Waverley Press publish a map giving a complete run-down of all the beats and the named pools, all the way from Cock Bridge to the estuary. It is well worth having.

The nets pick up a tremendous number of grilse

The weir above Strathdon

but if the river is high in July or thereabouts, as in 1979, the Don can receive a heavy run of these 5 to 7 lbs fish which will give excellent sport all the way up the main river and its tributaries. In the spring the salmon fishing will peak in mid–May, especially up to Monymusk. The Don also has a good run of real autumn back–end fish with sea lice. These will be seen in September and give good sport for many miles upstream.

Some of the big fish are coming back nowadays. One of 42½ lbs was taken from Parkhill on 17 April 1978. In 1980 one of 35 lbs was taken from the Sauch Pool on the Mugiemoss Beat on the 18 March on a black and yellow tube fly. This suggests that fly can be productive in the early months and that would be correct. But all legal lures are allowed on most beats although there are some waters where bait fishing (worm, etc) is prohibited. In these early months most anglers will spin a Yellowbelly devon, a black and gold, brown and gold or a black and orange devon about 2½ to 3 inches long. Some prefer the black and gold (Zebra) Toby spoon. But if the angler is fly orientated he will use a predominantly yellow one such as the Yellow Dog or Torrish dressed on a heavy tube. Hardly anyone uses the old traditional single iron these days – all hair wing tubes, and cheaper!

Some of the best fly waters are on Fetternear at Kemnay with its Mill Stream and Black Pot, their best pools; another Mill Stream is on the Kintore fishings and is most productive in lowish water; on the Manar fishing there are some lovely white water pools such as the Sheep Pool, Upper and Lower Wood Pools and, next one down, the Chapel Pool. Up at Kildrummy fly fishing is good by mid–May as stocks build up then. But it is on one of the nicest fishings on the Don at Monymusk that the fly angler comes into his own. When temperatures rise, 1½ inch tubes and down to even smaller lengths, produce the fish. The best pattern is the Stoats Tail but, naturally, anglers will have their own preferences. It is the size of fly that catches salmon which interests me. Very small flies will attract and kill salmon here. A Cinnamon and Gold (or Silver) on a size 12 double can do the trick as it did for one angler who took a 9½ lbs salmon on that fly from Ram Pot. My friend, Dr David Hawson, had a similar spectacular experience using a small No 12 trout Greenwells and successfully hooked and landed an 8½ lb salmon from Paradise Woods.

The Don is an 'open' river. There are vast stretches of very good salmon and sea trout water available to the public and these include excellent tributaries such as the Urie. Detailed information is listed in the guide *Fishing in Grampian Region* published by the region's Department of Leisure, Recreation and Tourism written and compiled by Harry Munro.

The Dee

River: Dee
Aberdeenshire/Kincardineshire
Season: 1 Feb–30 Sept
Best months: see text

The Dee has much in common with the Spey. Both are fast flowing rivers, beautiful fly water, both share similar origins in mountainous country, are snow fed (which has an important influence on the spring angling) and both are typical Highland salmon rivers, although the Dee, in its lower reaches, flows through the Lowland-type country.

Its main sources are from Ben Macdhui which is 4,000 ft high and from Braeriach also about 4,000 ft. This is why the depth of snow on those mountains is so important to the anglers and the salmon. Even in summer the sheer elevation and a catchment area of some 800 square miles gives every prospect of rainfall and there are many small tributaries to pick up local rain and feed the main river with a freshet.

The Dee is about 90 miles long and 50 to 60 miles of that is excellent water. Though there are fishable stretches in the top reaches, the cream of the fishing is to be found in the good middle waters, with famous beats from Peterculter up to Dinnet and Aboyne, all of which have the lovely streamy water which is so ideal for the fly angler. Over the whole river there are restrictions as to the permitted lure. By a gentleman's agreement one can fish fly and/or spin (but no bait fishing at all) up to around mid-April. After that it is supposed to be fly only although I know that this agreement is not strictly observed in high water on some beats.

In spite of its length, the Dee does not give very long periods of high water, but the season has got to be divided into two parts – spring and summer. In the spring (that is from 1 February to, say, mid-May) much will depend on the amount of snow in the head waters up in the Grampians and Cairngorms, and also on the temperatures. With very deep snow in the corries, well packed and consolidated from months of deep frosts, there will

be a snow-melt each warm spring day, which will cause two things; a small rise in water level and a similar small rise in water temperature. These are important factors and can have a very interesting effect on the salmon's 'taking' stimulus. These phenomena usually occur in mid-afternoon (depending on how far down the river the angler is fishing) and the outcome can be quite dramatic. It often means the difference between a blank day and success. Naturally, in early spring, the river can be virtually frozen over and unfishable; if there is a thaw during this period then the river will flood with 'sna' bree'.

By mid-summer, with all snow gone, rainfall becomes the important factor. If the river is at nil on the gauge then, after heavy and prolonged rain, say, on a Saturday, the river will peak on Monday and stay up for about a week if there is no further precipitation. At first, with the intense afforestation on Dee-side, there will be peat stain and, to some extent, the river will colour, but it has a shingly bottom and it will soon clear even if still at a high level.

When UDN struck the Dee in the mid-sixties, the massacre was terrible and had a severe effect on stocks – especially of spring salmon. But they survived, and over the last few years the spring runs have improved. 1979 was not quite so good as the previous three years but in 1980 the spring run was doing well although disease was appearing again by late April. The spring run peaks by mid-May and by that time all the beats from top to bottom are stocked with salmon.

Then come the grilse. They come alright, and in massive numbers, but a sadly small proportion gets into the river, unless there are good levels allowing them to negotiate the estuarial nets. The greatest havoc of all occurs out on the coast, by the stake and bag nets which annually decimate these heavy runs of fish. There is an autumn run but it is really of little consequence compared to the Border rivers.

How far up the river system a salmon will be taken on opening day, or during February will, of course, depend on the kind of winter. If the river is low and severely affected by hard frosts then salmon will not have ascended any higher than perhaps Park or Drum and at worst, Garthdee where they can lie comfortably in the long canal-like stretch known as the Manse Pool. It is always a holding pool but will not stop them if conditions

A grand day on the Dee near Ballater

are right for running. The pools at Peterculter, Park (north side) and Durris (south side) will stop them in very cold water. If it is not too cold then the early runners can be found as far up as the Banchory area and Buchts, Whinny Brae and Holly Bush could produce the fish. In fact, in a normal February there could be chances of success as high up as Kincardine O'Neil but best of all would be immediately above and below Banchory and down to Park. Even the legendary Cairnton could produce the goods in the early days of February. AHE Wood related in his letters how he fished for, and caught, salmon in February and March – and Cairnton is a bit above Banchory. By and large, the Banchory area, and downstream, is the best bet for a February salmon. However, such was the mildness of the winter in early 1980 that the Cairnton beat produced something like 130 salmon in February and about 90 in March – another example of the influence the weather has on the runs of salmon.

Again, depending on the weather conditions, and as temperatures begin to rise, so the fish will slowly push upstream until by mid-April they have reached Braemar and thus every beat, from top to bottom, will hold salmon. Here again, is another similarity between Dee and Spey. April is the big month. It is the month when the maximum stocks of salmon in the lower and middle reaches get on the move and migrate upstream in large numbers.

Around Kincardine O'Neil, and in April when the big move is on, the Ballogie Beat at Potarch fishes well. It is a medium water level beat but if too high, fish will pass upstream. Paradoxically, even in low water, as in April 1980, they still tend to do this. Nevertheless, 31 salmon for a week in April is not bad and that was the score for the last week of April 1980. But the next beat up, Carlogie, seems to do a little better, no doubt because it is more of a holding water. Here again, the lower levels of April 1980, helped. 40 fish for the last week of April that year was good, with seven salmon in one day by one rod. It is fly only on Carlogie and the Munro Killer on size 4 or 6 hooks, even in April, is very successful. Mind you, the water is crystal clear most of the time. Where restricted spinning is allowed, for example, on the Ballogie water, and even in lower than average water levels, a big 3 inch silver and copper spoon can be devastating. So here we are with a 3 inch spoon versus a No 6 fly and both doing well.

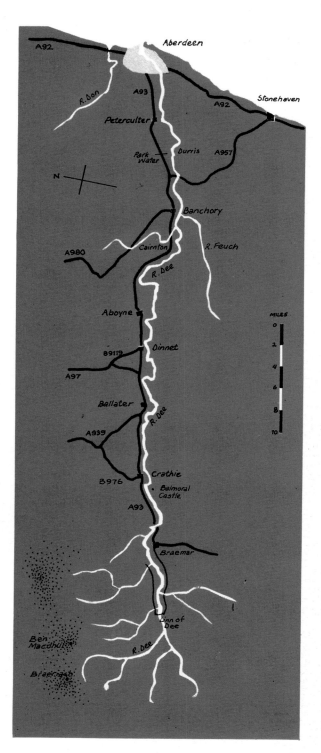

The Dee above Balmoral in April

Opposite top: The Invercauld Arms Hotel by the bridge at Ballater
Bottom: The tackle shop in Ballater reflects the proximity of Balmoral

The spring fish average about 12 lbs. One of 25 lbs will be a good fish but a number of 15 to 20 lbs fish are taken each year. One of the areas which consistently gives up the larger fish is above Aboyne. On the Glentanar water (south side) and the Dinnet water (on the north side) there is the Waterside Pool which is a big deep slow wading pool immediately followed by rough water known as Jocky Fyfe. It is really just one pool but big fish can be taken here from both the slow moving water and the fast water. Away down at Maryculter is another place for big fish where salmon come through broken water and appear to rest for a moment and it is at that time the lucky angler can catch one of the big ones. This is on the Kingcausie water on the Powberry Pool. But it is a 'hit or miss' affair.

Printed and published by the Waverley Press (Aberdeen) Ltd is a marvellous pictorial *Fisherman's Map of Salmon Pools on the Dee* which shows the beats and every pool on those beats. It is well worth having if only to follow the weekly or monthly angling reports in the fishing journals. However, although it is not possible to go over all the famous beats of the Dee, let alone the pools, I cannot but refer to one of the most famous of them all – the Cairnton Beat. This is not so much for the beat itself but for the man who fished that beat in the twenties and made famous at Cairnton the technique of the 'floating line' for salmon. Even today, one sees the majority of anglers in the summer months casting out at a perfect 45° downstream angle and mending, mending the line upstream to try to prevent the fly from dragging, which it would undoubtedly do if the current got hold of the belly of line between fly and rod tip. Failure to mend would allow the line to proceed first, followed by the fly whipping round at a considerable pace. This was anathema to Mr Wood. He insisted that the fly, so far as possible, should fish without drag. His other discovery

was that salmon will rise to a fly on the surface so long as the air temperature is greater than that of the water temperature.

Not only is the Cairnton Beat of the Dee renowned for the development of the floating line but on the Park and Durris beats two interesting discoveries were made – perhaps 'inventions' is the more correct word. Anyhow, it was there that the wooden devon was first used. Most anglers over the whole country, where spinning is permitted, use lead weights with wooden devons. But not on this part of the Dee. They continue to use the wooden devon just like a fly. They cast it out and let the current bring it round in a semicircle. This means that salmon can be seen actually taking the devon on the surface. This method has been used successfully on the Conon, but only infrequently.

The other 'invention' associated with the Dee was the introduction of the Riffling Hitch by an American, Lee Wulff, in 1962. The method is to tie on a fly with a half blood knot and then two half hitches over the head of the fly. The fly will now be unable to swim in the usual horizontal way but sit up like a dry fly and bob its way across the pool like a small animal. Since Lee Wulff, certain conditions have been found for the best use of this method. The water temperature must be at least 57°F; it must be very hot weather; the fly has to be one or

The Dee above Braemar

two sizes larger than the one normally used; and the line has to be a complete floater. I have seen my friend and colleague, Dr Stephen Innes, use this method when conditions permitted and when Stephen's salmon come at the fly fished this way they come with a tremendous bang and are nearly always well hooked. Lee Wulff was a great exponent of the single handed rod for salmon and the late Alan Sharpe of Aberdeen built him one to order – only 6½ ft! Harry Munro also of Aberdeen is a present day exponent of the small rod and he uses a 9 ft Heddon Pal rod to great effect, killing a lot of salmon each year with it. I must say, though, I prefer to use my 14 ft Sharpes spliced over the whole season – I wouldn't know what to do with my other hand!

Early in the season when spinning lures are used, the most productive are the devons in brown and gold, the yellowbelly and various other colour combinations. They are usually wooden with weights. Lengths will be from 2½ to 3 inches. The fly angler will use the big tubes and for the Dee they will be predominantly yellow or red which means a variant on the Garry Dog with plenty of yellow, red and blue hair wing. Black and yellow will be the next best tube and these will be 3 inches long, in brass for heavy and cold water, or aluminium when conditions permit.

Arthur Oglesby preparing to tail a Dee salmon

Later, when the water and weather warms up and out comes the floating line, or floater with a sink tip, the best summer fly up and down the whole length of the Dee will be the Stoats Tail. At first it will be about 1½ inches long but in the really warm and lowish water of July, August and September minute sizes will be used very successfully indeed. There will be other patterns, naturally, and the Blue Charm, the Silver Wilkinson and Thunder and Lightning are the best of the remainder.

The season starts on 1 February and closes on 30 September, and I have referred to the spring and summer seasons and the fact that salmon could be as far up as Braemar before April is out. It depends

on the weather and this was the picture in April 1980, when conditions were so mild that the first salmon off the Invercauld Arms Hotel water above Braemar was taken on 24 April. This hotel has a total of 9 miles of salmon water from Braemar up to Linn of Dee and for another 3½ miles beyond. They can arrange gillies, the hire of all kinds of tackle and even Landrovers.

Although salmon may be in these top reaches of the river in May the best months there are September, August and July – in that order. In 1979 14 salmon was the score for one rod for a week. There are three really good holding pools in the top water – big, deep and slow flowing – which hold fish from May on. Only a little wind is required when the water is low and they are therefore fishable nearly all the time. They are known as the Suspension Bridge, Linn of Dee, and Dalvoura.

By early September the fish are pretty red but give good sport. However, in early September, there is always a small run of clean fresh fish which suddenly appear up at Braemar. So, although a lot of red fish are caught, September can offer the angler the odd silver fish – even that far away from the sea and so late in the season. This great back-end sport applies to all the beats above and below Braemar. The Stoats Tail is the best fly, once again, but the Mar Fly, tied by Sandy Thomson of Mar Lodge, catches a lot of fish if used on a size 7 hook. Few big fish manage to reach Braemar and the average weight is about 10 lbs with the odd one just over 12 lbs thrown in.

Sea trout also run the Dee. They average 2½ to 4 lbs and one of 6 lbs would make news. They reach as far as Dinnet, Glentanar and Ballater but few go beyond. Best fly is the same as for salmon – a Stoats Tail tube but if using a double or single then the Black Pennell is the pattern.

There is a very reasonable amount of accessibility for the public on the Dee. Many angling clubs and hotels have water which they offer. The Grampian Regional Council's Department of Leisure, Recreation and Tourism put out a most comprehensive little booklet *Fishing in the Grampian Region* in which most of the available salmon waters are listed and addresses given. In addition, the Scottish Tourist Board and other organisations produce booklets listing the hotels, clubs and estate offices to which one can apply for information.

EAST AND SOUTH EAST SCOTLAND

The two main fisheries, Tweed and Tay, are divided by Edinburgh and the Firth of Forth. The more spectacular hill and mountain scenery away from these two rivers has to be searched for, but east of Perth are the lovely areas around Crieff and Comrie, just north of Gleneagles and, of course, on the eastern boundary of the area are the Trossachs and Loch Katrine. There was a time when salmon ran in large numbers up the Forth, but pollution in various forms put an end to the bulk of these runs. In spite of this, the salmon still determinedly make their way to the Teith which provides reasonable fishing in the Callander area and up to just above Stirling. Thanks to the work of the purification board the Forth water is improving – and more and more fish are finding their way through the de-oxygenated areas.

Around the valley of the Tweed, those with eyes for more than the fishing and with antennae tuned to the ghosts of the past, will not find it difficult to become absorbed in the atmosphere and still-living history of the Border country.

The North Esk and South Esk

Rivers: North Esk, West Water
Angus
Season: 11 Feb–31 Oct
Best months: Feb–Apr/Sept

River: South Esk
Angus
Season: 16 Feb–31 Oct
Best months: see text

The North Esk

If ever there was a 'changing scene' in the philosophy of its riparian owners, the North Esk provides the perfect example. Not so long ago very little information would have been available from the estates, because it was all very much a private fishery. The owners did not fish it hard nor did they let the public on to it in any big way. But giant strides have been taken over the past couple of years in opening up this beautiful salmon river to both local and visiting anglers.

The North Esk has great potential but for a long time it has been the target of the critics of commercial netsmen. For many years, going back to the days of Hodgson and Grimble, there has been a barrage of vituperation about the intensity of the estuarial netting of this river; the inefficiency of the various 'dykes' in or near the estuary which inhibit the free access of salmon to the river proper; and the awful army of nets – stake and bag – which, at low tide present a frightening picture as they stretch away into the distance from St Cyrus to Montrose. I have always believed that precious few salmon could avoid such a barrier. Now a little doubt has wormed its way into my mind. The North Esk and its immediate coast line has become and experimental ground for scientists from the Department of Agriculture and Fisheries for Scotland and they have produced many interesting papers on the movement and behaviour patterns of salmon.

What has caused me to pause and think has been their study of the coastal movements of salmon near and at the estuary, relative to the tide flow, by inserting in the fish's stomach an acoustic transmitter and tracking each salmon, with a receiver mounted beneath a small boat. Apart from information on the tide flow and its effect on salmon,

there has emerged evidence to indicate that salmon are able to avoid the bag and stake nets by some instinct about which we, at present, know nothing. Some of the fish actually swam between the leader and cleek, around the leader, then out between leader and cleek on the opposite side – thus avoiding the bag. Some salmon swam beneath the leader. I found this astonishing and so would most people who have seen the countless number of nets so close together. That was good news and the possibility was there that the nets were not making the terrible inroads to salmon stocks that had been feared. But the poor fish, when they get through the maze, have to reach the river and this can only be done by swimming up the estuary and negotiating the infamous 'dykes' and trying to dodge the estuarial nets.

If the river is coming down in flood then there is no real problem, but as soon as the flow is back to a summer level the salmon have great difficulty in getting through the dykes to the safety of the river. Morphy Dyke is one of the main culprits because there is thin water leading up to it with the inevitable consequence that shoals of salmon mass in the pools below during the periods of low water and are 'mopped up' by the sweep nets. No matter how skilful they were at avoiding the bag and stake nets on the coast they could not possibly keep clear of the curtains of estuarial nets. So, when I heard that the river proprietors had begun to commercialize their fishings, I was overjoyed to learn that they hoped to gather enough finance to put an end to the terrible effects of Morphy Dyke. It was hoped that, before 1980 was out, the work to ease this obstruction would be completed. The proprietors have formed themselves into an improvement association (and I am glad to hear that the commercial netsmen are represented) and already they have done just what their title suggests by improving the West Water by making a fish pass at a point one mile west of the village of Edzell. Other improvements along those lines are planned.

Gannochy Estate was one of the first estates to open its water in a big way and the results over the early months of the season clearly illustrate just how high water, usually experienced over February to early May, can allow the free passage of salmon through the estuary and clear of the dykes. The spring run of salmon is extremely good and fish can be taken on opening day (11 February) as

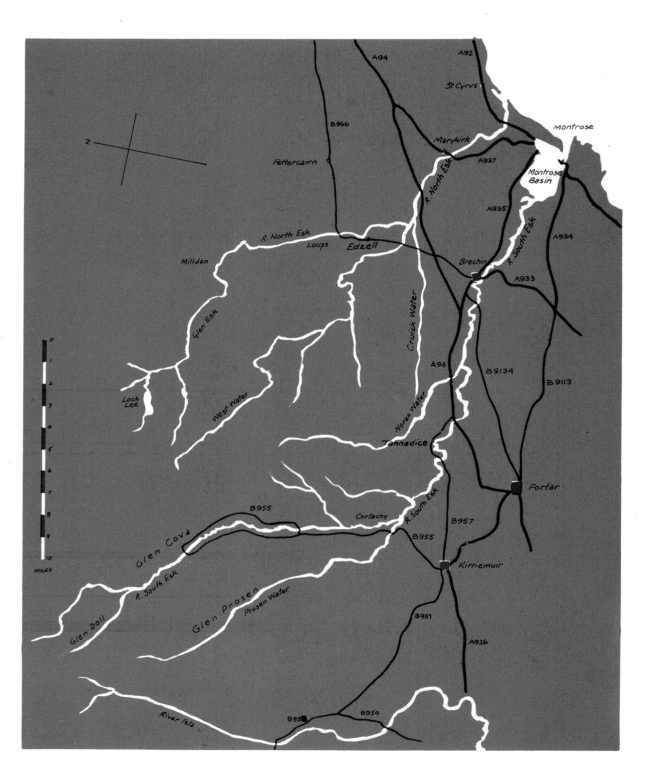

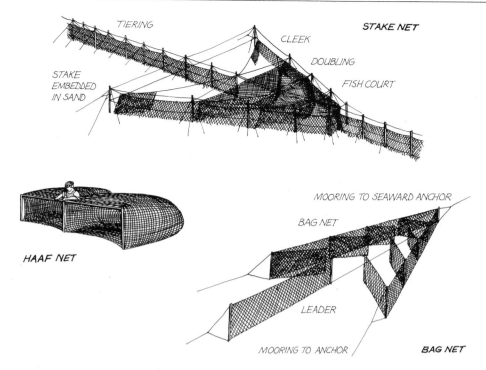

far up as the Loups Pool on Beat 1 on the Gannochy water.

But first, a quick look at the North Esk. It rises at Loch Lee and gathers up a number of small tributaries all of which are important spawning grounds for both salmon and sea trout. It is not a spate river in that if the level is low, then after 36 hours of heavy rain the river will fish for about a week. The West Water is the best tributary and is quite an angling river in its own right with prolific runs of grilse and sea trout (when there is plenty of water). Brechin Angling Club has stretches on it by courtesy of Dalhousie Estate, and this estate lets the upper Esk at Millden by issuing day permits through the keeper's house there (salmon do not get up that far until June). This estate also has three beats below Gannochy Bridge on the right bank and these are leased to the public although they are usually taken up by the same anglers. Gannochy Estate also divides its water into three beats.

Until May all the fishing is done over about 700 yards of the Loups Beat (Lower Beat). There is a fall over which no salmon will go until the water warms up, usually in May. The best pools on this very productive early water are the Caves, Major and Sand. This part of the river is in a gorge with a multitude of rocks, ledges and underwater snags which spell danger for tackle. This is the only beat where worming and spinning are allowed and such is the mortality rate in tackle that Mr Ramage, the head keeper, told me that now and again they get a

skin diver to go down to clear it out. Big fish are in these deep pools, as the skin diver can tell, but one would have to be lucky to land one. All the same, Mr Ramage had a 29 lbs salmon in the spring of 1980 from the Cave Pool. In fact, the spring of 1980 was pretty good with over 140 salmon to May – and all from this short stretch above Gannochy Bridge.

Part of the Lower Beat includes a fair bit of water above the fall but the two beats above the Loups are miniature Speys or Dees with beautiful shingly pools and runs and it is not surprising that it is fly only on these beats. Once salmon start to go over the falls into these upper beats the Loups goes off as fish stream through for the top waters. The Witches Pool is a lovely looking water but not as good as it appears. Upper Haughend and Lower Haughend are the best places on the Middle Beat with Craigoshina a very big pool. Best of all is probably the Rock Pool on the Upper Beat. As Mr Ramage says, the upper water has great sporting potential but one has to work for one's fish. Small flies ranging from 6s to 10s according to water levels are best in patterns such as Stoats Tail and Blue Charm and the tube seems to be preferred to singles, doubles or even trebles. Big fish can go over the falls but they do not readily take once they are over.

There is an autumn run of fresh fish but unless the water level is right for them they will not come up and as often as not they can be seen as late as

December. A good day in the spring could mean about eight salmon between three rods off the Loups but, up above, an average of one salmon per day per rod would be about right. Gannochy water is handled by Savills of Brechin and they put out a most comprehensive map showing access and all the named pools, with other worthwhile items of interest to the angler.

The North Esk was one of my earliest angling haunts as a very young and inexperienced angler. I remember one evening, after dining, strolling down to the bridge at Edzell to survey the scene where I had had a frustrating day, just in time to see a young lad 'tackled up' with a stout stick, even stouter nylon, hook and worm – but no reel or any other such refinements – retreating up the shingle and disappearing into the bushes with a fresh-run salmon flapping away like fury. There was I with expensive equipment on an expensive beat and a blank day. I remember that incident as though it were yesterday but I never ever had any thought of grudging the lad his fish. The moral was more important!

To reinforce my contention that this Esk is being progressively opened up, the Montrose AC has negotiated a lease for six rods on the Craigo stretch. The Links Hotel, Montrose, has the valuable Gallery Beat which extends for $1\frac{3}{4}$ miles with $1\frac{1}{2}$ miles of both banks. There are no restrictions and salmon are there to be caught over the first days of the season. The Hatton Pool is easily the best one and a lot of their fish come out of it. The hotel averages about 100 salmon and 300 sea trout per year and the best months are, as one would expect, February, March and April and then again in September. A good day would produce four or five salmon and fish up to 20 lbs can be taken. The hotel provides anglers with a very lucid map illustrating the pools, the access and the boundaries.

The season closes on 31 October and that final month can be good with the fresh-run back-enders.

This is a river which is coming alive; within a year or two it may present quite a different picture from the one which the writers of 80 years ago painted.

The picturesque village of Edzell is full of good hotels and the town of Montrose can offer even more. Estate cottages are often let with the fishing and fishing tackle can be purchased anywhere from Edzell to Montrose.

The South Esk

There are two Esks in Angus and Mearns – the North and the South – and of the two the South Esk is longer and probably offers more fishing to the public than its northerly neighbour, although the North Esk is changing for the better in that respect. The South Esk rises in the high tops about 3,000 ft up in the Grampians. It then follows down two lovely glens above Glen Doll – one, Glen Clova where the main river comes from and the other Glen Prosen which gives the name of the biggest tributary. Both rivers are helped on their way in Glen Clova by the Rottal Burn, which receives a late run of a few salmon and sea trout which spawn there, and the Moy Burn, a private water which is an excellent sea trout spawning stream. These sea trout are fished for – but privately. The Noran is another little late sea trout stream, but also private, as is the White Burn. These little streams are important for the well-being of the Esk because of their spawning potential.

The first 5 or 6 miles of the Esk after descending down Glen Doll (which becomes Glen Clova) are pretty slow flowing, with miles of bends and twists as it meanders towards Gella Bridge. Then its character alters as it becomes a river with rough boisterous water – thin at times, but with occasional pools. Below Justinhaugh the flow rate decelerates and from there the Esk streams its way through agricultural land with nice pools – ideal for the fly-only fisher, until it reaches Montrose Basin – a distance of some 40 miles from source to tide. Montrose Basin is a great tidal 'balloon' into which the Esk empties at Bridge of Dun and rushes out the other side on an ebb tide through the main channel at Montrose and so into the North Sea. At times therefore the basin will look like a loch whilst at slack low tide it will deflate and be empty except for a channel or two.

Coming off the hill without any lochs to absorb the river, when a spate occurs the Esk will be unfishable for at least one whole day – except, perhaps, for the wormers. But next day the water will be clear enough for fly and this second day will give the best fishing over the period of the spate. However, it takes eight to nine hours for a spate to reach Cortachy at the confluence of the Esk and Prosen and about 15 hours to reach the lower beats around the town of Brechin. There is a residual problem with sewerage pollution at Brechin but otherwise there is no severe pollution over the remainder of the river and it is regarded as a clean one.

Salmon run in the spring and when the season opens on 16 February there will be fish up to just below Brechin. The Dam Dyke at Kinnaird forms a temperature pool through which salmon will not go until that magical figure of 42°F is reached. The spring run, badly hit by disease after 1968, is improving. In fact, there is quite a noticeable improvement and over 20 salmon can be taken on opening day alone from the marvellous stretches of the lower beats. To refer back to the Dam Dyke it is an interesting feature (but not unknown elsewhere) that when the water is cold and fish are held up, as soon as it is warm enough they tend to go through these temperature pools very fast and straight upstream. Up at Aldbar and Craigeassie there are other dams but no serious obstacles and they do not hold up fish as does the lower one.

Cortachy would be termed 'the middle reaches' and salmon will be there by the end of March or beginning of April. Above Cortachy fish will really be on the move by mid–April and certainly in May. Sealiced salmon can be found as far up as the foot of Glen Clova. The mild spring of 1980 brought fish up to Shielhill, not far below Cortachy, and one was caught there before March was out.

Sea trout run early in this Esk (it is a much better sea trout river than the North Esk, I am told). But they are getting earlier, in fact, and the main run could be above Brechin by the end of May or early June. The sport is good, especially on the main river, and the average weight is about 1¾ lbs – anything over 3 lbs is exceptional but, all the same, an 8 or 9 pounder can occasionally be caught.

The grilse run starts in late July and there was a very heavy run in 1979 – but that was the year of very heavy precipitation. There is an autumn run of salmon but they do not have the characteristics of the back-enders of other rivers in that they do not come far up the river – to about Brechin or a little above the town.

The average springer will weigh 7 or 8 lbs but one of over 20 lbs can be taken although that would be a specimen. Grilse show the usual average of 4 or 5 lbs and autumn fish are larger at 15 lbs. But the best springer in 1980 was one of 27¼ lbs from the Montrose Angling Club's water at Bridge of Dun which came near the club's previous best at 29 lbs caught a few years ago from the same beat.

The best beats in the middle and lower reaches are private but there is an improvement association. There is also the Kirriemuir AC which has some very good fishing on the Esk from about 2 miles above Cortachy to the March Burn below Clova Hotel – some 9 miles and both banks. Part of their water is fly only and on other stretches it is fly only whenever the level is below a marker. They have some of the Prosen, too, about 1½ miles of both banks and then about 3 miles on one bank above that. This club produces a nice little map showing the pools, the access and even the lures and flies which are locally successful. The best pools include the Crooked Pool, the Mill Pool, the Red Brae and a pool with an unusual name Auchen Turc, the Gaelic for the 'field of the boar', probably going back to the days when wild boars roamed the area! The Gella Dam is a good holding pool. I will not dwell on the type of lures and fly patterns because the handout by the club gives full details. In 1979 the club water did well with 212 salmon and 393 sea trout from the Esk, 5 salmon and 29 sea trout from the Prosen and 28 salmon from the neighbouring lower Isla – a return to compare with the best of them. The secretary of the association is Harry Burness, 13 Clova Road, Kirriemuir. Day tickets (excluding Saturdays) and weekly tickets are available.

The lower beats for salmon in the spring often fish fly and one fly which is very successful is the Peacock Demon. This is like the Alexandra but has three hooks. I had not previously come across a fly lure that is so successful. I suppose it must look to the salmon like my own very long-tailed Blue Elver.

1980 was the big year for spring salmon. On the opening day 51 salmon were reported taken from the Upper Kinnaird Beat followed by some catches of upwards of 20 fish a day until conditions deteriorated. The total spring catch for the river is not known but it may have been a record one and was certainly above average.

From Glen Clova right down the river system to Montrose there are many hotels catering for anglers and in the towns and villages anglers will find all the tackle they will require.

There is a lot of finnoch fishing in the lower beats and below the Bridge of Dun, the Montrose AC offer daily tickets on their water from the bridge to the tide.

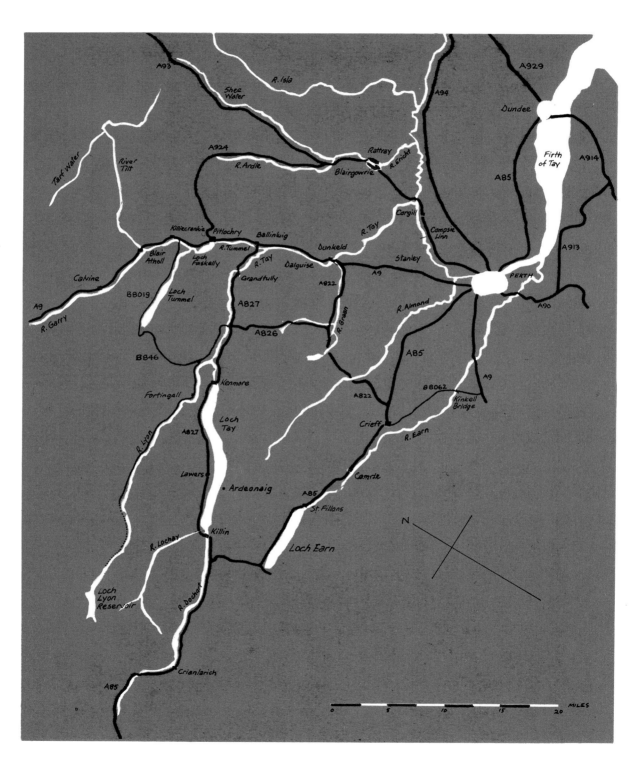

The Tay

Rivers: Almond, Dochart,
Garry, Isla, Lochy, Lyon,
Tay, Tummel
Perthshire
Season: 15 Jan–15 Oct
Best months:
Jan–May/July–Oct

The Tay is the greatest salmon river of them all and the largest river in Scotland. It has many tributaries that deserve a chapter each. In fact, the Tay and its tributaries could be the subject of a whole book, not only because of the tremendous salmon angling potential (a vital element in the local economy and tourist industry on Tayside) but also because of the scope it offers for research. It is not by accident that the Freshwater Fisheries laboratory is situated on its banks at Faskally.

The river is 123 miles long and is said to drain 2,400 square miles of Scotland. It rises on the slopes of Ben Lui. But that is away to the west of Crainlarich. What if you look north-east? Then you will see that the river Tilt rises away up in the Grampian Mountains just over the hill from the source of the Dee. Look east and you see the Isla, the Ericht, Ardle and the Shee draining the southern slopes of the Grampians and the plains of Strathmore.

Not only that, this is one river which has fresh-run salmon running from the sea every week and every month of the year. There is never a period without them.

If one examines the main river (in reverse) from bottom to top, the first main tributary is the Almond just above the town of Perth. Although so near the tide, it is not a spring river but summer salmon and grilse will run, given water. Its upper catchment area is trapped and diverted in another direction towards the Earn. The pool by the confluence with the Tay is known as Almondmouth and it is a good pool for salmon right from the 15 January when the season opens.

The next tributary of note, and a very important one, too, is the Isla where it joins the main river at Cargill. The Isla has its own reinforcements – the Ericht, the Shee and the Ardle. The Ericht is a very valuable salmon water because it has spring fish in it right up to, and beyond, Blairgowrie. The Isla also has good spring salmon fishing. The Isla is a slow, sluggish water with a sandy bottom and no obstacles to stop the springers. But it was not always so. There was a fall which was a temperature pool and this stopped salmon until warmer water arrived. Now the Isla and the Ericht have benefited from the blowing of Cargill's Leap for easier access. Cargill's Leap is in the region of Blairgowrie, just above the town. But the poachers have also reaped a benefit too, I'm told. There have been lots of poisoning incidents and sniggling since these premium early fish began to penetrate past Blairgowrie. Nevertheless, the spring fishing is now so much improved that one member of the Blairgowrie AC had around 100 salmon to his own rod, fishing from January to May on the club's stretch. Many an angling club would be proud to have that kind of total catch as their aggregate for a season!

As for the other rivers flowing into the Isla, salmon penetrate well into the hinterland; the upper reaches of the Ardle and Shee are the spawning areas and also give the back-end anglers some sport. The enormous and famous pool at the mouth of the Isla is known as Islamouth (not a very original name for such a renowned water). Very few people know how many fish come off this pool in a year but it is certainly in four figures! It is, in my opinion, the most prolific salmon pool in the whole of Scotland.

Moving on and up to Dunkeld we come to an enigma. The Bran joins the Tay at this point and, if you follow it all the way to Amulree and beyond, you would, like me before I knew better, look in vain for signs of salmon in this beautiful stream. But you will never see one because of an insurmountable fall at the Hermitage, Dunkeld. There is no project to blow this fall. So the upper Bran cannot have any upstream run of adult fish. What lovely fly water is going to waste. Below the fall there is more than a mile of very good salmon angling controlled by the Dunkeld and Birnham AC.

At Ballinluig, the Tay turns west and up to that huge reservoir, Loch Tay. There are three salmon streams here, the Lyon, the Lochy and the Dochart. More fish turn west at Ballinluig than go straight on up the Tummel to Pitlochry, where they meet

Frank Moir on the Pitlochrie Beat

with their first major obstacle – Pitlochry Dam and its salmon ladder. Anyhow, they will not ascend the ladder until late March or early April and, naturally, a big head of fish will have massed immediately below the dam by that time. So the pool immediately below the dam is a 'sanctuary' and fishing is not permitted there.

The Tay has the largest catchment area in Scotland (perhaps in the whole UK) so it was not surprising that the hydro board should cast its eyes in the direction of Tummel and Breadalbane. By Act of Parliament, it was allowed to dam, aqueduct, tunnel, build power stations, reservoirs, divert water courses and so on. But it also had statutory duties towards fish preservation, the most important of which related to salmon and sea trout. Where spawning redds were drowned it had to

build hatcheries; where dams were erected across water courses they had to build fish passes.

Inevitably, angling interests opposed the schemes but, whilst not going into the consequences in detail, I believe the Tay has got off lightly. The main fishings do not appear to suffer very much from the same dreadful fluctuations in water levels as other smaller schemes. Some gillies on the Tay say they can detect the minute alteration to the levels, say, below Dunkeld. But the Tay is too big a system for the discharge of water from Pitlochry Dam to have much effect – it tends to dissipate very quickly, especially after Tummel has met Tay at Ballinluig.

The dam at Pitlochry is the most important one because it is situated right in the middle of very good salmon water. Salmon will ascend the fish

ladder in April but by the end of the season the average number of fish up the Garry, Tilt and so on, will be around 6,000, although in some years the number can reach almost 12,000 as in 1973 or 9,000 in 1978.

In the Loch Faskally reservoir, just above the dam, about 30 salmon per year are caught by the boat anglers. At the head of this 'loch' the Tummel veers away to the west towards that part of Scotland well-known through the words of the song 'Sure by Tummel and Loch Rannoch and Lochaber I will go'. But not the salmon. No more than 200 will go through the Tummel pass and salmon angling is of little consequence west of that point. It is, however, the main area where hydro-electric operations are carried out, though hydro-electricity work is not the reason why so few salmon go that

way. Before the dams were built salmon angling was very limited. But it was an area of excellent redds for natural spawning and some say that that is the reason why there are no 'monsters' in the Tay today. Still, it contains important nursery areas and the smolts which produce the present day big springers are believed to grow and feed there before descending through the dams and to the sea.

So, at the junction of the Tummel and Garry most of the salmon take the right fork and ascend the Garry. There is a bit of an obstacle for them at Killiecrankie but, as soon as the water warms up they will race to the Tilt which joins the Garry at Blair Atholl. Strangely, the timing of the arrival of salmon in the Tilt is related to the number ascending the Pitlochry pass. If there is a big run through the dam then a fair proportion will proceed fast, to the Tilt and will eventually reach the Falls of Tarrf which is many miles up into the hills. Atholl Estates are beginning to open up the Tilt to the public. The remainder of the Garry salmon will eventually reach the fish barrier at Calvine and that will be that – except for spawning.

That, then, is the Tay and its tributaries – an enormous mileage of salmon water with huge runs of fish giving tremendous sport. No one can tell how many fish are caught in a season. Beats are strangely reticent to give their annual returns. I know of one place where the gillies are actually told not to disclose to their tenants what the previous tenants had caught. I wonder why? It is the same with net catches. It is a highly competitive river and there are netting stations all the way up to Almondmouth. But the size of the annual catches can only be a matter of conjecture without the statistical returns from the Department of Agriculture and Fisheries for Scotland. There is a growing demand that salmon catches for individual fisheries be made public on an annual basis and not kept secret for the statutory 10 years as at present. Even then no individual catches are disclosed, only the total for the whole system.

One of the most impressive features of this big river is that most of it is open to the public – there are very few strictly private waters. I've seen many publications up and down the country but I am sure the best of all is *Tayside for Fishing* published by the region's Leisure and Recreation Department. It gives details of every bit of water available to the public, all the hotels with their own stretches, all

The fish ladder and pass at Pitlochry

the angling clubs, the shops where one can pur-
chase tickets, and even how to fish and what tackle
to use in the different seasons relative to the species
one is fishing for. It was only 30p in 1980, wonderful value for money.

The Tay used to have gigantic runs of spring
salmon. They were also very large fish. The greatest of them all was that 64 lbs salmon taken by Miss
G Ballantine in 1922 from Caputh which was a
record then and will probably remain an all-time
one. There has been recent evidence that salmon
over 60 lbs could be caught once again. Recently,
one carcass from the Earn was examined by scientists and was estimated to have been between 60 to
70 lbs and an even longer fish found on the Nith in
1978 was probably heavier. The other interesting
feature to explain the larger fish in 1980 was the fact
that they were older fish – three winters plus salmon. So perhaps the old records are in jeopardy and
someone will break Miss Ballantine's record after
all!

Whether or not disease had anything to do with
it, or even the hydro-electric schemes, there has
been a diminution of these valuable spring fish both
in numbers and average weights, though in recent
years there has been an encouraging sign of a recov-
ery. 1979 started it with a very good run of springers. But 1980 surpassed all expectations. There
was one of the best spring runs for years. The
astonishing features of 1980 were the numbers and
the weights. The spring of 1980 saw the average
weight on one well-known beat rocketing from 8
to 9 lbs to over 17 lbs! This, of course, meant that
many fish of over 30 lbs were caught.

Another surprising feature is that sealiced salmon can be caught at the top end of Loch Tay.
They can appear above Pitlochry with sealice and,
believe it or not, sealiced fish can be in the Lyon as
early as April. But on opening day salmon can be
caught anywhere on the whole of the Tay, Loch
Tay, the Lyon (if it is not completely frozen over),
the Tummel below Pitlochry Dam and the Ericht.
It doesn't really depend on the weather at that time,
because January-caught fish may have run the river
from October and many back-end anglers will tell
you they've caught those so-called 'springers'
before the season closes on 15 October – or, to put it
another way, before the new season has begun!

All the same, the water temperatures have an
influence on the catches in the various beats. The

best and most expensive beats are in the lower and
lower middle reaches of the Tay. If the winter is
mild then the expected heavy salmon concentra-
tions in these lower reaches will quickly dissipate
and the relatively lower priced waters higher up the
system will benefit, to the detriment of the famous
beats and pools lower down such as Pitlochrie,
Islamouth, Catholes, Redgorton, Cargill and so on.
This was the situation in 1980 after one of the
mildest and driest winters and springs for years.
Upper beats bettered the lower ones from January
to May. Some years ago Stanley Weir was blown
and the natural barrier at Campsie Linn, which
tended to hold up running fish (it never stopped
them), deteriorated and was subsequently eased.
Now neither of these slight barriers is a strong
obstacle to salmon although both still show white
water.

From May there is a hiatus in the lower reaches
until summer salmon and grilse arrive in numbers
in July but this does not seem to benefit the lower
beats although the middle beats can be good in
June. The Tay season is really from January to May
and again late July to October. Most of the beats of
the middle and lower river take in their boats in
May and put them out again for the back-end until
the season ends on 15 October. These months,
early and late, produce enormous catches although
this is not to say the summer months are unproduc-
tive – they, too, can give good sport.

Up on Loch Tay the cream of the season is from
January to the end of May. The quarry is mainly
large spring fish and a boat can have as many as four
salmon in a day averaging in weight 14 to 15 lbs (in
1980) although most years produce at least half a
dozen over 30 lbs. Boats from the various hotels
troll the Rapalla or Abu Killer, the Kynoch Killer in
pink or orange, and an assortment of spoons. But
the angler, or his boatman, must know the loch.
The stranger could troll away for days without
making contact if he doesn't know the lies. Fir Bush
Point, Fiddlers Bay and the whole top end (west) is
good. For example, by May 1980, Killin Hotel had
nearly 100 salmon with an average weight of
14.2 lbs. Ardeonaig Hotel had three fish in early
1980 at 33, 34 and 34 lbs each. Much the same
results were reported from the other hotels which
made the 1980 spring season a memorable one.
Salmon will ascend the Lyon in numbers during the
spring so long as the water temperature is at, or

Below: The third Duke of Atholl and his family at Blair Castle on the banks of the Tay, by Zoffany

Opposite: Evening sport on Loch Tay

above, 42°F. Peter's Pool is probably the best one and there are always lots of fish in it. 1980 was so mild that salmon were caught as far up as Meggernie in April – the earliest there for years.

The Tay is such a big river that most anglers spin all the season through. Certainly from January to April there will only be the 'cranks' fishing fly. I remember fishing fly one day at the end of March at Caputh. Everyone else was spinning but, as the water level was relatively low, I though I'd show them! But all I got for showing off was a broken 14 ft Sharpes spliced rod by trying to cast the long distances required – even in breast waders. I think it is this inability to cover the water adequately with a fly rod that determines whether or not one spins or fly fishes. But even in the summer months when the river is low, breast waders must be worn to be able to cover the water with a fly. In the early months boats will harl a Rapalla or a Kynoch Killer. This is the method by which the boatman will start at the top and zig-zag gradually down the pool covering every inch of it. It's a pretty effective method but to my mind a boring one. Others will spin a brown and gold devon or other colour combinations, from the bank. One angler, Jimmy Stewart, still harls a huge single 8/0 or 10/0 fly on

the Dunfallandy Pool on the Tummel and catches the early salmon on it!

In the summer, though, there are plenty of anglers who use the fly. The Stoats Tail (as always), the Tosh, Munro Killer, Hairy Mary and Blue Charm from 6s to 10s, are the successful ones. But the majority seem to spin all the season and a lot of anglers use the natural prawn and shrimp. I, and a couple of friends were fishing Kercock one August day. The others fished prawn, devons and spoons without result whilst we had successes on size 10 flies. There are definitely times in the summer when salmon will prefer a tiny fly to a spun lure. I hear, though, that the lower beats have now banned prawning and this restriction seems to be spreading upriver.

The tide backs up the freshwater to Almondbank yet the town water at Perth can yield as many as 300 to 400 salmon in a good year – but low water is best for this fishing. There are various angling associations and hotels with their own or leased water. They are all listed in the guide to which I have referred. Most of them start on 15 January with every chance of success. For example, the very first fish of the 1979 season off the whole river system was taken from the Ferry Pool on Dunkeld House

Top: Spinning on the Tay at Dunkeld House   Bottom: A cast on the Kinnaird water near Ballinlung

Hotel's water. This fish was taken at 9.10 am on the 15 January and, if I remember correctly, winter was pretty severe that year. Some great days are often recorded in the early weeks of the season. In 1979 one famous beat produced 39 salmon in one day between 5 rods!

The 'big fish' beats are Kinnaird (where HRH The Prince of Wales sometimes fishes), Dalguise, Newtyle and the Murthly area – in fact, the lower middle waters. But 7 salmon for one day below Pitlochry Dam in May 1980 by a permit holder of the local angling club is not to be sneezed at either. This club, the Pitlochry Angling Club, owns its own bit of the Tummel below Pitlochry. Following their stated policy of making salmon fishing more available to local people the hydro board sold their fishings below the dam to the club. This is the right hand bank and the club have an annual average catch of 180 salmon. Permits for non-members can be purchased from the tourist office in Pitlochry. It is laudable that 50% of the availability is reserved for non-members.

There are no real runs of sea trout. The adjoining Earn is the great sea trout river. However, there are sea trout in the Tay – more than most people think,

but most only come as far up as Islamouth. No one would contend that the sea trout fishing on the Tay is spectacular although the finnoch fishing on the tidal water of the town stretch at Perth is very good.

Finally, to complement the very excellent guide book I mentioned earlier, there is a splendid map of the principal beats of the Tay, Tummel, Garry and Lyon showing every single pool. It is published by W Horlock of Glenrothes and can be purchased from any of the tackle shops.

The Earn

Rivers: Earn, Ledwick, Ruchill, Turret
Perthshire
Season: 1 Feb–31 Oct
Best months: Sept/Oct

The Earn is not really a tributary of the Tay. It only has two common factors – the same salmon fishery board and the sharing of a common estuary. It too empties into the Firth of Tay well below Perth. It flows out of Loch Earn and has three main tributaries – the Ruchill, Lednock and Turret. So it drains a considerable square mileage of western Perthshire. From Kinkell it winds and meanders its way through flat agricultural land, has a sandy bottom, undercut banks, and looks most uninteresting, except for spinning or worming. But above Kinkell there is a stretch of streamy water through red sandstone, the slabs of which present very bad and dangerous wading. Up at Crieff it is a bit sluggish in places but there is also some nice streamy water from there to Comrie and St Fillans.

The river is controlled to a certain extent by the power station at Dalchonzie so that below this point the level will rise when electricity is generated. From there to St Fillans there is also a compensation flow.

The Ruchill is the main tributary and is very rocky, streamy, with lots of white water, small deep pools and is a very exciting river to fish. Salmon and sea trout can be in this stream by July or earlier, if water levels permit. But in a spate it comes down very coloured.

This is another river system which is being improved by the resuscitation of the old River Earn Angling Improvement Association. The credit for this has to go to the secretary, David Liversedge of Comrie, who does most of the work and writes the annual reports. Although his figures are by no means complete (they never are in the angling world – or in the netting world, for that matter) in 1979 the Earn produced 1,557 salmon and 1,881 sea trout. Now, I know that 1979 was a very wet year, so I have averaged the known catches for the past 12 years and it looks like this: 960 salmon and 1,133 sea trout. The sea trout averaged 2 lbs which meant trout of 3 to 4 lbs and even a few at 5 lbs.

It is not exactly a spate river because of the hydro works but the lower reaches need a good bit of water. There will be a few fish in these lower stretches from 1 February (opening day) and they will give sport up to the end of March or April. After that there is little activity until the big runs come in September and October. But on the opening day a salmon can be taken even above Kinkell Bridge and by the end of March between 20 and 40 salmon can be caught. There is a bit of private water but also a number of angling clubs offer permits. For the most comprehensive of details as to what fishings are available to the public *Fishing in Tayside* at 30p is excellent value.

Most anglers use worm, some spin, few use the fly, yet others the shrimp and the prawn. Devons from 2 to 3 inches in brown and gold and various other colours are used and, if fly, then the Stoats Tail tube is best. For sea trout small tubes with red hair do well but so does the Stoats Tail. But there is no doubt that the Earn must be described as a great worming river.

The problems facing the improvement association are water abstraction by the water authority, freshets from the hydro-electricity stations and a feeling that 6 million gallons a day of flow in the Lednock is not enough and, if increased would enable salmon to ascend the Deil's Cauldron and open up a vast area of nursery streams for salmon and sea trout. Even so, the height of the fall would be a formidable obstacle. The association has a job on its hands.

The Tweed

Rivers: Eltrick, Gala, Leader, Teviot, Till, Whiteadder, Yarrow

Berwickshire/Peebles-shire Roxburghshire/Selkirkshire

Season: 1 Feb–30 Nov

Best months: Feb/Mar/Sept/Oct

Although the Tweed is the second largest river in Scotland (the Tay being the largest) it is, for me, the most fascinating river of all those that I have fished. It has many tributaries, all of which can affect the angling and the fish in numerous ways. It has no great lochs up in the headwaters, like the Tay, to impound significant quantities of rainwater to keep the river going in time of drought. As a result it can and does suffer long periods of low water.

The whole system drains something like 2,000 square miles. That is an enormous amount of territory – but look at its tributaries. The main ones are rivers in their own right. The Whiteadder, Teviot, Leader, Gala, Ettrick and Yarrow are all, themselves, reinforced by other substantial streams. Yet each of those I have listed drains more than 80 square miles. In all, the Tweed's catchment area of 2,000 square miles ranges from the Cheviot Hills in the south to the Lammermuir and Moorfoot Hills in the north. At Moffat in the Tweedsmuir Hills, is the source of the main river, just to the north of the Devil's Beef Tub.

Such an immense area of drainage creates its own sorrows. The Tweed and its tributaries drain all the agricultural land in the catchment area together with the afforested regions. These two factors have had serious and damaging consequences for the river. Agricultural and forestry interests have, for many years now, been going at it, hammer and tongs, digging drains which lead into the burns, streams and the main river. The result has been two-fold. Spates are short-lived and heavy. They also bring down fertilisers and other harmful matter from agricultural land, together with the acid washings from the afforested areas. Spawning redds can be destroyed, burns silted up making access difficult for ascending fish, and fly life and

other food supply may be killed off, making life difficult for parr (young salmon). Fortunately these problems are being tackled and there are now consultations between all the bodies concerned with a view to easing the consequences of widespread drainage.

There are other problems for the Tweed salmon. One is monofilament drift-netting, legal and illegal. Salmon bound for the Tweed and other eastern Scottish rivers are known to migrate down the middle of the North Sea, turn back north, hug the north east English coast and finally reach Berwick. Off Northumberland there are a number of licensed drift-netters (illegal in Scotland) who lie in wait for the migrations of salmon. They are alleged to be doing to Scottish salmon stocks what they did to their own supply of salmon, which used to home on the Coquet and Tees but are now substantially fished out. There is much pressure either to phase out these licensed drift-netters or to legislate to make it an offence to use monofilament nets.

These are political problems, of course, but the Tweed Commissioners have stepped up their protection cover in the 140 square miles of sea which they control beyond the estuary at Berwick. They have a 39 knot patrol boat which has been reasonably successful in containing illegal netting. In 1979 the Commissioners confiscated 300 nets along the coast. The Department of Agriculture and Fisheries for Scotland has co-operated and the result of this additional help has meant that there has been a change of emphasis. The larger boats no longer risk a £50,000 fine with, more seriously for them, the confiscation of the boat itself. Now it is the small boats which are doing the damage, because they are more difficult to intercept and are not so expensive to replace.

An examination of the records over this century will reveal how the runs have fluctuated. For periods, the spring runs were heavy, but over recent years the trend has definitely been in favour of the autumn runs. Nevertheless, these trends have come in cycles and it has been an interesting object of speculation whether one lot of autumn fish will eventually become spring fish. I know of no other Scottish river that has fluctuated so markedly. This is what makes the Tweed such an enigmatic river and one which has attracted so many investigations and surveys by scientists.

Spring, summer salmon and grilse runs have

155

Opposite top: A bend on the Tweed near Dryburgh Abbey
Bottom: The infamous nets on the Northumberland coast

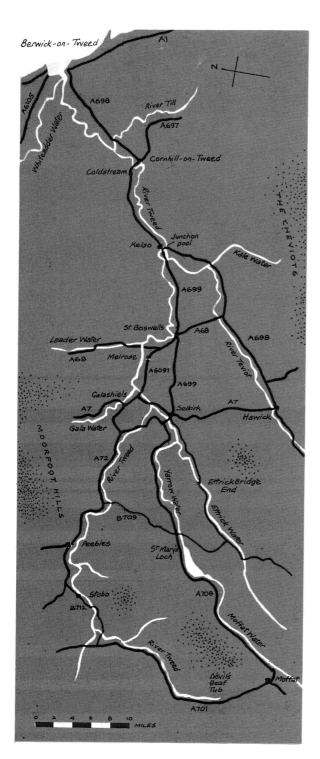

been poor. 1979 was a very lean year but, all the same, there was probably just a little indication over the years just prior to 1979 that the summer fish were that bit more numerous. However, the grilse catches were reported to be well below average if taken over a five year period.

The Tweed's main problem occurred in 1966/67 when disease (UDN) erupted on the Border rivers and then spread north to embrace nearly every Scottish salmon river. The carnage was dire and, without a doubt, stocks of fish were seriously decimated. Since those early days the disease, while ever-present, has not taken the same toll of salmon that it did in the beginning. It is persistent though, and, now and again, the outbreak can still be severe, especially around spawning time. The Tweed survived disease. By 1973 there was a marked reduction of diseased fish before and during winter spawning. The marvellous feature was that these fish were the progeny of the adults which had been affected by disease some years previously. That seemed to be the first break-through. Since then there have been the ups and down in the disease pattern but, on the whole, there has been a steady improvement.

I have tended to paint a gloomy picture of the Tweed. But it has weathered the storm although no one can be complacent – there are too many greedy forces at work, home and abroad, who care nothing for our salmon – only the making of a 'fast buck'. This is why we need much more stringent domestic and, more especially, international controls aimed at the limitation of salmon netting in international water. Nowadays, with the disease not quite as virulent as it was, with better protection measures on and off the coast and with good management, the salmon stocks have not only survived but have improved slightly. The autumn is certainly the best time but there are still questions to be asked. Where have all the big fish gone for which the Tweed was renowned? Until 1979 the scarcity of the big fish puzzled all the experts. Was it because of the nets? Were all the big fish taken and did only the smaller fish manage to escape through the nets? I do not know, but just when we were thinking that 1979 was going to be another year of few back-end big ones, up they came over the final two weeks of the rod season and the list of large fish caught by rod and line for 1979 suddenly showed a large increase over the immediate previous years.

Jim Hardy at White Dykes on the Junction Beat

Interestingly enough, the story was the same on the other two back-end Border rivers, the Nith and the Annan. So one wonders what were the common factors?

The Tweed is too large a river to allow discussion in detail of all its beats, many of whose names are world-famous. Who hasn't heard of Birgham, Junction, Floors, Mertoun, Dryburgh, Pavilion, Bemersyde or Drygrange? The list is nearly endless and all are magic names. For me the finest is that middle beat, Mertoun, at St. Boswells. It was on that water that I was introduced to the cream of autumn angling. I was told that very long rods, quick sinking lines and big brass tube flies had to be used – otherwise I would catch nothing. I was in no doubt at all that this equipment, and fishing the fly extremely slowly, would catch fish – that was the way it was done. I was using a 14 ft Sharpes spliced rod, a sinking line but just a two-inch tube fly. But there is one thing I just cannot do and that is leave the fly alone. I must have it coming round faster

than the current. I know this is anathema to most anglers but it is the way I fish and I get the fly to 'swim' fast by recovering the line by hand. Anyhow, my way with autumn salmon worked, and worked well. In two days, that first week of November, 21 salmon were taken and all were sealiced. That was my first experience of real autumn salmon fishing.

I said the Mertoun was one of the middle beats of the Tweed yet, in November, all these fish were sealiced. Over recent years it has become quite apparent that salmon have developed a nasty habit of travelling rather fast upstream. It has been happening in all salmon rivers and the reason is almost certainly the presence of disease. Even in spring the middle and upper beats have been more productive than the lower waters and, as I have shown, it is the same in the autumn. There is nothing to be done about it but be thankful, if you are fortunate enough to have a rod on middle or upper waters. Yet the Junction at Kelso, where the Teviot joins

Ed Zern of *Field & Stream Magazine* at Upper Hendersyde

the Tweed, remains a great pool. Not only that, it is well up the league table for what big fish there are in the Tweed. If there is a fish in excess of 30 lbs then the Junction, Sprouston and Gledswood are some of the beats which are likeliest to produce it.

Nearly all the famous beats offer some fishing to the public but, of course, salmon fishing being at a premium, there are waiting lists. However, quite a large number of angling clubs have salmon water which can be very attractive. There are too many to list but I can recommend the informative detailed guides to the Tweed which the tourist bodies publish annually.

The Tweed opens on 1 February and does not close until 30 November and has, therefore, the longest season of any river in Scotland. Before the nets come into action on 15 February it is fly only throughout the whole of the Tweed. Some beats insist on fly only over the entire season. All the November fishing is fly only. The main tributaries all have their runs of salmon. The Whiteadder has

spring fish but is mainly a sea trout stream. The Teviot has salmon as far as Hawick and above. The Leader has some salmon but is reputed to be of little consequence. The Ettrick is good as far as Ettrick Bridge. The Yarrow is good salmon water up to St Mary's Loch and the Tweed itself provides salmon sport up to around Stobo, above Peebles. Naturally there are no rigid boundaries and the action will vary according to local conditions.

The Till is entirely English in that it rises on that side of the Border and flows into the Tweed at Tillmouth, also in England. Tillmouth Park Hotel, Cornhill-on-Tweed owns 2 miles of this water and offers it to guests. It also has 4 miles of the south bank of the Tweed divided into five beats. All the beats are fished in rotation. The hotel does a very comprehensive guide and map of the fishing, indicating the beat boundaries and the named pools. The Till should have salmon in it by early March and easily the best pool is the Mill Pool. June is the best month. The five beats on the Tweed produce big fish. Largest was one of 43¼ lbs from The Pot, in 1972, by Lady Burnett. This was a true November fish the cast of which can be seen in the hotel. In 1979 the best salmon of the year was one of 28 lbs taken on fly in October from Haller Heugh on Beat 1. The autumn is the best time for these hotel beats on the Tweed.

There are many hotels shown in the local guides which cater for anglers – too many to list individually. Some, like the George and Abbotsford Hotel at Melrose, own their own fishing whilst others will offer salmon angling by arrangement with the local associations or even act as agents for owners.

I have referred to the Tweed Commissioners. This is a democratic and representative body of local people who bring together the two quarries, salmon and brown trout, and provide the management of the river. The council is made up of 81 persons, 38 of whom are riparian owners of fishings and 43 others who represent the local authorities, angling clubs, and so on. Since its inception this integration has worked very well and they have learned to look to the river as their main concern, without any self interest. The council is privately funded, raising revenue from assessments of fishings of riparian owners and contributions from angling clubs. They make all decisions relating to good management, husbandry and fish protection and do an excellent job.

WEST AND SOUTH WEST SCOTLAND

Just as the previous region has Edinburgh as its gracious pivot, so this region is divided by the huge, busy, boisterous but less attractive city of Glasgow – yet within a short time after crossing the Firth of Clyde the traveller can be winding his way around the banks – still, miraculously, bonnie – of Loch Lomond. South of Glasgow is Galloway, home of artists, goal of thousands of holidaymakers who would never dream of going elsewhere. There are numerous small rivers, mostly accessible with day tickets, which mainly fish best from midsummer onwards – and they include the Urr at Dalbeatie, the Dee at Kirkcudbright, the Fleet at Gatehouse, the Cree at Newton Stewart and the Luce at Glen Luce. These are mostly spate rivers but each of them has its own enthusiasts who would exchange them for no other.

Above Loch Lomond comes the real fishing country, spectacular and with miles of lochs, hill passes and solitude. Here can be heard (in Robert Louis Stevenson's words), 'the infinite melancholy piping of hill birds' – where 'the winds are austere and pure.' Not too austere though, for the area is blessed with the influence of the Gulf Stream, and there are parts where trees and flowers flourish with almost tropical intensity.

The Annan

River: Annan
Dumfries-shire
Season: 25 Feb–15 Nov
Best months: see text

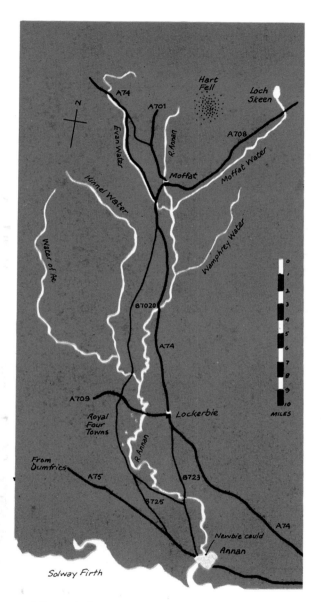

This is a big river. It is big in the context of the quality and size of its salmon. It is big, too, in respect of the length of its season (25 February – 15 November). These are not just arbitrary dates – it really does have spring salmon in February and genuine back-enders in November with fresh-run fish in between, during the summer months.

It is about 50 miles long rising from two separate sources in the north and north east in the drainage areas. The Moffat water begins by flowing out of a little lochan called Loch Skeen at the Gray Mare's Tail and another little burn below Hart Fell. The other main source is the Elvan originating near Leadhills which parallels the A74 to the north west of Moffat. Eventually the Annan is reinforced by its two tributaries, the Ae and the Kinnel, and the aggregate flows out through the estuary to the Solway Firth below the town of Annan.

In spite of the fact that these upper sources spring from the Lowther Hills, it is not a fast flowing river. The only stretch where one can find a fall is on the Kinnel water. Otherwise the main fishing pools are big and sluggish although there are, inevitably, some pools with a little white water.

Because there is, unfortunately, no big loch or reservoir in which to impound water up in the catchment area, the Annan is a spate river. The extensive forestry work compounds this characteristic. The drainage associated with forestry makes for a very quick run off of any rainwater. The consequence is that, after heavy rainfall, there is at least one day of unfishable conditions with the water coming down very red. Following that, the levels are high for a few days without colour, and spinning or worming are the usual methods where these are allowed. (Some beats have marker posts to indicate when worm and spinning are prohibited and fly-only becomes the rule.) However, when it fines down, out comes the fly rod (at least, for some) and salmon will become interested in the fly. But by this time, though, the fish will have used the spate and be found in all the big holding pools. If it is an autumn spate, the very top stretches will be the most likely place for them.

The river, as I have indicated, has a so-called spring run. I say 'so-called' because February is still winter and perhaps these fish ought to be termed 'winter fish'. No matter, though, when the season opens on 25 February they are there and seemingly in reasonable quantity. About 3 miles up from the tide there is a cauld, or weir. This obstruction is Newbie Cauld and creates what I call a temperature pool, that is, a pool with a rush of water through which salmon will not swim until the water temperature has risen to a level of their liking – well up in the 40°s F. The consequences are that from opening day in February to about May all the salmon taken during those early weeks and months are from below the cauld. There might just be an exception to that in a year of abnormally high temperatures but it would be unusual.

So long as the cauld remains in its present state and nothing is done to ease the passage of salmon through it the sport will be confined to the pools below. Indeed, on opening day there are usually enough fish to give a lucky angler three or four fish to his own rod. Bailiff Burns has seen as many as 20 or 30 salmon taken on that one day alone. Sometimes well over 100 salmon can be taken over the early weeks. Until March or April the stocks build up below this weir and the Cauld Stream and Craigdale Pat's Bridge Pool are the most productive places. But it does not take long for salmon to become dour and soon they are difficult to catch unless these 'lodgers' are being reinforced with new arrivals. If the cauld goes, or is eased for the passage of salmon, profound changes will result for the angling both below the cauld and above it.

The spring runs have their ups and downs. From May to late June or July there is a hiatus and few people bother to fish. Everything goes quiet until the summer runs commence. These have been reasonably good over a number of years although, very recently they have been poor. 1979 was a very lean year for them. The commercial nets were down by one third of their average catch that summer. The summer months are chancy affairs. They may have poor runs anyway or the summer may be dry resulting in drought conditions (this is a spate river, remember) but there will be fish about and they will be well up the river by then.

However, the Annan is most noted for its autumn run and its big back-end fish. Although the average weight of these fish is 13 lbs (compared to 10 or 11 lbs for spring fish) some specimen salmon are always taken. In 1979 one of 38 lbs and another

of $32\frac{1}{2}$ lbs were caught in November – bars of silver and sealiced. Local observers say that the autumn runs have been increasing. Throughout September, October and November thousands of these fish come streaming up the Solway with a good proportion bound for the Annan. 1978 and 1979 were especially prolific and, in the latter season, the commercial nets missed out because the run started just after the nets stopped on 9 September. This was one reason for a real bonanza for river anglers that year. During the last weeks until the 15 November the Annan is one of the most productive rivers in the country, along with its neighbour, the Nith and, of course, the Tweed. Over that period one can rely on good water levels although, as has already been stated, in a spate river the first day or two of high water may be unfishable.

Whatever the reasons, worming and spinning, where permitted, are the popular methods of catching salmon throughout the season. But there are beats which insist on fly only and where this is the condition the beat is usually beautiful fly water. One of these is Hallheaths Estate water where the river is streamy and just perfect for fly angling. This beat is some 3 miles long on the right hand bank. Over most of the river worm fishing is employed by many anglers over the first couple of days of a spate and then spinning comes into its own. A Yellowbelly devon, 2 to $2\frac{1}{2}$ inches in length, is the most successful spinner. But for those anglers who prefer to flyfish, and there are those who use fly all the season round, the Yellow Dog tied on a tube and the Stoats Tail, also as a tube fly, are the two best flies. Sizes are pretty consistent at $1\frac{1}{2}$ to 2 inches for both spring and autumn fishing and in the summer tiny 8s and 10s in the same patterns will attract salmon. In the big sluggish pools there is ample scope for 'backing up'. This is a method of fly fishing designed for the Highland fly-only rivers especially productive in the spring and again in the autumn. If the current cannot move the fly in an attractive way then the angler can induce movement by casting at the tail of the pool and walking a few steps upstream. However, in a heavily fished beat he will be unlikely to get away with progressing upstream instead of down! So the next best way to deal with the situation is the one I employ myself and that is by recovering line (hand lining) in order to bring the fly across the pool quite fast. This method works well in these big slow waters.

Salmon and Sea Trout by HL Rolfe

The Annan is broken up into many beats. Most of these are owned by estates but nearly all offer fishings to the public in one way or another. The two main tributaries, the Ae and Kinnel, are two major spawning streams with lots of back-end fish and are private.

From Annan road bridge down to the estuary the Annan Angling Club has the fishing and daily permits are available for visitors from the club's own premises in High Street, Annan. Above the bridge, Newbie Estates have that all-important part of the river which includes the water from Newbie Cauld downstream to the road bridge. They have the right hand bank and offer this fishing to the public. Permits are dispensed by Mrs Clark, Newbie Mill, Annan. The left hand bank is private. This highly valuable stretch below the cauld is where most of the salmon are taken over the first 10 weeks or so of the season and it is gratifying to note that the public is accommodated – even if limited to 10 permits. I make no apology for singling out this beat.

By May, or better still, July and on to the end of the season, one has to look at the middle and upper reaches. There are numerous bits and pieces of stretches available to the public through estate offices or from persons who offer holiday cottages with fishing. The Annan Angling Association has negotiated a number of permits on a fair number of beats and the Royal Four Towns have $3\frac{1}{2}$ miles of water offering day and season tickets. This water was given by Charter by Robert the Bruce to the Royal Four Towns of Hightae, Small Holmburn, Greenhill and Heck.

My only reservation with the Annan springs from the comparison between it and the Nith. While the Nith is a highly organised river with a well-developed stocking programme, the Annan has no such policy. The fish come, spawn and presumably continue to reproduce themselves rather successfully without much help from anyone. Nevertheless, it is a river which offers good fishing in the autumn and one of the few rivers these days with fresh-run sealiced salmon well over 30 lbs. There are not many salmon streams which one can fish with real hope of catching the fish of a lifetime. But the Annan is one.

Availability to the public is comprehensive but rather confusing. Interested parties could do no better than acquire the publications by the various tourist organisations for the complete list with terms and conditions. Apart from the ones I have mentioned in the text the following will be some sort of guide.

A number of permits embracing quite a few beats are handled by Messrs McYarrow and Stevenson, Lockerbie. Smiths Gore, 64 Warwick Road, Carlisle, also handle a number of fishings with availability to the public.

The Red House Hotel, Wamphray, Moffat, offers salmon fishing to guests and so does the guest house of Elmhill at Moffat, where there are also offered self-catering flatlets. The Upper Annandale Angling Association have a limited number of season permits from J Black, 1 Rosehill, Grange Road, Moffat. The best time up there is from about August on to the end of the season.

The Nith

Rivers: Cairn, Nith
Ayrshire/Dumfries-shire
Season: 25 Feb–30 Nov
Best months: Sept/Oct

Like its neighbour, the Annan, the Nith is about 50 miles long. In fact these two Border rivers have a great deal in common. They are spate rivers and both have substantial numbers of real autumn salmon ascending in September, October and November. They have almost the same length of season – except that the Annan closes slightly earlier on 15 November.

The Nith begins life away north in Ayrshire near Dalmellington and flows down the valley past New Cumnock, across the boundary into Dumfries-shire at Kirkconnel, through Sanquhar, Thornhill and finally the county town of Dumfries where it falls over the caul (weir) and thence to tidal water to dissipate into the Solway Firth. On the way down it picks up many tributaries but the most important one, from the angling and fish nursery point of view, is the Cairn which joins the Nith at Newbridge.

Like the Annan the descent to the sea is minimal and there are few fast-flowing stretches. A great number of pools are sluggish in character. It is also a spate river and, like its neighbour, the first day of the spate is quite impossible for angling because of clay-like opaque water. But on the second or third day the water clears and this is when the wormers are out in force. Within a few days the level is back to normal. Again, the similarity between these two Border streams is uncanny because they both suffer from flash floods caused by the same topographical features. There is no reservoir up in the headwaters of the Nith to impound enough water to keep the levels going and there is some afforestation which, together with agricultural drainage, allows for very quick runs off from the hills after heavy rain. However, the influence of these features has been the subject of controversy and some Nith authorities contend that they do not have a significant effect on the river. Be that as it may the river is a spate one and the high levels last but a few days. In other words the length of the 'fishing time' is nothing like it used to be before the massive forestry and agricultural drainage programmes were commenced some 30 or 40 years ago. A good proportion of the river is slow flowing, as I have said. In the upper reaches at Sanquhar it is quite canal-like and the most turbulent water can be seen at Drumlanrig Gorge. When the whole river is running at a normal height there is virtually no white water at all. Therefore, there are numerous large stretches of water which will hold salmon.

The largest tributary is the Cairn. It is about 15 miles long in fishing water and the confluence with the Nith is just above the town of Dumfries. This is an important tributary because it provides good sport for salmon. It is also noted for its sea trout and brown trout with which the Dumfries and Galloway Angling Association frequently stock the water. This association owns most of the Cairn which is also a spate river and will come down very peaty. However, it will clear just as quickly, in contrast to the parent river which can run dirty for days.

The Nith and Cairn are well organised. A lot of work goes into their administration with the end products demonstrated in the careful balance of stocking. Expert advice is taken as to the restocking policy. Should more brown trout be introduced to certain parts of the system? Should sea trout stock be planted out or perhaps more salmon fry, or a combination of all three? Vital decisions are made after consultation with Scotland's best advisers in this field. The people responsible for the excellent husbandry and management of this river are all the members of the Nith Fishings Improvement Association, constituted in 1934. This body incorporates proprietors and the Mid Nithsdale Angling Association, the Upper Nithsdale Angling Club, the Dumfries and Galloway Angling Association and the Nithsdale District Council. The hard working secretary, who produces the most comprehensive annual reports, is James Fyfe, of Dumfries, himself an expert angler and part-time angling journalist. This body of most knowledgeable people has done such a magnificent job that an HM Inspector of Salmon and Freshwater Fisheries for Scotland once said that the Nith

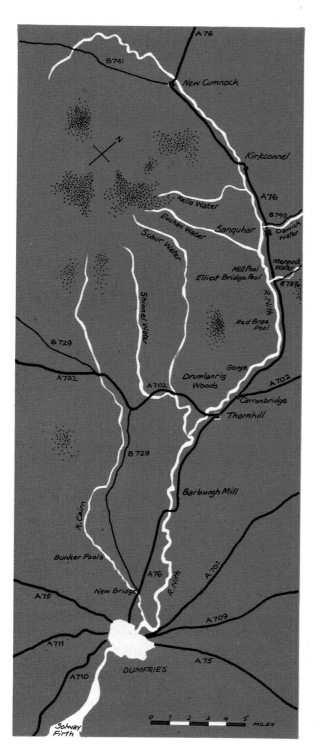

was the best managed river system in Scotland.

It was noted at the beginning of this chapter that the Nith is renowned for its runs of true autumn salmon. The same cannot be said for the spring run. Only about 15 years ago there was quite a marked run of spring fish but now these salmon are extremely scarce. At the present time there will be less than 50 springers caught over each individual month of March, April and May. Even in June there will be only a few salmon caught by rod and line.

One would expect a decent summer run of grilse and salmon but, again, this has not been the case these last few years. July, in 1978, produced less than 100 fish. But the picture changes dramatically in August because it is this month when the harbingers of the late summer and autumn runs commence to run the river. The catch returns begin to rise and between 150 and 200 fish can be taken that month. But the peak months are September and October and the latter ought to be the best month of the whole season. During October the back-end run is at its heaviest. The consequences of disease, however, have meant that September has edged October off the top of the league table. The reason appears clear enough. Although October salmon are fresh-run and sealiced, the sudden drop in water temperature at the end of September almost certainly results in the escalation of disease and it is a well known fact that these fish will run very fast through the disease-ridden lower and middle reaches with only one thought in mind – to spawn.

The Border rivers were the first to suffer from UDN (Ulcerative Dermal Necrosis) in 1967/68 and it caused a disaster in salmon stocks; only recently have stocks held their own and begun to recover. Nowadays, the onset of disease is late on, in October, and is accelerated if the water temperature falls quickly. It is often a race against time. Will the salmon manage to spawn in reasonable numbers before disease overtakes them? It is a worrying time for most river authorities.

The few spring fish that come back to the Nith cannot, and will not, ascend the caul (weir) in the town of Dumfries until the water temperature exceeds at least 42°F. The tide comes up as far as the caul but the barrier is there and it is usually April before fish will go through. As soon as they do ascend the weir they can be found as far up as Sanquhar by about mid-April. Later, sealiced fish

Trout fishing at Thornhill on the Nith in August

can be caught as high as Thornhill – some 15 miles above the tide.

Nowadays, an average spring fish will weigh around 12 lbs and in the autumn a fish of 20 lbs is a very good one (they used to be much larger). But in 1979 fish up to about 30 lbs were seen in this river in November and, even in December that year, there was a run of big, clean salmon. This has caused speculation that perhaps the close season for salmon should be put back somewhat.

The Nith is pretty well open to the public. What is known as the 'town water' extends from the estuary to one mile above the caul. In the middle sixties 200 salmon could be caught from this water but now it is down to just over 150. The best pools are the Purls, above the caul, where a large proportion of the spring fish are taken, and the Wee Green which is below the caul. The Caul Pool is not allowed to be fished, for obvious reasons. The Wee Green needs steady water. It is a high water pool. Above that water comes the stretch owned by the Dumfries and Galloway Angling Association. They also have most of the river Cairn. The association have erected markers which, when the river falls to a certain level, indicate that it is time for fly-only angling. This part of the Nith has long deep holding pools, with some rough water, but it needs good high levels to fish well. Fortunes vary on these beats. 200 fish in 1975 was the best season over the past 12 years or so and in 1978 it was about 170. Success ultimately depends on good heavy rainfalls.

On the Cairn there are two outstanding pools called the First and Second Bunkers Pools. These are the best ones on this tributary. But on the Nith this association's best and most productive pools for salmon are Denholm's Wood, Mouth of the Burn and the Stag Pool. All are deep, hold many salmon and can be fished more or less any time.

Above that fairly productive water are private stretches; then comes the Mid Nithsdale Angling Association which controls quite a stretch of water between Barburgh Mill to Thornton with a couple of small private beats within. There are plenty of holding pools here with the odd stream but lots of flat water which is very open with no, or few, trees. Fish are later getting up this far but their average catch return is about 150 to 200 although, before disease came, over 400 salmon were taken in a season.

I have singled out the two best pools on the stretch controlled by the Mid Nith AA. These are the Scaurfoot Pool – a nice pool with a lovely neck for the fly angler and Red Brae which is a tremendous holding pool. Many salmon come out of those pools each season.

When the level is over the 1 ft mark worm and spinning are allowed. Below the mark, it is fly only. The main marker is at Drumlanrig Bridge, on the private water, for better accuracy.

Mr McKune, the association's president, started the fish hatchery in 1949. 20 years later the capacity was increased to 300,000 eggs and for six years they planted out those alevins. Now, they are reaping the benefit. In the late back-end of 1979 there was a tremendous run of autumn fish – all of which were the result of efforts of Mr McKune and his many colleagues. A nice little success story for the Nith.

Progressing up river we come to the Drumlanrig water which is mainly private but to a limited extent is also open to the public. The factor at Drumlanrig Estate Office, Drumlanrig, Thornhill, would confirm the possibility of procuring a rod. As far as sheer length of river is concerned the Upper Nithsdale Angling Association has the longest stretch of river, from above Drumlanrig all the way up to around Cumnock in Ayrshire, about 17 miles in length. Tickets are available to the public but salmon are not to be found up there until well on in the season although sea trout can be caught as early as June. These beats produce a lot of back-end fish with a steady increase in catches since disease decimated the stock back in the late sixties. In the pre-disease era over 500 salmon were taken and in 1978 they were climbing again to over 300 fish.

Again, I have chosen to mention the two best pools on this beat. One of them is the Eliock Bridge Pool which can be fished at almost any time and any level and holds a large number of fish. On a par is the Mill Pool which also can be fished at any time and is a very good holding pool. Mr Hammond, the vice-chairman, told me that for the past 10 years they have worked out a nice system whereby the wormers and spinners can have their chance on the beat and the fly-only anglers also have their stint. He said the club was satisfied that there was something for all tastes and methods.

To catch salmon on the Nith one can worm, spin or flyfish. There are restrictions, of course, on most

Nithsdale Hotel, Sanquhar

beats with regard to the method relative to the water level and even hook sizes are printed on some permits. The dark flies do well here in contrast to the Annan where yellow flies seem to be preferred. Here, the Black Doctor and the Thunder and Lightning are firm favourites.

With well over 1,000 salmon, including grilse, in recent seasons this river cannot be described as being an insignificant one but when one looks back to 1966 and notes the annual catch at well over 2,500 one realises the terrible havoc that disease wrought with the salmon stocks. But on the credit side anglers have the consolation of good sea trout runs, with about 3,500 caught in 1978. But, here again, in 1966 the total was 9,500. Still, they are recovering. One sea trout of 8 lbs was taken in 1978 which indicates that some, at least, are surviving annual visits to the river to grow to that size. If good administration and management can improve this river then the Nith Fishings Improvement Association will do just that.

The Nith is a well endowed river from the point of view of public accessibility mainly because the big local associations control many miles of it. Although I give some information on where permits are issued, I do not give the cost for the reason that it changes annually, in most cases. However, a day permit will cost from £3 to £5; a weekly permit at around £15 to £20 and, in some cases, a season ticket is available.

The tidal stretch at Dumfries and a short bit above the weir can be fished by applying to the Director of Finance, Municipal Chambers, Dumfries. This water is best in the spring and autumn.

Permits for the rivers Cairn and Nith (Dumfries and Galloway AA) can be obtained from D Mac-Millan, 6 Friars Vennel, Dumfries. These beats fish from June to October and restrictions on method of fishing depend on water levels.

Mid Nithsdale AA issues permits c/o A Coltart & Son, Shoe Shop, Thornhill. Worming and spinning allowed only in flood water and there are no day permits on Saturdays. This water could be good in March and April and certainly in October and November.

Upper Nithsdale AC issues permits to visitors who must stay in the district and must be previously introduced by letter from the secretary of the visitor's own club. There are no day permits on Saturdays and best months are from May to the end of the season. Permits can be obtained from the secretary, W Forsyth, Sanquhar. This club, in addition to the Nith, can also offer fishing on the tributaries of Kello, Crawick, Euchan and Mennock waters.

The George Hotel, Thornhill, issues permits for the Nith. Mennockfoot Lodge Hotel, Sanquhar, issues daily and weekly permits. Nithsdale Hotel, Sanquhar, issues permits by arrangement with the local association. Buccleuch and Queensberry Hotel, Thornhill, as well as issuing the local association's permits can also offer private estate water on three two-rodded beats and they also run angling courses in April and again in November.

The Ayrshire Rivers

Rivers: Ayr, Doon, Garnock, Girvan, Irvine, Stinchar
Ayrshire
Season: 25 Feb–31 Oct
(Ayr, 11 Feb–31 Oct)
Best months: Sept/Oct
(Ayr, July–Oct)

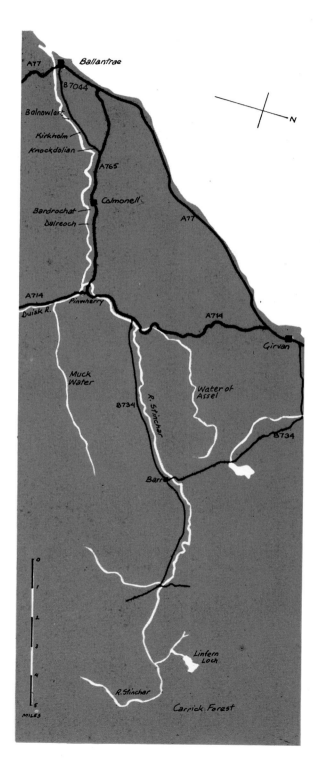

There are six salmon rivers within the old county boundary of Ayrshire, the Garnock, Irvine, Ayr, Doon, Girvan and Stinchar. All are spate rivers to a greater or lesser degree and it is usually April before a salmon is caught in the earliest of them. The common problems are pollution from sewage and industry which the treatment plants are not quite coping with and pollution from disused coal mines; afforestation which is common to nearly every Scottish river system and over-netting in estuaries and the adjacent coasts. There is, of course, the ever present curse of illegal drift netting at sea affecting the runs to all rivers.

River Stinchar

Of the six rivers the Stinchar is, at present, the best. It is the most southerly and is described as being the elite Ayrshire salmon river. This is not too surprising because it is the cleanest of them all and is well clear of effluent-producing industry of any kind. In addition, the estuarine nets are operated with a degree of conservancy and the river is stocked every year – good salmon husbandry has maintained stocks during difficult times.

It decants out of a little loch called Linfern in Carrick Forest some 20 miles to the north of Ballantrae where it flows out into the lower Firth of Clyde. On its way it picks up two tributaries, the Duisk and the Assel. There is no reservoir to hold any reasonable quantity of water, so the Stinchar is a spate river. There are large areas of afforestation in the upper reaches with the usual inevitable consequences of flash spates. These are remarkable for the suddeness of their arrival and the shortness of their duration. For example, in a matter of hours after heavy rain starts to fall, the river is up to spate level. If there is an overnight spate then at 8 or 9 o'clock in the morning the river will be unfishable but by noon the level will be down enough to allow fly fishing. This demonstrates the worst feature of afforestation drainage.

There is not much of a spring run of salmon. It is a particularly good late river; the reason for this may be that there will almost certainly be consistently high water levels at the back-end. In 1979 a 30¼ lbs salmon was taken on worm, late on, from the upper reaches. So it has big fish, too. Nevertheless, a few spring salmon will almost certainly be around in April. In 1979, my friend Jack Paton of Prestwick, had the first salmon of the season on 12 April on the Knockdolian Beat some 3 to 4 miles above the tide. At the confluence of the Duisk and the parent stream, at Pinwherry, the prime beats are from there to the sea at Ballantrae with Knockdolian, Kirkholm, Bardrochat, Dalreoch and Balnowlart the best of them. It is a lovely river hereabouts with shingly pools, streamy water – just ideal for the fly. Indeed, Knockdolian and Bardrochat Beat are fly only and, apart from early spring and at the extreme back-end, the floating line with a sink tip is invariably used.

It is such beautiful fly water, overall, that it is not surprising that the majority of anglers appear to prefer fishing the fly to other legal lures. As it is also a spate river it is important to find out quickly the preferred colour schemes for fly patterns. Conveniently the season can be divided into two sections with regard to colour. Up to about mid-June the Yellow Dog is a pretty successful fly with the Stoats Tail a good second. However, I must call this Stoats Tail the 'Stinchar Stoat' because the difference between the original and the Stinchar one is the added touch of a hot orange throat hackle.

But best of all, and most successful over the whole season, is the Esmund Drury General Practitioner fly. It really comes into its own after a spate and before the water clears. It can be used all season and in sizes from 2s to 10s depending on the height and colour of the water. As I have described elsewhere, I personally like to have my GP moving rather fast; it is exciting to see a salmon bow wave start up some yards away as it makes a dash for the fly. That is my method with the GP but in Ayrshire the GP is seldom fished on the floating line so they miss out on the bow wave and swirl. In other words, it is fished deep. Fishing it my way I feel that the vibrations set up by the long 'whiskers' arouse

the curiosity of salmon, together with the quick movement of the fly which probably resembles the action of a prawn or shrimp. Whatever the reason the GP is a most productive fly on the Stinchar. The local anglers, who tie their own, use dyed pig's bristle for the 'feelers' or 'whiskers'.

As it is the best of the Ayrshire rivers, it is not easy to get on to the Stinchar. When one can sometimes get a beat I am afraid it will not be in the prime months of September and October. These will tend to be booked solidly. Permits for the Bardrochat and Knockdolian Beats can be applied for through Michael Barnes and Partners, 14 Alloway Place, Ayr, or the Keeper's House at Knockdolian and Bardrochat Estates.

The Boarshead Hotel at Colmonell has a half mile stretch down from the village. It has the right hand bank and only two pools. Four rods are allowed at £3.50 per rod per day (1980). The opposite bank has been given by the proprietor of Knockdolian Estate to the local angling club and this little bit of water is improving all the time as trees and bushes are felled and pruned for better accessability.

The majority of the pools on the Knockdolian Beat are good – it's that kind of water. But if pools have to be named then Mathews Weil, the Scaur, Shacksiston, Blackstone, House Run, Mermaid, Bank Weil, McCallum, Sallochan and Kirkholm will bring a lot of memories to a lot of people. On the Bardrochat water the most productive pools are the Dub and the Bridge Pool but local anglers will tell you that the others must not be ignored.

On a really good day, with everything just perfect, these beats can produce a daily bag of 30 salmon or more and it would be unfair to ignore the Cray Weil Pool on the Kirkholm Beat which is another great Stinchar pool.

The town of Girvan is 8 to 12 miles from the best of the river and, there, one can find all the amenities of hotels and tackle shops. But Ballantrae, Colmonell and Pinwherry are all convenient to the Stinchar. The season opens on 25 February and closes on 31 October.

River Doon

I believe the Doon to be the most exciting Ayrshire river. Not that it is free of problems like the lucky Stinchar but because great events have been, and are, taking place – events designed to improve the river and restore it to its former glory.

The Stinchar at Colmonell

Firstly though, a look at the river as it is, from a topographical view. It commences at Loch Doon away to the south west nestling in the forest of Carrick, and from there it flows some 20 miles to the sea approximately one mile south of the estuary of the river Ayr. Although it is a small river it has great potential. It descends past Dalmellington, through a tiny loch called Loch Bogton, past Patna, Dalrymple, Minishant and through Burns country at Alloway and so to the sea. It is a picturesque river with attractive streams and pools. Who has not heard Burns' 'Ye Banks and Braes o' Bonnie Doon'?

Loch Doon is dammed but it has a fish pass with an installed fish counter. Salmon are allowed into the loch where there are a vast number of spawning burns. Prior to the building of the dam there used to be a spring run of fish and now there are great hopes of a revival of the spring run just so long as the smolts can descend successfully through the dam, into the river and down to the sea. This is sometimes the great problem with dams and fish passes – salmon will go up and through alright, but so often smolts refuse to descend. Expert advice has been taken on this problem. There is a compensation

flow from the dam at Loch Doon which is discharged over two days. However, there were moves to have this flow over a 24 hour period in order to give a really good spate, or freshet, instead of the 2 ft rise which the two day flow usually provides.

Firmly behind the Doon there is now (from 1978) the River Doon Angling Improvement Association. Even although only a couple of seasons have passed, as I write, this body of dedicated anglers has performed miracles. One of the great difficulties for the river was the severe netting of a long estuarial pool at the top of which there is Greenan Dam which inhibited the easy passage of salmon. Thus a very large head of salmon and sea trout were there for the taking and big inroads were made into the stocks by the commercial netsmen. The first priority of the newly formed association was to seek approval for an improved fish pass in Greenan Dam. The fishery board agreed and, in February 1979, the job was done and almost right away the rewards were evident with a 7 lbs salmon on 14 April at Barnford.

The new fish pass above the estuary has resulted in the netsmen virtually ceasing to fish the tidal

pool although, in response to the association's request, the netsmen had agreed to fish their nets only once per week in the estuary pool till the end of April. With the improved fish pass, salmon get through the dam fairly easily now and into the sanctuary of the river above.

After 1966/67, when disease decimated grilse and salmon, stocks were in jeopardy. While all the other Ayrshire rivers have been comparatively disease-free for the five year period from 1975, the Doon was not so fortunate. However, the spawning was good in 1979 and disease showed a remarkable improvement. It was important, therefore, to restock and the association appreciated this and is trying to find a site for its own hatchery. During this time it is undertaking a stocking programme with eyed ova brought to the fry stage in the Girvan hatchery and transporting them up to the Doon for planting out. It should be mentioned here that all credit must be given to Adam Milroy, the secretary of the improvement association, who virtually runs the hatchery.

The spring runs of salmon are, at the moment, of little consequence but, as I have said, great hopes are pinned on the efforts of the association. Certainly the odd fish can be caught early in the season, which begins on 11 February and closes on 31 October. Thus fish would be taken on the lower reaches probably just above the estuary or as far up as the Dalrymple beats, shortly after the opening of the season.

The grilse come in June and July and can give good sport but, here again, the Doon is like the other Ayrshire rivers these days – a back-end one. There is a very good autumn run with fish up to over 20 lbs. One of 22 lbs was taken in the Patna area in 1979. In big water these fish will run straight through. In 1979, for instance, a year of continuously high water levels, the nets fished disastrously, the low and middle beats fished only with a degree of mediocrity and the upper reaches scored well.

Another problem for both salmon and anglers on this river was the intensity of poaching. One of the first acts of the new association was to appoint 12 water bailiffs and gain additional assistance from the police. Immediately these had an effect and quite a number of convictions were successfully secured. These bailiffs have also reduced the 'putty hunters'. I did not know what that term meant but apparently a 'putty hunter' is a despicable fellow who poaches in burns with gaffs for gravid fish and uses the roe for bait! My friend, Jack Paton, who told me of this term, said that 'You Highlanders must be Simple Simons as far as putty hunters are concerned!' However, this kind of poaching has also diminished – another excellent reward for the new association.

Above the tidal stretch the river is privately owned or syndicated up to Dalrymple. But there is then the Dalrymple Angling Club which leases a stretch for its own members. Above that, it is privately owned again up to the Dalrymple AC water. Most of the upper water is controlled by clubs; the Dalmellington AC, Kerse AC and Patna AC – all of which offer fishing to the public. In the main there are no restrictions as to legal lures but some private beats are fly only in low water. The best of these beats are Swallow Braes, Doonholm, Nether Auchendrane, Monkwook, Cassillis Estate, Smithston and Skeldon. The pools on the Doon are numerous and the majority are not named.

Flies are much the same as for the other Ayrshire rivers but one very popular fly on the Doon is the Blue Charm. Some anglers use a single hook in sizes 4s, 6s and 8s whilst others use the doubles or trebles in which case a 6 or an 8 is the appropriate size. But the Stinchar Stoats Tail, the Tosh and even the GP can entice a salmon in any height of water so long as the hook size is related to the level and water temperature.

Permits can be obtained from Hollybush House Hotel, Hollybush. Fly and spinning only are allowed. Tickets are available from Dalmellington AC, Kerse AC and Patna AC. It would be advisable to enquire at the village post offices where permits are issued as addresses will vary from year to year. These clubs do not impose any restrictions – all legal lures are permissible.

September and October are the best months for salmon and the association in its report gives an interesting breakdown on good fishing days (GFD). This clearly shows, as one would expect, that October is the most reliable month for water. In 1979 there were 22 GFD in October and in 1978 there were 22.

This river will go from strength to strength as a result of the work done by the improvement association and October, and even September with 21 GFD in 1979, could prove a good bet for the late angler.

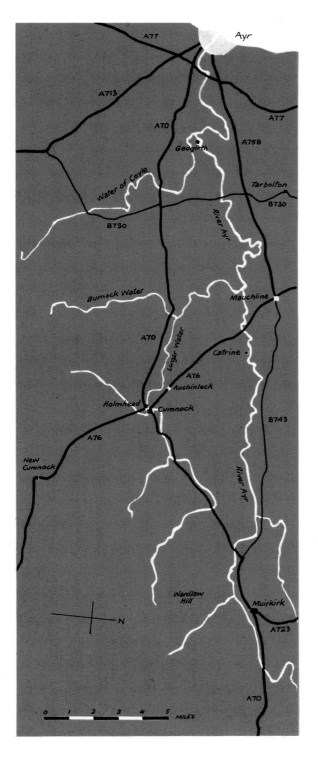

The county town of Ayr is conveniently only two or three miles away with all its hotels and tackle shops.

River Ayr

The Ayr itself has the largest catchment area of all the six salmon streams. It tumbles down from Wardlaw Hill between New Cumnock and Muirkirk and then picks up its main tributaries of Lugar Water and Water of Coyle. The whole system drains central Ayrshire.

It is very scenic in places, particularly in the Failford and Stair stretches. There is quite a variety of water with deep holding pools, lots of white water and, in the middle reaches, a sandstone bed which is rather dangerous for wading. Lots of dams abound, most of them man-made during the industrial revolution for water abstraction and which now serve no useful purpose. Most of these weirs and dams have fish passes but the majority are inefficient, hold up ascending fish and help to increase 'sniggling' and other poaching activities.

The catchment area is large enough to make the Ayr just a little more than a spate river. In other words, although it is classed as one, the spates take longer to get going compared to the others and when they do get going they can last for three to four days whilst the rest have spates lasting just a few hours. This is an important factor. It has a flow approximating to the Nith and with proper salmon husbandry and the institution of an efficient improvement association in co-operation with the riparian owners the Ayr could rival the Nith as one of the best salmon rivers in south west Scotland.

But there are problems. Pollution rears its nasty head and the river suffers to a certain degree from the disused coal mines situated upstream. The purification board classifies the Ayr at 7 to 10 on the Trent Biotic Scale. This means that it can be fairly clean and will contain a wide variety of animal life such as the Stone Fly and the May Fly which are pollution sensitive. If the classification drops too low then the fly life will disappear.

Still, the salmon keep coming in spite of the threat of pollution and the advent of UDN in 1966. Disease bit into the stocks very deeply. The grilse runs were hard hit and so were the spring runs. Nowadays the river is mainly a back-end one with the sport best from July to the end of the season on 31 October. All the same, on opening day on

The Cree, a small Ayrshire river, drains Loch Moan southerly to Wigtown Bay

11 February, an odd remnant of the springers can be caught. The early angler often has a go in the town of Ayr itself. There, quite near the town centre between two weirs a salmon can be picked up by members of the Ayr AC or further upstream, from the Craigie Pool. Above this big pool there is a dam which used to hold salmon back thus making the Craigie Pool a very valuable one as a holding pool. Then it was breached by a big spate and now the pool holds fish but not in the numbers it used to do. The nets come off on 26 August and thereafter the back-enders appear in numbers, just so long as there is water. Some of these back-end salmon are reasonably large but perhaps not the specimen fish of the Stinchar or the Nith and Annan. In 1979 one of 24 lbs was taken at Annbank.

As I said, the season closes on 31 October but it is a well known fact that during November and even in December the big 'gray-backs' ascend the river. There is always much controversy about these fish coming into any river after the season closes. Do they reproduce their own kind? Do they dig up the redds of the more valuable earlier fish? Are they just useless and should they be taken out before they do any damage to the fish which come within the rod season? All these questions are worth considering and answering. One answer could be that, during UDN, these fish, ripe with spawn, were the salvation of the salmon stocks. They spawned rapidly before succumbing to the disease. There may be truth in that because some of the small west coast Highland streams did not have much disease because their salmon came late on, spawned and sometimes even got away before UDN hit them.

October is the best month of the season especially in the middle and upper reaches. Like most other salmon streams these back-end fish usually run very fast as though they just have to get up there to the spawning redds.

For those who prefer to fly fish, the Brown Turkey, the Tosh, Blue Charm and the GP are all good flies in sizes according to the season and height of water. 8s and 10s in the summer and early autumn, then larger sizes as the water volume increases and the temperature drops. Some anglers prefer the complete floating line – others, the floater with the sink tip. I use the floater with the sink tip all the time except, perhaps, very early in the season when large heavy tubes are necessary.

Spinning is productive, especially in water which

has not cleared after a spate and the Yellowbelly, black and gold devons are popular as are the spoons such as the black and gold Toby. A No 3 Mepps in gold or copper is also a good lure.

Most of the beats do not impose any restrictions as to lures so long as they are legal. The bottom beats are controlled by Ayr AC which has that big important pool called the Craigie which can fish all the time. Day tickets are available from Gamesport, Sandgate Street, Ayr. It is mainly an angling club river but there are a few private stretches. Stairaird is one and Lord Glenarthur offers a limited number of tickets. Ayr AC also has another 1½ miles of water at Gadgirth; Mauchline AC has a substantial stretch; Ladykirk AC also has a good stretch and so has the Muirkirk AC. Auchinleck AA offers salmon fishing, too. It is a river which is widely available to the public.

The town council of Ayr has some fishings in the town water and offers these through the Director of Finance, Town Buildings, Ayr, for salmon as well as other species. Best months are April, May, August and September for this bottom beat. Auchinleck AA offers permits through J McColm, 21 Milne Avenue, Auchinleck, or J English, 1 Darnconner Avenue, Auchinleck. Ayr AC issues permits through Gamesport, Sandgate Street, Ayr. The post offices at Mauchline and Catrine also offer permits.

The town of Ayr is a large town with two main tackle shops and a superabundance of hotels and restaurants and, up country, there are Tarbolton, Mauchline and Catrine.

Salmon fishing ceases about the village of Catrine but the two tributaries of Lugar and Coyle have a very late run of back-end fish which, although fished for, use these small streams for spawning purposes. The Catrine dam has been a bone of contention for many years due to the 'snigling' activities which take place despite the efforts of club committee members. The same applies in certain parts of the Lugar and Coyle.

The Girvan has recently been the victim of a pollution disaster and its future as a salmon river is very much, at the time of writing, in the balance.

Finally, two minor Ayrshire rivers, the Garnock and the Irvine. On both the fishing shows signs of improvement and on both day permits may be obtained locally.

Loch Lomond

Rivers: Blane, Endrick, Fruin, Levon
Dunbartonshire/Stirling
Season: 11 Feb–31 Oct
Best months: Sept/Oct

I am one of the few fortunates to own a copy of Lamont's *Loch Lomond*. It is out of print but it makes fascinating reading, describing the loch as it was some 50 years ago. The most interesting feature of his book is the description of the problems at that time, problems which we are still experiencing today, of pollution, poaching, and even disease.

But to go back in time it was after the Pleistocene period that the loch was finally given its present-day look, when the Ice Age reluctantly released its grip. It was left with a division in the form of a geographical fault running from Balmaha on the east side, to Arden on the west side as a direct consequence. Southwards from this line to Balloch, at the bottom end of the loch, the depth gets progressively shallower, whilst to the north of this imaginary line the loch is deep with rugged outcrops, with gullies rather than burns, and certainly no streams of any importance except the Falloch at the very top end.

Below this imaginary line, the surrounding country is broader, with wide valleys, compared to the fjord-like structure of the loch higher up. These broad valleys provide the streams such as the Endrick and Fruin rivers where salmon spawn and find the necessary nursery areas. The Ice Age certainly left beautiful and varied scenery, dominated at all times, and from all angles by Ben Lomond; hence the emotive words of the song 'By yon bonnie banks and by yon bonnie braes . . .'

Loch Lomond water, because of its rock formation, has always been pure and of high quality. According to the Clyde River Purification Board's own recordings the loch water remains at a high quality level and their 21 sampling stations show no significant changes. Localised and short-lived pollution may be suffered from time to time from

camping sites and the like, but these are quickly remedied at the board's instigation. There are no peat beds to reduce alkalinity level. The only temporary discolouration is from the Endrick (and its tributary, the Blane) which can cause quite a reddish tint for miles beyond its estuary after a spate.

Another legacy of the Ice Age was the formation of the great banks of silt, sand and boulders which give marvellous fishing grounds for the salmon angler. The Pilot Bank above Ross promontory is a typical instance of this valuable legacy.

It is also fascinating to think that Loch Lomond once emptied into the sea at Dumbarton, before there was a river Leven. The loch is only about 26 ft or so above sea level and were the land surface to subside by 25 ft, high tides would flow into the loch as they now flow into the Gareloch and Loch Etive. That they did at one time, about the end of the last Ice Age, is proved by the presence of sea-shells. Perfect specimens of these in the clay beds on the north side of Inchlonaig were found by Lamont.

What Lamont could not have foreseen was the building of a controversial barrage at Balloch where the loch becomes the river Leven. The Central Scotland Water Development Board applied for, and received, authority to tap Loch Lomond water for the domestic and industrial requirements of Central Scotland. After a public enquiry, the scheme went ahead and was completed in 1971 and, ever since, anglers have complained that the effect of the barrage and the impounding of the water has been bad for angling in the loch, and, even more so, in the Leven.

The barrage is so constructed that there are seven gates hinged at the bottom and raised and lowered by steel wire ropes. When the loch drops to control level (26 ft above ordnance datum) five gates are fully raised while the other two control the flow of compensation water. A fish pass with two pools is provided at one side of the barrage through which there pass 12 million gallons of water per day. But, I am told, most of the time the fish don't use the pass but go over the compensation water gates when the river is under control.

The statutory compensation flow into the Leven must be not less than 130 million gallons per day plus freshets of not less than 1000 million gallons which will occur sometime over each 30 day period. The Loch Lomond Angling Improvement Association decide when the freshets should be

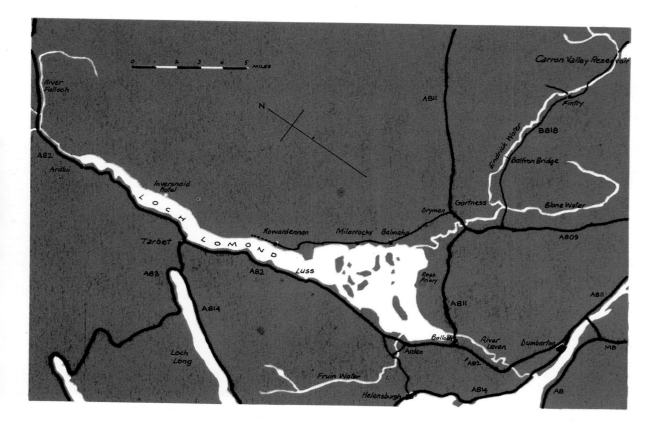

used and they do this in co-operation with the Clyde River Purification Board. From experience, a freshet appears to do most good covering the period from Friday evening and lasting through Saturday. This is felt to give the best results both for angling purposes and for giving the fish good access to the loch.

As for the river angling, the Leven is subject to extremely sudden and drastic falls in levels whenever the barrage gates are operated and it is not unusual for the flow to drop from a rate of 800 million gallons per day to 160 million within a space of three hours. Conversely, a corresponding rise can be experienced in a similar period. The flow can actually alter by as much as 550 million gallons in the space of only one hour! Prior to the erection of the barrage rates of flow between 800 to 250 million gallons per day were very common. Anywhere between these flows produced the best angling conditions but only because they would remain fairly constant for several weeks at a time. As any

salmon angler knows, gross fluctuations of level will upset salmon, spoil angling conditions and severely try the patience of anglers. As a result, the sale of Leven permits has dropped dramatically. During the angling season the river is down to compensation flow 58% of the time and anglers are just not interested in fishing the river when it is as low as that or if they cannot be sure from day to day or hour to hour what the river level is going to be.

So far as fishing in the loch is concerned, there is also controversy – the common complaint being that the level is left too high (but this may often be attributable to high rainfall). John Grant of Glasgow who knows the loch as well as any living person, contends that the effects of the barrage are serious so far as salmon fishing is concerned. The banks where Ian Wood (the founder editor of *Trout and Salmon*) once caught seven salmon on fly in a day are no longer easily identifiable – but it could just be that the angler has not yet adapted to the different levels and different patterns of fish runs.

The bonnie, bonnie banks of Loch Lomond

Over the past 12 years the first salmon off the loch has been taken in March on eight occasions and usually near the south shore between Balloch and Balmaha. It will be caught on a trolled bait, and the gold-dyed sprat, as a rule, catches this first fish, but as soon as the first one is taken anglers switch to the blue and silver toby spoons, followed by the Kynoch Killer with its reddish and purple body. I do not know why this is the pattern, but it is the way it is done on this loch. Certainly by 1 June salmon will take a fly over the banks; from 1 May the Endrick Bank is restricted to fly only for the remainder of the season. This famous bank extends from the stables at Ross Priory along the shore to Balmaha and, as is the salmons' way in lochs, they lie close in-shore in shallow water. Apart from Rossdhu Bay, on the west side, off Rossdhu House (which is private fishing), the whole loch is available to the angler.

I have mentioned the best drift, the Endrick Bank (or, at least, it used to be the best but has been less prolific in recent years), which is about 3 miles long. The other good drifts are the south side of the island of Inchfad, very close in, the north side of Inchlonaig, also very close in, Luss Points, the north east side of Inchmurrin and also the south west to a small extent off the same island. The Black Rock at Millarochy Bay is also well known. These are the best and most prolific drifts but the improvement association put out a very comprehensive map of the loch which clearly indicates the names and best angling stretches.

As for fly fishing, John Grant's own successes are on the Invicta, Mallard and Yellow and the Grouse and Claret. The sizes of hooks depend on the wave – the bigger the wave the bigger the fly. Sizes will therefore range from 10s down to 6s. The Invicta should be bushily dressed on a gold hook or, when using a silver hook, lightly dressed. The heavier dressed fly is the dropper, with the slimmer fly on the tail. The significance of this procedure is that the bushier fly on the dropper becomes more lively on the water surface. This local expert has made a study of his own loch, and the flies to use in all conditions, but no doubt, others have their own choices. I personally would have just two flies on my cast: either a 6 and an 8 or an 8 and a 10 – depending on the wave.

In recent years salmon of up to 34 lbs have been caught. Most are caught on the trolled bait or lure but one of 27 lbs was caught on fly a few years ago. Sea trout in double figures are again being taken now that UDN is on the wane.

The two main rivers for angling are the Leven and the Endrick although the Fruin also produces some good fish. The Leven is the communication from loch to sea and, as previously stated, it is not

the angling river it used to be. All the same, there are still a few salmon running in the spring and an odd fish or two can often be taken in February. But the spring runs have been getting progressively poorer each year. In May 1979, however, there was an encouraging sign when one angler had 10 salmon in a week. Again, the improvement associa-

tion issues a very good map of the Leven showing all the named pools from Balloch right down to the Burgh of Dumbarton – some 5 miles. It is tidal up to Dalquhurn Point which is well above the town of Dumbarton. In recent years a few big fish have come off the Leven with a best one of $33\frac{1}{2}$ lbs.

The Endrick is the main salmon angling stream

of the whole system. It rises in the Fintry Hills north of the Carron Valley Reservoir. As far as angling is concerned it fishes up to and beyond the village of Fintry, about 20 miles from Loch Lomond. Here again, the improvement association issues a map of the river indicating some 42 named pools. It is a spate river and, by the geographic nature of the whole Endrick valley, when it comes down heavy it brings with it a tremendous amount of reddish tinged water. This is due to the valley having a bed of old red sandstone which causes the discolouration during the period of the spate. The upper reaches provide the spawning redds for salmon and sea trout but below that the river winds its way rather slowly through flat agricultural land. But, at Gartness, one comes to the tourist attraction of the Pots of Gartness where the salmon congregate before making their leap up the rush of water. Not only tourists come to this beautiful but vulnerable place – so do the poachers. The bailiffs have their work cut out in keeping a watch on the salmon, swarming, at times, in the Pot.

The first salmon run into the Endrick will be in July at the earliest although it used to be May. Even this run is dwindling these days and September and October are now the best angling months. The first pool to come on would be the Meetings at the confluence of the Endrick and the Blane, which is a spawning and nursery stream. Above the Pots are Clay Lynn and Drumtian both worthy of mention as is the run above the latter, the Ford Flats. The two pools above the Ford Flats were destroyed by the digging for gravel. The Oak Tree is a holding pool but the Black Lynn is even more so. There is not much else until Balfron Bridge is reached. Further up, at Fintry, the Manse and Greystone Bridge are fishable with a good pool just below the bridge.

Salmon will take in this river right into darkness and my friend, David MacDonald of Glasgow, who knows the Endrick as well as any member of the association, told me one of his most successful flies for salmon is the Kingfisher Butcher tied on a No 8 low water hook. The trouble with this river is that it can be a 'pea soup' river in early morning and within two hours it can be right down. David MacDonald tells me that there will be perhaps two hours of good fishing then all goes 'dead'. So the most successful angler is the one on the river at the right time – a short-lived 'right' time.

One other river flowing into Loch Lomond is the Fruin on the west side above Arden and the first salmon can be there in July. But it is also a spate river and gives something like one hour's fishing as it starts to clear after a spate. The Bends, half a mile above the main road bridge is good and then one has to go to the top end to fish the Black Bridge and one other pool. It has over 4 miles of fishing, but has only eight or nine decent pools. Small tube flies such as the Stoats Tail, Hairy Mary, and Yellow Dog (when the river is still coloured) are best. The improvement association has the Luss water, too, a small stream but overgrown with trees; the river Falloch at the head of the loch is private.

Boat hiring is centred mainly at Balloch, Balmaha, Luss and at the many hotels on the periphery of the loch. Anglers can hire a boat with or without engines when the loch and rivers open on 11 February until they close on 31 October.

My account of Loch Lomond would be incomplete if no further reference were made to the Loch Lomond Angling Improvement Association; indeed it would be a crime to omit details of such an august body of dedicated people who, for the past 100 years and more, have acted in a capacity like the Tweed Commissioners or as a local district salmon fishery board (there being no such body for this loch and its tributaries). Over the years the association has leased fishings from the riparian owners and has looked after the policing, developing, management and restocking of the loch and its environs from its own hatchery which can take 250,000 eggs stripped from fish of the Endrick, Leven and Fruin. In addition, salmon eyed ova are bought from other areas to safeguard the association's own restocking programme. A bailiff force is employed which was at full strength in 1979, and as a result a great number of poachers have been caught, with nets confiscated and some individuals charged and convicted although the courts still tend to impose paltry fines.

When it held its Annual General Meeting in February 1980, the association had completed 79 uninterrupted years since it became a permanent body looking after Loch Lomond and its tributaries, for the benefit of local anglers and visitors – a valuable local amenity and an important part of the tourist industry. The association will be only too happy to respond to enquiries from intending fishing visitors.

The Awe and the Orchy

Rivers: Awe, Orchy
Argyll
Season: Awe, 11 Feb–30 Sept
Orchy, 11 Feb–15 Oct
Best months: Awe, Feb–Apr
Orchy, July–Sept

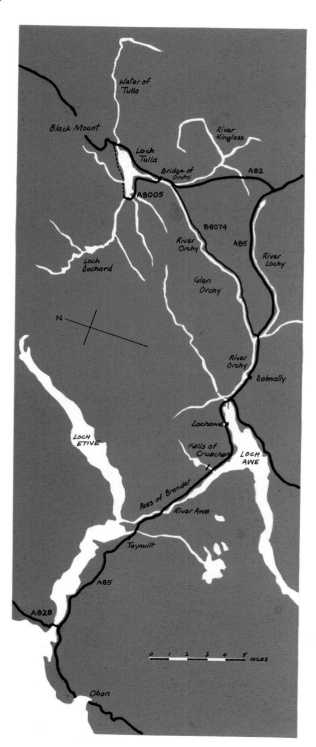

This is an account of a river system which, before being 'hydroised', was one of the foremost salmon systems in Scotland with good spring runs and very heavy salmon. Many fish of over 40 lbs were taken in the 'old days' and two salmon of over 50 lbs were taken on fly. But with the building of the hydro-electric scheme on the Awe and the incorporation of the barrage across the river some 4 miles upstream, the early salmon angling has deteriorated above this barrage. Fish do not ascend through it into Loch Awe and up into the Orchy until the end of May. In the pre hydro-electric days salmon used to be in the Orchy by March and April – then the best months of the season in that river. Critics say that not only are the fish later but are fewer, and the days of the big ones are gone. However, that is a common enough complaint today in most rivers. A redeeming feature is that the grilse runs are now heavier.

The Orchy flows out of Loch Tulla on the Blackmount and down to Loch Awe – a distance of some 10 miles. It is joined by the little river Kinglass near Bridge of Orchy. The Orchy is a beautiful stream with bubbling, tumbling water, lovely pools and magnificent falls about halfway down. A single tracked road runs very close to the river on its way through Glen Orchy which is one of my favourite glens in the Highlands.

It empties into the east end of Loch Awe which is 23 miles long and the loch, in turn, contracts itself to form the Pass of Brander and so through the barrage into the river Awe. This barrage was built near the top of the river and has a Borland fish lift. The Awe resembles something like its old self with a very swift flow through broken water but with some excellent pools which hold the salmon before they go up the barrage.

Although salmon can come into the river quite early in the season, which commences on 11 February and closes on 30 September (the Orchy goes on until 15 October), they will not go through the barrage until May. So these fish build up in numbers and the early harbingers tend to go stale. Nevertheless, the sport below the dam can be good and there is a slight suggestion that the early months are getting better.

River Awe

The Awe below the barrage is, surprisingly, open to the public. I know of only one section which is completely private and that is from the barrage down the north bank (right hand) but the left bank is available through Bell Ingram of Edinburgh, who work a three beat system with anglers rotating down two beats on the left bank and then a third beat opposite the second one. Below that there is a short beat called the Muckairn Beat and finally there is the Inverawe and Lorne Beat which is about 2 miles in length. There is also the tidal Polfearn Pool which the Oban and Lorne Angling Club lease.

It is fly only over this short river and the usual large tubes are used in the early months. It does not really matter what colour combinations are used – the springers are usually keen to take anything just as long as they are new and fresh into the river. The early months of the season are probably best because once the fish lift is open the salmon go streaming through to the loch and up the Orchy, followed in July by the grilse.

It is difficult to get figures of the number of fish caught by rod and line but what is known is the number of salmon which ascend the barrage. The hydro board publishes the number annually and it is a fluctuating number. Over the years, though, the average works out at 3,600 salmon. According to the records, 1976 was the best year with 4,389 fish but the number can drop to just over 2,000.

Just above the barrage the hydro board issues permits for a short stretch of river/loch. It is difficult to call it a river because it is at the same level as Loch Awe as a consequence of the barrage, but one can spin here as well as fly fish. In Loch Awe the fishing is 'free' in that no permit is required. Salmon and sea trout can be caught on the trolled lure. The usual spoons, sprats and devons are also used. Because of the late arrival of the fish the salmon

fishing is not what it used to be – but it is still worthwhile. Boats are necessary and the whole periphery of the loch abounds with hotels geared for the angler, with boats for hire and sometimes the services of a gillie – essential if the angler is a newcomer to the loch.

River Orchy

The fishing on the Orchy could be better than it is. At the moment anything goes. Any legal lure is used and far too many anglers use prawns, worms or spin. There have been unsuccessful moves, recently, by the river proprietors through their association to try and restrict the use of worms and the spinner. The answer could have been to make certain pools and stretches fly only and I believe that is what will happen.

Because it is now May or June before salmon arrive (given a spate) small flies are used. I have found that my little No 8, 10, or even 12 Esmund Drury Tosh is as good as any. But a small black fly is successful such as the Marsden which I like because of its longish tail. It is dressed with a black floss, silver-ribbed body. Wings are one and a half lengths of the hook in black goat hair with a scanty mixture of yellow and blue hair – all goat. I have used this fly and found it good for salmon in most rivers.

The only completely private beats are from Allt Kinglass up to Loch Tulla. One way or another the whole of the rest of the river is open to the public. A fine description of what is available, and where to enquire, is listed in the leaflet by Alan Church, Croggan Crafts, Dalmally, who also stocks tackle.

The first salmon which run in May, if there is water, tend to go right to the Iron Bridge Falls where they can be caught in the Pulpit and Gut. It is there that the first ones will be caught – even before the bottom beats. With the first spate in June, fish will be over the falls and searching for Loch Tulla. Best months are July, August and September. On the lower beats the Black Duncan is a very good pool close by the Glen Orchy road and the Bridge Pool down at Dalmally is another.

The pools above and below the Falls of Orchy are good. Inveroran Hotel's beat has four good ones – Canal and Shepherd above and the Falls and Upper Boat Pool below. But it is on the private water, where they tend to fish fly only, that one sees just how much more successful fly is compared to

Fishing the Awe

the worm or spinner. They can get 10 salmon in a good day up there by using nothing but small flies. The Ladies Pool is one of the best and the Otter is a favourite for some.

In the vicinity of the falls some of the pools are in rocky gorges and there is little else one can do but spin or worm. I have emphasised the advantages of fly fishing, but only because the river could be so much more productive if less worming and spinning were done.

Fishing on the Orchy is available from estates and hotels and some rods also go with the rental of chalet accommodation which is fast becoming the most popular way to acquire a lease of salmon fishing in the Highlands. But there are plenty of hotels within easy reach of this system, from Oban and Taynuilt, Loch Awe-side, Dalmally and Bridge of Orchy.

Salmon for the Table

"I say, Waiter, this Salmon Cutlet isn't half so good as the one I had here last week."
"Can't see why, Sir. It's off the same Fish!"

'This dish of meat is too good for any but anglers or very honest men.'
IZAAK WALTON

THE delicious flavour and rich texture of salmon have ensured its popularity since ancient times. We make the most of its season from February to November. *The Lady's Companion* of 1753 contains directives for making a 'sallad with fresh salmon' complete with apples, onion, oil, vinegar, pepper, lemon slices and capers.

In the Middle Ages there were many meatless days, Lenten and otherwise. A happy compromise was 'Calver Salmon', probably pickled fish. Today a salmon and fruit pie could be prepared with fresh salmon, and lose none of its basic medieval appeal. There is an interesting recipe in *To the King's Taste* by Lorna Sass (John Murray). Salmon also lends its name to a high fashion colour, a compound one produced by the mix of pink and orange, a splendid tribute to the lordly river fish.

Salmon is not exclusive to Scottish rivers; yet salmon caught in them has an exclusive indeed superior quality to all other salmon. From a culinary and gastronomic viewpoint Scottish salmon has the hallmark of perfection. And, moreover, when the fish is in prime condition its nutritive value is high, and it approaches meat closely in its sustaining qualities. The irony is that salmon is at its most succulent also when it is at its most indigestible. Gourmets may appreciate it most while the fatty curd remains between the flakes of its flesh for up to 12 hours, but it is certainly more wholesome when it has been kept a day or two.

Enthusiasts who cook salmon whole should invest in a fish kettle. This is a specially shaped rectangular implement eminently suited to its cooking process. The poacher comes complete with a strainer. It is a costly item and fortunate is the salmon lover who has inherited one as a family heirloom. Stockists of fish kettles include Fairfax Engineering, Finchley Road, London NW3 who stock poachers between 50, 60 and 70cm and Richard Dare, 93 Regents Park Road, London NW1 who have poissonnieres measuring between 40cm and 80cm, and who can also provide salmon smokers to order. If your fish kettle is not big enough for the fish to be cooked whole in a horizontal position, either cut it in two, or choose a centre cut from a larger fish. A slice cut in this manner from the centre – about 12 inches (30 cm) long – is known as a 'trongon de saumon'.

The sea trout (*salmo trutta*) is cooked, exactly like salmon, although it is generally served boiled. Sometimes called finnoch trout, it is in season May – July and usually cooked whole.

Choosing Salmon The entire body should be covered with small yet brilliant scales. Dullness denotes that the fish is either not fresh or in bad condition. Look out for firm rosy gills. While salmon can bow in at vast weights, a smaller fish is ideal for culinary purposes. A short round fish with firm flesh is the preferred shape. Because of the narrow rectangular shape of salmon and sea trout they are reasonably quick to cook. Once boiled, let them cool in their own created juices.

The freezer life of salmon is six months if whole or four months if cut into steaks. While smoked salmon is intact, it will keep whole for eight months, but sliced, only for four months. Salmon is good deep-freeze material.

Hot smoking of salmon or indeed any fish, is really a method of barbecuing, whereas cold smoking is the method by which we most often encounter salmon. Cutlets and fillets are best for hot smoking. Hot smoke boxes are manufactured by Brook's Original Home Smokers, 88 Windsor Road, Southport, Merseyside, who also supply wood chips and smoking powder.

From River to Table First catch. Then despatch. The salmon fisherman has an exacting task on hand from the moment he has caught his salmon or sea trout to the moment he has it prepared and packaged for travel to a distant table.

When the decision to keep the salmon or sea trout is made, the angler's first consideration should be the care and cleaning and dressing of the fish. If the intention is to keep the fish, line a wicker creel or dampened canvas bag with wet grass, or spearmint and watercress leaves if available. Sea trout will remain cool in such a container for many hours. As soon as practicable after killing, clean the fish. Make sure that the gills are completely removed. These spoil first and even the tiniest bit remaining can ruin not only one fish, but an entire catch if they are packed together.

In order to freeze and ship salmon, place each one carefully in a plastic bag. This material is available in various sizes in rolls, with one end that is presealed at the factory. Be sure that the fish remain flat in the bag for shipping. Fill the bag with enough water to cover the fish. Before the end of the bag is twisted and knotted check that the air pocket in the bag is eliminated. Look for leaks. If they are in evidence, use another bag. This method freezes fish solidly in a block of ice. It keeps fish indefinitely if freezing is properly maintained, and prevents freezer burn which destroys the optimum flavour and texture of freshly caught salmon.

For shipping, look for a sturdy carton (preferably one that tinned food was shipped in) and neatly line it with at least a dozen layers of newspapers (see *Cartons* below). Then each block of ice containing a fish is wrapped in several layers of paper and packed in the carton. After the carton is packed, the top is lined with more newspapers which further act as an insulator. The carton is then closed tightly, and secured with rope. Be sure that the return address is plainly visible on the carton if it is to be shipped. Fish packed in this manner will remain solidly frozen for at least eight hours on the warmest of days, and should, ideally, soon be enjoyed by the fortunate recipients or deep frozen for later use. The fish should be slowly thawed in a pan of cold water before cooking preparations.

As far as transport from the river to the table is concerned the individual fisherman does not enjoy as varied facilities as commercial concerns sending salmon to retail outlets. For commercial purposes, refrigerated transport is used. The majority of road haulage services do not have refrigerated compartments, and those that do appear to prefer keeping them for large commercial consignments. Alas, Post Office guide rules do not allow for Royal Mail special delivery which would be swift, but only for parcel post which, in my view, could prove too slow.

However, there are two ideal methods of transport available to the private fisherman.

Red Star Parcels via British Rail Labels are provided, and the salmon is taken from the local area to the nearest station. Overnight travel is recommended for cool conditions. Recipients are notified, and can collect their salmon from their local station early in the morning.

By Air British Caledonian Airways inform me that fresh salmon must be packed in dry ice, particularly for long journeys. For short journeys such as Glasgow/London, wet ice is sufficient provided it is packed in a leak-proof container.

Cartons Tillotsons of Manchester manufacture aquacartons which are waterproof, lightweight and ideal for salmon. Mainly they are produced for commercial consignments, but outlets can be found in Edinburgh, Lochfyne and elsewhere.

Smoked Salmon There are three major salmon smoking houses in Scotland. These are Highland Seafoods at Boddam, near Aberdeen, Pinneys in Dumfries, and Macfisheries' Smokehouse in Fraserburgh, which is used by Marine Harvest (Unilever) under contract. It is usually the larger fish which go for smoking.

Pinneys Smokehouses are picturesquely located in a set of whitewashed Scottish farm buildings at Newport Farm, Brydekirk, Annan. All is character in the facade, but the interiors are cool and spotless, especially equipped for salmon curing. The approach to the actual task of smoking the salmon is traditional. Suitable fish are chosen in the summer months. Enormous care is taken at this point to ensure a superb end product. Pinneys pride themselves on using a traditional cure – utilising salt, sugar and the smoke of carefully chosen hardwoods. This mild cure is favoured, in order not to mask the intrinsic flavour of the fish.

Mail order is prompt, and customers' own salmon is smoked on the premises at reasonable cost and with great personal attention. Pinneys smoked salmon is air-freighted to the United States, the Far and Near East, South Africa and, of course, Europe, where chilled or refrigerated road transport is also used. Ideal expanded polystyrene boxes are used for air-freighting.

Finally, remember that smoked salmon is not preserved salmon, and its refrigerator life is like any other perishable. A side normally weighs between 3 and 4 lbs. Smoked salmon is a perfect Christmas present, indeed the perfect present for all seasons. MacGilvray, a Glasgow-based firm, make a speciality of Christmas presentation boxes, including the magnificent 'Chieftain's Choice'. Salmon and smoked salmon are both great favourites with the Jewish community. Alan Flax & Co. Ltd. is a typically excellent North London firm (459 Finchley Road, London NW3) which specialises in smoked salmon.

Ice is a great cooler for salmon, and it must be made from water that is drinkable. Ice is its own thermostat and it maintains fish at a temperature just slightly above the point at which it would begin to freeze. Whatever ice is used – it can come in block, crushed block, and small pieces – too much can never be utilised to keep salmon fresh. If frozen salmon is thawed it will spoil as readily as unfrozen wet fish, and, therefore, must be chilled until required. Salmon should never be overheated during the thawing process, otherwise its keeping qualities will be destroyed. The reason for freezing salmon is to lower the temperature to halt spoilage. So when the frozen salmon is cold stored, it should approximate the quality of fresh salmon. Freezing and cold storing can only maintain the condition, not actually improve it. Delay between freezing and cold storage should be absolutely minimal.

Smoked salmon, destined to be kept for more than a few days, should be frozen and cold stored as soon as it has cooled after removal from the kiln.

The cold storage life of frozen salmon is by no means indefinite. Eventually, albeit slowly, deterioration will take place. A fatty fish such as salmon does not keep as well as a white fish such as cod. Smoked salmon keeps less well than fresh salmon. Stale or inferior salmon should never be frozen and cold stored.

Here are a few recipes from my collection that can be tried at home.

Plain Salmon

If salmon has been poached in water, it is not uncommon to serve it with a boatful of this liquid, and baked potatoes. The ideal method is to bring the salmon slowly to boiling point in the kettle, then let it cook the appropriate number of minutes, according to its size, and, finally, to allow it to cool in its own liquid.

Roast Salmon

Select a 6 lbs cut of salmon, flour it lightly, and wrap it well in herbed and buttered paper. This can be cooked in a Dutch oven or on a spit.

Boiled Salmon Cutlets

Cut one inch thick cutlets of salmon. After washing and drying put them in kettle (or saucepan) with enough boiling fish stock to cover. Simmer gently for 10 minutes. Drain the cutlets well. Arrange them on a folded damask napkin on a hot dish, so that one cutlet leans against another. Garnish with potatoes, olives, and scalloped cucumber, serve with piquant sauce.

Grilled Salmon

Cut salmon slices $1\frac{1}{2}$ inches thick, brush them with oil, dust with salt and pepper. Grill for about 20 minutes, turning the slices frequently and rebrushing with oil each time. They will be crisp and brown when served.

Poached Salmon Court-Bouillon

Poach six salmon steaks an inch thick in two cups of white wine court-bouillon to which has been added the juice of a lemon. Let steaks simmer for 10 minutes when fish will flake easily, and can be arranged and served piping hot with Hollandaise sauce, or chilled with cucumber mayonnaise.

To make a white wine court-bouillon combine a quart of water and a quart of dry white wine and bring the mixture to boil with a tablespoon of salt, two carrots and two onions, finely sliced. Add a few peppercorns and cloves, a bouquet garni and simmer it for 30 minutes. Court-bouillon makes the fish tenderer. Cook the fish in the liquid. Overcooking will render salmon over-tough.

'Matting' freshly caught salmon

Salmon en Papillote

Marinate two salmon steaks for an hour in sweet oil to which has been added parsley, onion, shallot, and mushrooms, all chopped super fine. Season with a bay leaf, salt and pepper. Oil a paper bag large enough to contain both salmon steaks. Put in the fish, now removed from the marinade, and cook in a moderate oven. Squeeze on a little lemon juice before serving.

Potted Salmon

Pound 1 lb salmon in mortar with 2 oz butter, half a teaspoon of ground cloves, 2 teaspoons of anchovy essence, dashes of cayenne and black pepper, and a teaspoon of lemon juice. Spread on thin slices of bread and butter. Cover with other slices and press firmly down. Garnish with watercress.

To Salt Salmon

Cut fish down, take out inside, remove the scales and wipe it with a dry cloth. Rub it well with common salt, and let it remain on a large dish for 24 hours to drain. For about 12 lbs of fish take $\frac{1}{4}$ lb pounded salt petre, $\frac{1}{4}$ lb coarse brown sugar, and three handfuls of common salt. Mix them, and rub well into the salmon. Leave it in a large dish, and rub the pickle into it every day. It will be ready for use in three weeks. Add a little bay salt.

Variations on a Salmon Mayonnaise

Remove the skin and bones from a cold boiled salmon, and mix the flesh with a sauce vinaigrette. Arrange this mixture, salmon shaped, on an oval platter.

(a) Pipe thick mayonnaise into a lattice pattern all over the salmon. Garnish with lemon and tomato slices and hard-boiled egg slices decorated with sliced gherkin in the middle.

(b) Cover the salmon mix with mayonnaise, and serve with lettuce and red cabbage salad, garnished with tomato and hard-boiled egg slices.

Salmon mayonnaise can also form part of elaborate hors-d'oeuvres.

Salmon Trout in Aspic

Select a fish about 2 lbs in weight. Make a quart of fish broth with separate cuttings. Use this as a base to construct a court-bouillon and then combine with an equal quantity of Chablis. Cover the fish when it is laid in the fish kettle. When it is cooked, cooled, and strained, paint with liquid aspic jelly, and add more set chopped jelly as a surround. Serve with a tomato and basil flavoured mayonnaise.

Ways of Presenting Smoked Salmon

Smoked salmon should always be featured in a delicately presented hors-d'oeuvres; it can be the chief ingredient in a chilled soup, and in a quiche; it is best carved with a long and sharp knife. Traditional accompaniments include fresh brown bread and butter, a pepper mill holding black peppercorns and lemon wedges.

Small tomatoes can be stuffed with ground smoked salmon, anchovy paste, grated onion, lemon juice, and chopped parsley.

Form smoked salmon into rolls and garnish with slices of egg and tomato.

At the Romantik Hotel in Schlopwirt near Salzburg smoked salmon is served in very thin slices, with lemon and toast. Alongside is a bowl of whipped cream flavoured with freshly grated horseradish.

Index

Picture Acknowledgements

The Ashmolean Museum 12; Reproduced by kind permission of His Grace the Duke of Atholl 150; E T Atkinson 115, 118/119, 167; A B Beattie 132; British Tourist Authority 26, 58; Arthur Brook 38; W Brown 62, 70/71, 83, 87, 90, 93, 107, 171; R V Collier 102/103; House of Hardy 42, 47, 48/49, 50, 146/147, 158; Highland Trout Company (Scotland) Ltd 55; Copyright of the Hornel Trustees 54; Eric Hosking 66/67; The Mansell Collection 8, 13, 37, 163; Roy Miles Gallery 11; National Gallery of Scotland 16; Arthur Oglesby 15, 19, 21, 22, 35, 47, 120, 122, 123, 137, 148, 152/3, 154, 159, 183; Private Collection 51; Punch Publications Ltd 184; Scottish Tourist Board 14, 97, 99, 110, 135, 151, 175, 178/179; Robert Speirs 168; John Stidolph 18, 122, 125, 127, 129, 134, 136, 157; Syndication International 94/95; John Tarlton frontispiece, 74/75, 76, 79, 80/81, 82, 84/85, 105, 131, 152/153, 189; Ronald Thompson 31, 33, 34; John Topham 45, 69, 77, 104